THE FIFTH MODERNIZATION

THE FIFTH MODERNIZATION

CHINA'S HUMAN RIGHTS MOVEMENT, 1978–1979

Edited by
James D. Seymour

With an Introduction by
Mab Huang and James D. Seymour

1980
HUMAN RIGHTS PUBLISHING GROUP
A division of Earl M. Coleman Enterprises
Stanfordville, New York

Library of Congress Cataloging in Publication Data
Main entry under title:
The Fifth Modernization
  Bibliography, p.
  Includes Index.
  1. Civil Rights—China—Sources. I. Seymour,
James D.
JQ1516.F53   323.4'0951   80-14531
ISBN 0–930576–38–1

© 1980 Earl M. Coleman Enterprises, Inc.

HUMAN RIGHTS PUBLISHING GROUP
A division of Earl M. Coleman Enterprises, Inc.
Conklin Hill Road
Stanfordville, New York 12581

Printed in the United States of America

CONTENTS

PREFACE

This book is comprised largely of translations of unofficial documents from China which were written during the political thaw that the country enjoyed between November 1978 and March 1979. The editor is responsible for the italicized introductions to the sections and documents, all footnotes, and occasional clarifying remarks enclosed in brackets. The original authors played no part in the publication of this English version of their works. All royalties are being contributed to nonpartisan organizations engaged in promoting human rights in East Asia.

The documents are complete unless otherwise indicated. Where omissions have been made, the reasons usually have to do with considerations of space and avoiding duplication of types of material. In a few cases, the physical condition of the originals was so poor that certain passages were illegible.

Some of the translations have been taken from U.S. Joint Publications Research Service (JPRS) microfiche. These have often been substantially rewritten without indication. Other documents were translated especially for this book by Steven K. Chen, Mab Huang, Arthur Li, Maddy Lynn, James D. Seymour, the International League for Human Rights, and the Chinese English Language Service. Details about translation and sources are given in the first end-note to each document.

I am grateful to the numerous people who assisted in this project (not all of whom agreed with the thrust of the introduction). Those who provided criticism and assistance are Robyn Bem, Lawrence Chang, Parris Chang, David Eisner, Victor Falkenheim, Mab Huang, Kenneth Lieberthal, Nataline Seymour, and Tso Wong. Of course, they bear no responsibility for this volume's shortcomings.

J.D.S.

New York, 1 April 1980

INTRODUCTION

By Mab Huang and James D. Seymour

During the 1970s there occurred an international revival of interest in the subjects of civil liberties and economic rights, together known as "human rights."* In Europe this culminated in the 1975 Helsinki accords and follow-up efforts such as Czechoslovakia's "Charter 77." In Asia the most notable development was the restoration of civil liberties in India. For the United States, the election of Jimmy Carter as president marked a turning point in the conduct of American foreign policy, with the subject of human rights, if not always at the forefront, at least being factored into the policy equation. During all of this, however, people tended to forget about the quarter of humanity that is China. Somehow, the People's Republic was conceived of as "different." Western governments might need public criticism to function properly, but in revolutionary China, it seemed, there was no need to hear from the people. Some (but not all)[1] of the prominent "China watchers" insisted that liberal democracy would not,[2] and perhaps should not,[3] come to that land.

On the surface, this view is rather compelling. It would be rash indeed to predict the advent of liberal constitutionalism anytime soon in that country. But if China does continue as a dictatorship, the explanation will probably be a familiar one. Like other dictatorships, China owes its existence to the power relations within the system more than to any unusual features of the political culture. Arguments to the contrary fail to take into account the drastic changes which the last half-century has seen. It is one thing to say that it will be difficult to realize democracy, it is quite another matter to say that the Chinese people have no interest in it. We believe that such contentions were consummately and eloquently rebutted by the events of the winter of 1978–79.

---

* Although we are in accord with the prevailing international view that human rights embody both civil liberties and economic rights, the emphasis in this book will be on the former. The reason for this is that there is no real controversy in China on the question of whether people's basic economic needs should be met (though there is disagreement on the best way to meet these needs, and on the extent to which they are in fact being met). In other words, both the writers of the essays in this volume and the men in control of the Party and government agree on the importance of the Four Modernizations, which are designed to bring China into the twentieth century in the material sense. What is at issue is the "fifth modernization"—political democratization based on protection of individual civil liberties.

For a period of five months, from November 1978 to March 1979, China presented the world with a startling spectacle: a democratic movement which, while centered in Beijing (Peking), engulfed cities throughout the nation. Posters demanding democracy and human rights appeared in Shanghai, Guangzhou (Canton), Hangzhou, Guiyang, and even Lhasa in Tibet. There were also a score or more of activist organizations, many with their own publications. The latter appeared irregularly and were generally poorly printed, but they often contained social and political expositions that were more candid and incisive than those commonly found in the official media. Despite their varying philosophical orientations, the organizations formed a kind of loose coalition and tended to stress certain common themes centered around demands for democracy, civil liberties, employment, and meeting basic economic needs. At the height of the movement, large demonstrations were held. There was a sense of excitement and urgency, and at times the atmosphere was electric. A new era in Chinese politics seemed to be dawning.

In a negative sense, the democratic movement was a protest against those responsible for the long years of deprivation of human rights, of humiliation and suffering—especially during the Great Proletarian Cultural Revolution. The victims of injustice, and their supporters, rose to confront the authorities and expose their immorality, incompetence, corruption, and abuse of power. People demanded that wrongs be righted, and that the reputations and positions of mistreated individuals be restored. They visited government offices and resorted to all available means to publicize their complaints. But in a positive sense, the movement pointed to the future, to the day when China would be at peace with itself and the world. On that day, China would be a fully modern nation, not only economically but also politically, for the people would then enjoy a full range of civil liberties and thus be in control of their government rather than vice versa.

But the movement, at least in its unrestrained form, proved short-lived. Indeed, almost as soon as the first journals hit the streets there were signs of an impending crackdown. As winter turned to spring, more and more dissidents were arrested. The government-controlled press took to the offensive, attacking the whole idea of civil liberties as bourgeois and inapplicable to China. Eventually the movement was effectively suppressed. But fortunately the literature of the movement has survived. It tells us much about the range of opinion found among the Chinese people and reveals a rich texture of social thought that hitherto one could only guess existed. Although the present volume cannot document the whole panoply of ideas spawned by the movement, the essays which follow are a representative sample of the democrats' opinions regarding social, political, economic, and cultural goals for China.*

A number of relatively programmatic statements were produced, speaking to both concrete policy problems and lofty philosophical issues. The most succinct and broadly accepted statement is the Nineteen Points of the China Human Rights League (Document 16). In demanding civil liberties and economic rights, the league takes a remarkably cosmopolitan position, quite at odds with the narrow nationalism that has characterized much of Chinese political thought in modern times. Declaring solemnly that "we are citizens of the world," the broad and free international exchange of ideas and goods is urged, as well as the freedom to study, travel, and work abroad.

Other statements are even more militant. The manifesto of the Thaw Society (Document 15) is sharply critical not only of traditional Chinese political culture but also of Marxism and Mao Zedong's teachings. For meeting the needs of the nation, the Thaw Society proposes the adoption of new philosophical, political, economic, and ethical systems, based on the teachings of the founder of the Chinese Republic, Sun Yat-sen. The group is also partial to Rousseau's concepts of human rights and to Christian civilization, the latter because of its doctrines of peace, forgiveness, tolerance, and love.

However, the purpose of this introduction is not to convey the content of the documents in this volume, but rather to provide information necessary to their understanding. We shall first sketch the historical background and contemporary context of the democratic movement, then trace the movement itself from its beginnings to its suppression, and finally give our own assessment of its meaning. The documents will speak for themselves.

Historical background. Traditional Chinese politics is invariably described as authoritarian. Although this view is not incorrect, it would be a mistake to assume that the Chinese have always been content to be despotically ruled. On the contrary, China has a strong tradition of resistance to oppression, and a substantial body of protest literature.[6] Furthermore, traditional Chinese culture was not without some element of liberalism and sanction of popular assertiveness. Village politics was generally

---

* This book is concerned with the "fifth modernization"—politics and certain aspects of political economy. However, it should be pointed out that the 1978–79 thaw was broader than this in scope. There were, for example, significant developments in the visual arts and literature (including science fiction).[4] Also, various issues which we would probably think of as nonpolitical came in for discussion. An example was the call for sexual liberation.[5]

less despotic than national politics, and even national politics enjoyed some "constitutional" constraints and legitimate liberalism. Among China's authentic heroes were men who bravely stood up to challenge authority. Sometimes these were generals or rebels, but often they were political figures working within the system.

The culture tended to sanction such behavior. To be sure, the philosophy of Legalism was often little more than a rationale for totalitarian rule. But Legalism did not prevail, and the most popular schools of thought, such as that based on the teachings of Mencius, were much more benign. The Taoists were often philosophical anarchists who advocated a kind of laissez-faire in both politics and economics. Confucianism is more difficult to categorize, but many Confucianists (of which Mencius was one) inclined more toward liberalism than authoritarianism.[7] Most notable in this respect was the seventeenth-century scholar-official Huang Zongxi. Huang, whose father had been a victim of political persecution, was a strong advocate of the rule of law.

> Only if there are good laws will there be leaders who govern well. Inasmuch as "unlawful laws" fetter people hand and foot, even a person who might be capable of governing well is likely to be suspicious and arbitrary. Of course, a *good* leader will realize the full intent of the law anyway; what law would do additionally is prevent the human suffering which results from rule by tyrants. Thus, I say that only good laws will ensure good rulers.[8]

In the notion of "unlawful laws" one can almost see the seeds of modern constitutionalism, which would have checked arbitrary government and thus protected the citizenry. Unfortunately, the seeds never sprouted and (not coincidentally) Confucianism began to die.

The demise of Confucianism was occasioned (but not caused) by the advent of Western imperialism. This was unfortunate timing, because it gave rise to opposition to the West and everything it stood for. True, many of the new breed of intellectuals were educated in Western schools and came to appreciate the view that individualism can unleash a dynamic which can enrich the total society.[9] And Woodrow Wilson's Fourteen Points convinced many that China need no longer fear imperialism. But in the wake of the "betrayal" at Versailles, and also under the influence of the Russian Revolution, many Chinese came to believe in a future shorn of Western-style liberalism.

These crosscurrents came together, and then parted, during the movement which took its name from the demonstrations of 4 May 1919. The immediate impetus of the May Fourth Movement was the Chinese government's failure to stand up to Japan and the West and obtain the nation's due in the World War I settlement. But the movement developed into an intellectual renaissance, a period of the free exchange of ideas. What these various ideas were need not concern us here,[10] but it is important to note that Chinese of all political orientations look back upon this liberal period with nostalgia. The authors of the documents in this volume often refer to the May Fourth Movement, in the apparent belief that China again needs a period of intellectual ferment and exploration, free from the stultifying effects of imposed ideology.[11]

Neither the Chinese Nationalists (Kuomintang), who reigned until 1949, nor the Communists, who ruled thereafter, showed much interest in promoting civil liberties or establishing the rule of law. However, many leaders (including Mao Zedong) indicated that they realized the price China was paying (economically and otherwise) for the lack of free expression. Thus, the heavy repression of the early 1950s[12] was gradually eased, and in 1957 there was a "blooming of the hundred flowers." Mao's intention was to have a period of freer expression which would help the Communist Party to correct some of its internal shortcomings. At the same time, the older "bourgeois" intellectuals would be encouraged to play a greater role in the nation's economic and cultural development. However, it soon became apparent that there was greater disenchantment with the new order than had been realized, and so there followed a renewed repression in the form of the Anti-Rightist Campaign. Hundreds of thousands were imprisoned or otherwise punished—some until the 1978–79 thaw.

The next period of relatively open politics was the Great Proletarian Cultural Revolution, which began in 1966.[13] This time it was not the older intellectuals who spoke out, but rather the younger people who considered themselves good communists. These people, often organized into bands of Red Guards, were determined to wage Mao's war against Soviet-style politics and economics ("revisionism"). In this, they had the blessing not only of Chairman Mao but also of four powerful leaders: Mao's wife Jiang Qing, journalist Yao Wenyuan, army commissar Zhang Chunqiao, and the young rising star, Wang Hongwen. These leaders (who would later be denounced as the "Gang of Four") and their radical followers plunged the nation into bloody chaos, costing the lives of at least 400,000 people.[14] Once again, an attempt to open the political system failed to lead to the hoped-for benefits.

Thus, it was during the Hundred Flowers period and the Cultural Revolution that China enjoyed the freest flow of information and ideas. True, those who sought to express themselves did not often have access to the press and radio. However, there was one medium that was available to anyone who could write and was possessed of a modicum of courage. Although the wall poster predated Communist rule in China, the medium came into its own as an important means of political communication only around 1957. By now most Chinese were literate, and many were curious for more information and analysis than was available in the usually sterile official press. At the same time, the more radical elements in the Party found posters a useful way to mobilize the population. Free from the constraints and vested interests of professional journalists, posters were seen as a way to "undercut the bourgeoisie,"[15] even though they were more difficult to censor than newspapers and the broadcast media. Under the influence of Mao and his followers, the country sometimes almost seemed to be papered over with them. This was especially true during the 1958 post-Hundred Flowers movement, and again during the Cultural Revolution. Some posters were spontaneous, some were part of orchestrated campaigns. Because factions would resort to poster writing to wage political warfare against each other, politics sometimes became relatively open—at least if one could understand the arcane language often employed. Still, writers of offending posters were always subject to arrest, and the medium was never truly free until the winter of 1978–79.[16]

Two developments in the mid-1970s deserve to be highlighted. First was the appearance in Guangzhou (Canton) in November 1974 of what became a famous essay. Entitled "On Socialist Democracy and the Legal System," the series of posters was signed with the collective pen name "Li-Yi-Zhe." The writers used the current campaign against the late Lin Biao as a vehicle to demand the rule of law and democratic government.[17] "The masses," said Li-Yi-Zhe, "demand democracy and a socialist legal system. They demand revolutionary rights and human rights." These, it was explained, were necessary to protect the masses from the inflictions of arbitrary despots. Li-Yi-Zhe condemned the prevailing system, under which "shackles, barred windows, leather whips and bullets" awaited those who spoke out. In the summer of 1968 in their province alone, they said, more than a million people had been "imprisoned, put under control, or struggled against." Accused persons, they complained, were not allowed fair trials. "When authorities fail to produce evidence, even after protracted periods of imprisonment and licentious maltreatment, they confuse a clear case until it becomes an unresolvable mess, and then use this as an excuse to perpetuate the case. Political detention camps (which one of the writers knew from personal experience) were described as "scumhole cow pens."[18] Unsurprisingly, the authors were arrested, and a massive campaign was waged against them. They did not regain their freedom until the time of the 1978–79 democratic movement, which they had helped to inspire.[19]

In 1976 the deaths of Premier Zhou Enlai and Chairman Mao Zedong occurred. During the course of the year a bitter power struggle took place, and until autumn it appeared that Deng Xiaoping, the leading moderate, would be the loser. On April 5, during the Qing-ming festival, there was a violent demonstration at Tian-an-men Square in Beijing (see Document 67). According to some reports, hundreds of thousands of citizens participated.[20] Although the April Fifth Movement, as it came to be known, spread to many parts of the country, it was quickly repressed, with many of its participants arrested as "counterrevolutionaries."[21] The original purpose of the April Fifth Movement was to commemorate Zhou Enlai. However, official accounts later claimed that its target were the leftist leaders then in control of the government. (Two days after the incident it was announced that they had dismissed Deng Xiaoping from all of his posts.) But the writers of the essays in this volume have a somewhat different interpretation of the events. For these people, April Fifth marked the opening salvo of China's democratic movement.[22]

The Context. Both as a protest against the deprivation of rights and freedoms, and as a program for the future, the democratic movement was closely related to the rapidly changing political scene in China in 1978. Certainly it was linked to the struggle for power within the Chinese Communist Party. But more fundamentally, at issue was the question of what developmental strategy the nation should pursue. By now, Deng Xiaoping had been rehabilitated and held the vice-premiership. His political platform was built upon the Four Modernizations—the drive to upgrade China's agriculture, industry, defense, and science and technology. This signified a sharp break with the leftists and the politics of the Cultural Revolution, and many democratic activists supported him. Thus, early in the democratic movement, Deng gave encouragement to many of these dissidents, at least in part to increase his leverage against his rivals in the Party hierarchy.

These developments took place against the background of an extremely complex situation. Put simply, even though the radicals (officially dubbed the "Gang of Four") had been removed from all top positions, they still had many sympathizers in the Party and bureaucracy. Deng Xiaoping needed to consolidate his political base and strive for political unity. In March 1978 a new constitution was promulgated, once again promising popular participation in public affairs and more rights and freedoms for the citizenry.[23] An ambitious ten-year economic plan was adopted, which heralded "tremendous economic and technological change" and a better life for the people.[24] Within the span of a few months, a series of important national conferences were held on such subjects as science and education.

But before China could get moving forward again, a change in the nation's intellectual and emotional climate would be required. Thus, in May, Deng issued a challenge to leftist ideologues by boldly proclaiming "practice" to be the sole criterion for testing truth. As a philosophical doctrine, this may not appear particularly sophisticated or exciting, but in the context of the times it had very serious implications. For Deng was implying nothing less than that the oracular Thought of Mao Zedong might not be sacrosanct after all, and at the very least it could be improved upon. Thus, in policy matters, Deng was seeking freedom from ideological constraints. But even this was not the biggest political gamble Deng took.

The most remarkable development to follow the death of Mao Zedong involved the rehabilitations of China's many political outcasts. Among these were perhaps 110,000 who had been imprisoned in labor camps since the 1957 Anti-Rightist Campaign. These people were often liberals with precisely the kind of professional experience Deng needed to realize his Four Modernizations. And there were many others—men and women who had made both rightist and leftist political "mistakes," and had been punished for them, some since the early 1950s. Of course, there were those who could only be rehabilitated posthumously; either they had died natural deaths or had been executed. But Deng insisted on setting the record straight for these people also, and the press was filled with belated obituaries of people who had been "persecuted to death." The leadership itself does not seem to have known how many people were to be affected by the "reversal of verdicts." Said Chief Justice Jiang Hua in October 1978: "We still have no accurate statistics on the exact number of unjust and wrong verdicts. But one thing is certain: the number of such verdicts is considerable."[25]

The rehabilitations were essential if Deng was to convince the Chinese people, and especially the intellectuals on whom the Four Modernizations would depend, that China was to become a land of law and respect for citizens' rights. But predictably, there was much resistance from the leftists. Many of these people still occupied the middle echelons and did not welcome their newly-rehabilitated colleagues. And for those leftists who had met with serious political troubles of their own, it was clear that there would be no "reversal of verdicts." Indeed, all during this period the government was busy herding them into prisons. Furthermore, there were many in the Party and bureaucracy who wondered what their fate would be after their victims reemerged. Reprisals from the latter were feared by local officials, who at the same time worried that, should the political winds shift back to the left, there would be charges of having "shielded bad elements," of undoing the accomplishments of the Cultural Revolution, or of "negating military control."[26] Reports of "lingering fear" came from all over the country.[27] Nonetheless, Deng continued to insist that the victims' names be cleared and that they (like Deng himself) be restored to their position in society.

By the fall of 1978, the pace of Deng's political maneuverings quickened noticeably. In mid-November, the Beijing Communist Party Committee announced its long-awaited judgment on the Tian-an-men Incident, which was now declared to have been a "revolutionary act of the masses."* This completely reversed a two-year-old decision of the Politburo. The new judgment was taken as a signal that the changes for which the Tian-an-men demonstrators had struggled were finally at hand.

Before turning to the democratic movement itself, however, more needs to be said concerning the environment in which it took place. For one thing, political stability within the Party was not easily achieved. The big question was: Would Deng be able to move fast enough to retain the support of the public, without moving so far to the right that Party members and cadres (often Cultural Revolution recruits) would become altogether alienated? In December it became clear that this shrewd politician had succeeded. The Third Plenum of the Eleventh Central Committee marked the consolidation of Deng's forces and the final acceptance of the Four Modernizations as the blueprint for China's future. Deng managed to avoid a confrontation with his nominal superior, Chairman Hua Guofeng, while he packed key Party positions with Deng men like Chen Yun, Hu Yaobang, and Wang Zhen. Old disputes between Deng and the leftists were resolved in his favor, and "practice," rather than radical ideology, was certified as the "sole criterion for testing truth."

Thus, whereas Mao Zedong would have insisted on "politics in command," it was now to be economics in command. The economy, the Party leadership asserted, was to be managed sensibly and rationally, in accordance with economic laws, and with emphasis on incentives, productivity, and the use of new technology. The managers, workers, and peasants were all promised more freedom and material rewards so that they would work hard for the state.[28] And for the first time, Western nations and Japan were assigned a significant role in aiding China's economic development.

This brings us to foreign affairs, and here Deng's performance was especially striking. His role in the final stage of the successful negotiations with the United States in establishing full diplomatic relations, and the announcement of his scheduled visit to the United States, further enhanced his influence and prestige. No less remarkable was the break with Albania, which had been China's only real ally during the Cultural

---

* Seven months earlier, on the eve of the second anniversary of the April Fifth demonstrations, a few posters had appeared, atacking leftist Beijing Mayor Wu De for his role in the earlier suppression.

Revolution. Now the way was paved for the final rapprochement with the most liberal of communist countries, Yugoslavia. These foreign policy developments were to have considerable impact on the democratic movement. It is no coincidence that the two countries most favorably mentioned in dissident writings were the United States and Yugoslavia. This was in part out of conviction, in part out of certain misconceptions of how life really is in these countries,* and in part because these were the "safest" foreign models to laud, now that the government's relations with the two countries were so friendly.

At home, Deng Xiaoping pushed ahead to broaden the base of political support, particularly among those to the right of China's political center. (The attacks on and arrests of leftists continued.) The campaign to reverse verdicts went on. More and more Party and government leaders were restored to their former positions of influence and power, including Peng Zhen, a former member of the Political Bureau and mayor of Beijing, and Lu Dingyi, former deputy prime minister. During the New Year's celebration they appeared at the Great Hall of the People—with none other than Wang Guangmei, the widow of the once infamous chief of state, Liu Shaoqi.

The Party leadership also decided to make concessions to the business class, former landlords, and rich peasants, so that they would contribute to the modernization effort. At a meeting in Beijing with two hundred former entrepreneurs, Ulanhu (Ulanfu), a Politburo member and head of the United Front Department, told them that their assets and bank deposits would be returned with interest, their professional titles would be restored, and their children would not suffer discrimination in schools and jobs.[29] Likewise, the former landlords and rich peasants could reclaim their "citizens' rights." It was explained that most of them "have undergone remolding through manual labor for two or three decades, and the great majority of them have become laboring people who earn their own living." Therefore, "if they have not engaged in misdeeds," their punitive designations as landlords, rich peasants, counterrevolutionaries, and bad elements should be removed, and they should be treated as equals.[30]

In the pursuit of economic and technological cooperation with foreign nations, the government bureaucrats acted with zeal. Hardly a day went by without the announcement of some kind of joint project or plan to

---

* Many of the dissident writers either mention Yugoslavia favorably or sound very much like Milovan Djilas. (Wei Jingsheng is an example of the latter.) A few months after the democratic movement was suppressed in China, Djilas was returned to prison in Yugoslavia. The Chinese writers seem unaware of the true state of civil liberties in that country.

import new technology. Japan, the United States, and European countries all vied to do business with China. Credit in the billions was negotiated. The best-known commercial proposals included a hotel chain involving Pan American Airways, the importing of Coca-Cola, and the building by the Japanese of a giant steel complex near Shanghai.* Chinese military delegations were also dispatched to inspect sophisticated weapon systems in Europe, giving hints that China was about to purchase arms.

All in all, the effect of Deng's leadership and policies was unmistakable. People felt freer and more relaxed, and to a limited degree, lived better. They had more consumer goods available to them, and now more people could see foreign movies. They could indulge in their choice of hairstyles and perhaps have some say in decisions affecting their education and jobs. In many cities, Western-style clothing, as well as dancing parties, were the craze, especially among youth. Foreigners were sought after as friends—something unthinkable during the previous xenophobic decades.

Thus was the stage set for the launching of the democratic movement.

The Outbreak.   The movement had its beginnings in November 1978 when a spate of posters appeared in Beijing. Many of the posters told of the humiliation and suffering people had experienced at the hands of the Party and bureaucrats. There was expressed a deep sense of resentment against the political persecutions of the Cultural Revolution and a strong yearning for rights and freedoms. Some posters appeared to reflect divisions within the Party leadership. For example, one accused Mao of "metaphysical thinking" in his later years and asserted that the radical group had made use of him to purge Deng after the 1976 Tian-an-men Incident. Then, two posters called for an investigation of this incident so that those responsible for the suppression and cover-up could be brought to justice. The investigation, it was said, should be completely impartial and undertaken by a committee drawn from all major organs of the Party and state. Such posters clearly supported Deng and were implicitly a challenge to Chairman Hua Guofeng, who was implicated in the 1976 suppression.

Before the end of the month, the movement had spread to far-flung parts of the country. For example, in Guiyang, in a remote part of southern China, posters appeared praising American-style democracy. It was charged that China's development had been stymied by superstition, whereas the United States, which had no idols or superstition, had enjoyed

---

* In the end, almost all of these projects were scaled down, delayed, or abandoned entirely.

two centuries of progress. Representatives of the Guiyang group traveled to Beijing where they told a European diplomat: "Everyone in China knew that the Cultural Revolution was a period of fascist dictatorship, but at that time no one dared say it. Now we want real freedom, human rights and democracy." He and others also expressed great enthusiasm for Deng and goodwill toward America and Great Britain.[31]

Toward the end of November, two public rallies for democracy and human rights took place in Beijing. On November 27, a group of people gathered at what was becoming known as "Democracy Wall" on Changan Avenue.* The American journalist Robert Novak had promised to report to them on an interview he was to hold with Deng Xiaoping. Novak did not keep his appointment with the demonstrators, but he sent a colleague who announced that Deng had declared the posters "a good thing." This drew a cheer from the group. But spirits were dampened considerably when it was also announced that Deng had termed some of the statements in the posters incorrect and, in particular, had considered certain criticisms of Mao unfair.[32] The crowd, now numbering between three and four thousand, nonetheless proceeded to march to the Monument to the Heroes of the People at Tian-an-men Square. The atmosphere was joyful and festive. The crowd shouted slogans in praise of Deng Xiaoping, the late Zhou Enlai, and even Hua Guofeng. A participant observed, "This is the first time in the history of People's China that a spontaneous demonstration like this has been held."

Two days later, more than ten thousand people turned out at Democracy Wall to read posters and listen to speakers. They again marched to the monument at Tian-an-men. Speakers calling for democracy and human rights were cheered. An excited young man in the crowd said to a foreigner, "You are witnessing the greatest thing to happen in China."[33]

What was the reaction of the Communist Party to these developments? The left was not heard from, but we can surmise that its views were a mixture of chagrin and jealousy that such bourgeois liberal phenomena were being tolerated and that, while the rights of the democratic activists were being respected, a repression of the left was underway.[34] But what counted

---

* "Democracy Wall" was a 200-yard brick wall surrounding a bus yard at the intersection of Changan Avenue and Xidan Street in downtown Beijing. Thus, it was often called "Xidan Democracy Wall." Comparable materials appeared elsewhere in Beijing, including Tian-an-men, Wang-fu-jing, and Tai-ji-chang.

On 6 December 1979, the authorities ceased permitting the posting of unofficial material on these walls. Thereafter, Beijing's dissident posters were only to be permitted in Yuetan Park, a residential area three miles west of the center of town. However, the following month Deng Xiaoping announced that the constitutional provision guaranteeing the right to put up posters would be abrogated altogether.

was the view of the Deng group, and for the time being the vice-premier was taking a benign view. In late November he insisted that the unofficial media would be permitted to flourish, notwithstanding any minor embarrassments that they might entail. The right to publish by means of wall posters, he pointed out, was guaranteed by the Constitution. Foreigners might be titillated by them, but nonetheless he had no intention of suppressing the authors or denying the rights of the masses to express their views. "Sometimes it is necessary for us to be urged along by them."[35]

Conversely, it is quite possible that the democrats, or certain elements among them, were being encouraged by one or more factions in the Communist Party, who may well have used the late–1978 wall posters to promote (or at least reflect) their interests in the ongoing struggle within the Party. It was at least convenient for Deng to have the democrats attacking his opponents on the left (though determining just how instrumental "public opinion" has ever been in Chinese politics is problematic*). Indeed, many of the ideas we attribute to the dissidents had actually been aired within Party circles before being plastered on Democracy Wall—particularly on such subjects as legal reform, free discussion, and curbing special privileges of cadres. Of course, there had been such talk many times before, but now those promoting these ideas within the Party could demonstrate that they were developments that a significant sector of the public eagerly desired. They were thus later emboldened to reproduce in the official press toned-down versions of what had appeared in the democrats' publications, thereby completing the cycle.

In short, there was a sort of symbiosis between Deng and the democrats. But in the long run their interests would necessarily diverge, for Deng was primarily interested in enhancing his political power and promoting economic development. The democrats were not fundamentally interested in enhancing anyone's political power and did not want to see

---

* The role of public opinion in dictatorships is one on which there is little agreement among political scientists. Some see it as negligible; others argue that it is essential in order for dictators to sense, manipulate, and take into account the national mood. Most would agree that the situation varies from country to country. There is one school of thought which holds that a certain amount of dissidence is functional from the standpoint of ruling elites. It may act as a kind of safety valve, trial balloon for new programs, or measuring instrument to let the regime know where it stands. It may also serve to legitimize the political system by demonstrating that the human rights provisions contained in almost all constitutions are not meaningless, and that the ruling group can permit some dissent without being threatened.

In China, popularity has always been important to the Communist leaders. In Deng Xiaoping's case, in particular, the wall posters and journals which are the subject of this book were certainly not harmful to his position, though the role they played in the inner-Party power relations lies beyond the scope of this work.

economic modernization divorced from political democratization. The message conveyed by the poster writers was clear. Reacting against the many years of political persecution, people were determined to achieve a modern political system based upon respect for human rights.

The High Tide. In the final weeks of 1978, simultaneously with Deng Xiaoping's apparent triumph, the democratic movement became increasingly visible and spread nationwide. Though the participants were from a wide variety of backgrounds, they had certain things in common. They were mostly men and women in their twenties and early thirties. None of them had a good education in a formal sense (such was not obtainable in China during the Cultural Revolution). None of them had been abroad, and only a few had any real familiarity with the West. Their "education" had been gained in the "school of hard knocks," and they knew much about the dark side of Chinese politics. Many of them had been victims of political persecution. From their personal experience, they were convinced that China needed a drastic change in the way politics was conducted, and that rights and freedoms were both desirable in themselves and essential for the nation's modernization. Thus, there were calls for various civil liberties (which had always been promised by China's various dormant constitutions). People demanded freedom of speech (see, for example, Document 17), freedom of the press (Document 18), freedom to read material of one's choice without harrassment (Document 19), freedom to send and receive mail without interference or censorship (Document 20), and the inviolability of the home from arbitrary invasion by the police (Document 21).

Not that they agreed on all issues. Their different social backgrounds, philosophical perspectives, and personalities affected their attitudes and positions to a substantial degree. From the beginning there were divisions over such issues as support for Marxism and Mao Zedong's Thought, assessment of Deng Xiaoping's policies, and the degree of militancy which should characterize the democratic movement itself. Hence, the latter became fragmented into more than a score of different organizations which never achieved more than loose coalition. Some of these organizations requested the authorities to recognize and support them materially—without success in almost all cases. Others worked with the peasants who came to Beijing to seek justice and the satisfaction of basic economic needs. And some linked up with activists elsewhere in the country, transmitting news of the movement to the provinces.

Although the medium with which the democratic movement was launched was the wall poster, by year's end many of the fledgling organizations were publishing journals. These were not only sold but were often affixed to walls, just as posters were. The journals were published without the formal approval of the authorities and under the most difficult of circumstances (see Document 61). Most dissidents were laborers, teachers, or clerks. The writers among them were only amateurs for whom it was not easy to find either the time or the money required to put out publications. Materials and equipment needed for printing were generally controlled by the authorities. Thus, most of the journals were poor mimeograph copies made from handwritten stencils, and they appeared very irregularly.

Nevertheless, the printed medium did have many advantages over posters. Not only was it conducive to more thorough explorations of complex questions, but it was easier and safer for a reader to take and read a journal in private than to risk being observed reading posters in public. And of course, a printed journal had a much wider readership than a poster could, though it is difficult to determine how many people read the dissident literature. The publication with the largest circulation was probably *Masses' Reference News* (see below), which was said to have printed twenty thousand copies of its January issue. Other journals certainly had much more limited runs (some of only a hundred or so), but copies tended to be passed from hand to hand, providing for a greatly expanded readership.[36]

The leading organizations and publications were *Exploration,* the Chinese Human Rights League, *Beijing Spring, April Fifth Forum,* the Enlightenment Society, the Thaw Society, *Today,* and the above-mentioned *Masses' Reference News.*[37]

Exploration was the most militant of all publications. It carried many articles highly critical of Marxist ideology and of the Chinese government. Included in its issues were several insightful articles on the subject of democracy and modernization (see especially Documents 12 and 30), shocking exposés of political prisons (Documents 54 and 55), and, just before the publication's demise, a direct attack on Deng Xiaoping (Document 51). The moving force behind *Exploration* was a twenty–nine–year–old man from Anhui Province, Wei Jingsheng.

Although Wei Jingsheng strikes us a typical (and classic) Chinese intellectual from a bureaucratically well-placed family, he was actually an electrician by trade. He was from a "good" family, meaning that his parents and their siblings were old revolutionary cadres. His father, a deputy director of the State Capital Construction Commission, was an ardent Maoist who had insisted that young Jingsheng memorize the Thoughts of the Master. If the boy did not learn a page a day, he received no dinner. It is small wonder that such a strict upbringing should produce a rebel, especially when the boy's mother seemed to convey a somewhat different message of kindness and compassion for the poor and unfortunate.

When the Cultural Revolution broke out in 1966, Wei Jingsheng was in his early teens. Like millions of his peers, he plunged into the revolutionary tempest. He was even received by Mao in one of his meetings with Red Guards. Being by virtue of family background "naturally red," he was able to join the United Action Committee, a Red Guard group composed of children of high-ranking government officials in Beijing. For a time this group was a power to be reckoned with in the capital. During the latter part of 1966, however, it was criticized and then suppressed by the Party's Cultural Revolution Group, headed by Chen Boda and Jiang Qing (Mao's wife). Wei was subsequently arrested and spent four months in jail.

After his release Wei was assigned to work as an electrician in the Beijing zoo. But his experience had left a profound effect upon him, and he undertook to study politics. For one thing, he sought evidence against leftists such as Jiang Qing. But he also read up on Marxism and socialist thought. Through family connections he had access to *Reference News,* the internal government publication normally unavailable to the public. Through this he was able to gain some understanding of international affairs and conditions in foreign countries.

In 1969 Wei enlisted in the army and was thus provided with an opportunity to travel around China and learn of conditions firsthand. When he was discharged four years later, he declined an opportunity to become an official and returned to his job at the zoo. But soon he was witness to the events of 5 April 1976, which we have described. These made a strong impression on Wei, and he became convinced that China wanted and needed a new kind of politics. He now began spending much of his time at the home of a Tibetan friend, where he wrote essays on the subject of democracy.*

Wei became the most outstanding individual spokesperson for the democratic movement. No one else could match the daring and sharpness of his writing. But he does not appear to have had a broad and solid base of political support. In contrast, the Chinese Human Rights League was a large coalition, and to the extent that the democratic movement ever spoke with one voice, the league was that voice. It was founded on 1 January 1979 in Beijing, and immediately published its famous Nineteen

---

* *New York Times,* 20 October 1979.

The name of this friend is unknown. The fact that she was a member of a minority nationality underscores the cosmopolitan nature of Wei's interests and concerns. It is unusual for a Han Chinese to socialize with other races.

Points (Document 16). This statement, and also an open letter to the government on the subject of legal reform (Document 23), made the league very well known.

In the beginning, the league lacked any outstanding or famous leaders. The first to achieve renown did so only through her being arrested—the first participant of the democratic movement known to have achieved this distinction. Fu Yuehua appears to have been a kindhearted and dedicated but otherwise undistinguished figure. She graduated from high school in 1968 and for a long time thereafter was unemployed. Finally, in 1972, she found a job as a construction worker. The next year, she reported, she was raped by a Party secretary. Although the case against the man was dismissed, Fu continued to insist upon his guilt. The whole episode converted her into a political activist. Thus, in the winter of 1978–79, when many peasants came to Beijing to register their complaints and seek justice,* her sympathies were with them. She identified their fate with hers and was determined to help them. She worked to organize them, and on January 8 they staged a remarkable demonstration, tying up traffic for an hour. (During her October trial, the judge declared that she must have been the demonstration's leader inasmuch as she had marched at its front. She replied: "If I had been in the back, you would be saying that I controlled it from behind a screen, and if I had been in the middle you would be saying that I was in the mainstream."[38] It was all more than the authorities could tolerate, for here, unmistakably, was the proletariat rising up against the self-styled "dictatorship of the proletariat."

The least "dissident" of the unofficial journals was *Beijing Spring*. It was rumored to have at least the tacit support of Deng Xiaoping. At any rate, it did receive assistance from the government's Foreign Languages Press and thus was able to print as many as ten thousand copies, which generally sold out quickly. The organ carried news, political commentaries, poetry, and stories.

Most of the people associated with *Beijing Spring* were young people who had taken part in the 1976 April Fifth demonstrations and suffered reprisals as a result. Indeed, many of them had met originally in prison, and their comradeship was later reinforced as they worked together to "reverse the verdicts." Among these were Han Zhixiong and Wang Jun-

---

* Numerous so-called "peasant demonstrations" occurred during these months. Most of the participants appear to have been genuine rural folk, but some appear to have been former urban youths who had been required to settle in the countryside. Now they returned (usually, illegally) to the cities, calling themselves peasants while they in fact sought to remain in cities. The term "peasant" in this book refers to both groups, as it is usually impossible for us to distinguish between them.

tao, both of whom became prominent in the Chinese Youth League, and poet Li Zhousheng.

The April Fifth Forum took its name from the 1976 incident, but was founded in November 1978. It was another moderate group, with its publication (of the same name) taking a middle position on the issues of the day. Committed to promoting democracy and human rights, it also tended to support Deng's economic programs. After the suppression of the movement, the forum continued to be an important source of information on the fates of the dissidents. The group, for example, revealed what transpired during the trial of Fu Yuehua in October 1979.[39]

The Enlightenment Society was founded by a group of former Red Guards who had been sent from various eastern cities to work in the inland provincial capital of Guiyang. There they typically served as either laborers or schoolteachers. The society took its name from European history and was very cosmopolitan in its outlook. It is perhaps best known for its letter to U.S. President Jimmy Carter, seeking the latter's support for their human rights cause (Document 57). Although the organization had a branch in the capital, it was the least Beijing-oriented of all the major democratic groups. Because it was relatively representative of China generally, a large number of the documents in this volume are drawn from the society's publication, *Enlightenment*. Their best known writer was Huang Xiang, the author of several epic poems (Documents 67, 68, 69).

The Enlightenment Society was not militant enough for some of its members, who formed a breakaway group called the Thaw Society. Its most prominent members were Li Jiahua and Lu Mang.

Whereas the above organizations and publications were founded by young people with limited formal education, there was one publication which owed its existence to a Beijing University professor, Xia Sunjian. Xia's journal was called *Masses' Reference News,* the title taken from the government's internal *Reference News.* Xia supported Deng and the Four Modernizations, and the war against Vietnam. His journal deplored the emergence of "radicals" in the democratic movement who were attempting to achieve democracy overnight. Democracy, it was pointed out, had taken Western nations centuries to achieve.

Finally, *Today* was a literary review published by a group of amateur writers in their late twenties and early thirties. The publication was dedicated to the promotion of a literature which reflected the spirit of the new era. It featured poetry, short stories, literary criticism, and translations from foreign works. The short stories usually depicted life during the Cultural Revolution.

A further word is in order concerning the relationship between the democratic movement in the capital and the movement nationally. As we have indicated, although it was Beijing that was always in the limelight, the movement was by no means limited to that city. What was crucial was the interaction between the capital and the provinces. Thus, while developments in late 1978 were largely confined to Beijing, people around the country soon began picking up on its themes. They also introduced new themes, such as freedom of residence and the right to adequate food.

In late December, a group of twenty-eight youths who had come from southernmost Yunnan Province gathered at Tian-an-men and distributed leaflets about their plight. They claimed to speak on behalf of fifty thousand people who had been sent from the cities to work on state farms. The conditions on these farms were described as intolerable, with the exiled citizens being "cheated and oppressed" by the local authorities.[40]

Then, on January 8, as we have noted, several thousand farmers from various provinces marched through the capital under the leadership of Fu Yuehua. They demanded democracy, human rights, and most of all, food. It presented a moving scene—as grim and solemn as earlier demonstrations by Beijing youth had been festive. The farmers' banners read, "We don't want hunger," "We don't want to suffer any more," and "We want human rights and democracy." They said they had been mistreated by insensitive local officials and appealed to Deng Xiaoping for help. His answer, as we shall see, was to arrest their leader.[41] In frustration and anger, the farmers took to the streets again, although in smaller numbers. A hundred or so shouted, "We are tired of being hungry," and "Down with oppression." At one point they attempted to enter Zhong-nan-hai, the residential compound of top officials, and confront Hua Guofeng with their grievances. They were held back by military guards, who were quickly reinforced. The demonstration drew about a thousand onlookers. The farmers announced that they would not leave the capital until they had been able to present their demands to Hua or otherwise achieve satisfactory results.

By the end of January an astonishing thirty thousand or more farmers had trekked to Beijing to protest living conditions and seek help. While there, they survived as best they could, sleeping at the railroad station or in other public buildings. Although the government did not generally interfere with them, the winter weather was bitter, with the temperatures dipping to –20 degrees centigrade. Eight people died from cold and hunger. In the words of Agence France Presse reporter Georges Biannic, many of the demonstrators "were straight out of a Goya painting—sick, on crutches, dressed in rags and tatters, and wretchedly poverty-stricken."[42]

Elsewhere in the nation the movement made its presence felt. Urban youths who had once been settled in the countryside and had returned home (often illegally) demanded the right to live and work in the major cities. In Shanghai, several thousand of them marched on the local Party headquarters, besieging it for several hours. As the winter wore on, the demands escalated, but the authorities, were unable or unwilling to meet them. Riots occurred, resulting in injury to some officials, damage to public property, and disruption of transportation. But what drew international attention was the demonstration on March 16 on the occasion of the Boston Symphony Orchestra's first China concert. Once more, the returned youth insisted on the right to resettle in the city. To foreign bystanders they announced that they wanted to see Mayor Peng Chong to demand that he implement Central Committee instructions on improving living conditions. They said that they were seeking to better not only their own situations, but also those of people who had been sent off to remote areas a decade earlier and were still there.

In Hangzhou, dozens of posters appeared in the wake of the Third Plenum of the Eleventh Central Committee. One called for unofficial meetings to be held to discuss democracy, the problems of political persecution, and poor local leadership. It was asserted that people had the constitutional right to discuss openly the affairs of state. Another poster demanded "the right to live as human beings." It said that the people should be guaranteed three meals a day, and that "when one finally turns thirty and can get married, it should be possible to have a small room with a bed." The complaint was made that too much of a person's limited leisure time was taken up with politics. "There should be a social life other than meetings." A third poster criticized Mao Zedong. "It would be un-Marxist to expect a revolutionary leader to be free of any shortcomings. . . . Chairman Mao was our leader, but after all, did he not have his faults? Did his instructions not contain mistakes?"[43]

In Guangzhou (Canton), posters appeared demanding a review of the Li-Yi-Zhe case. Students, workers, and professional people also published a number of unofficial journals. The best known of these was the *Voice of the People,* which supported socialism and also advocated human rights and a viable legal system. There were also demands that the three local Li-Yi-Zhe heroes, whose cases we have discussed above, be released from custody. One poster asked, If verdicts on high-echelon individuals could be reversed, why not those which had been meted out to lesser souls? Around the first of the year, the three were indeed freed and subsequently fully rehabilitated. On April 1, the local journal *Future* sponsored an officially-approved meeting at which Wang Xizhe of the Li-Yi-Zhe group spoke. Wang praised Deng Xiaoping as a great revolutionary statesman and urged everyone to fight for the people's welfare and democratic rights.[44] But events elsewhere in the country indicated that it was now too late.

The Crackdown.   In a sense, the suppression of the democratic movement was under way from the very beginning. As early as November there were unpublished instructions to the effect that people should stop mounting posters critical of Hua, and that there should not be inflammatory demonstrations calling for democracy. This may all have been part of the tug-of-war between Deng and his rivals within the Party; and the democratic movement was not immediately affected. But, by January, Deng's rivals were no longer in a position to trouble him, whereas the democratic movement had achieved such momentum that it was a phenomenon to be contended with. There were signs that the Party was divided on how to deal with the problem, but before Deng's trip to the United States it was decided to take action.

In the early morning of January 18, plainclothes police went to the home of Fu Yuehua and took her away, ostensibly for questioning. The next day her father inquired about her at the Public Security Bureau, which denied knowing about the case. Only toward the end of the month did the government concede that she had been "provided with shelter for the purpose of investigation"—a euphemism for detention.[45]

The reaction to the news of her arrest was dramatic. Immediately posters appeared denouncing the arrest and demanding not only that she be released but also that her captors be punished. Her most emphatic defenders were *Exploration* and, of course, her own Human Rights League. On February 8, a number of democratic activists presented themselves as journalists at the police station where Fu had first been taken. The group raised questions about the legality of her arrest, and the police officer in charge, somewhat annoyed, questioned their right to inquire into the matter (Document 64).

But more arrests followed, and there were other signs of growing official hostility toward the movement. Before a meeting of the Municipal Communist Party Committee, a high-ranking leader accused the democrats of banding together to create disturbances, of publishing "underground literature" with the aid of foreigners, and of "impairing the state system." Such people, it was warned, needed to be reeducated. In response, protests appeared in various democratic organs, including one joint statement by seven of the groups (Document 62). *Exploration* rebutted the attack point by point, not only defending civil liberties but praising foreign observers who had shown interest in the movement.[46] This view was echoed by a poster writer: "Foreigners . . . who care about the democratic movement and show sympathy and real interest are the true friends of the Chinese people. . . . We thank them from the bottom of our heart."[47]

The democrats' valiant self-defense, however, did not deter the authorities. Instead, in the wake of the disturbances in Shanghai, the government was determined to prevent a breakdown in social order and was seeking ways to establish political stability. The bitter memories of the chaotic Cultural Revolution haunted the leadership. Least of all could anarchy be afforded at a moment when war with Vietnam was imminent. Thus asserted *People's Daily*: "We want a kind of democracy that will benefit the majority of people. It must promote socialism, normal social order, productive relations, and normal working conditions." The paper condemned those who had taken advantage of democracy to damage the public interest. These people could not be tolerated; they should be punished according to the law."[48]

On March 16, at a meeting of Party leaders, the vice-premier finally had his word. Deng declared that some people had simply gone too far in their demands, and he especially attacked those who had complained to Americans about China's human rights violations. But he stopped short of calling for suppression of the whole movement. "Everyone says that we should disband the human rights organizations, forbid people to attack the Party, and close down Democracy Wall. My opinion is that we should let people put up posters. Whether the poster movement survives or dies out naturally, we can avoid making the masses angry with us."[49]

Whatever Deng's real intentions, the bureaucrats had heard enough and launched an all-out attack against the dissidents, with *People's Daily* blazing the way. Whereas in January the paper had been saying, "Let the people say what they wish; the heavens will not fall," it now lashed out against those whom it labeled "counterrevolutionaries." "Where there is proof against people, we shall deal with them according to law. Where we should arrest, we shall arrest. Where we should hold an open trial, we shall do so. We cannot be weak."[50] *Workers' Daily* argued that human rights were already respected in socialist countries, and that no domestic campaign or foreign help was required to secure them.[51] But most of the press took a harder line than *Workers' Daily*. *Beijing Daily* insisted: "We should not take the worn-out weapon of human rights—which has long been window-dressing for reactionary bourgeois dictators—as a remedy for the problems of a socialist country."[52] The newspaper of the Youth League agreed, calling human rights and individual freedom outdated notions, and accusing the late liberal philosopher Hu Shih of having parroted American reactionary pragmatism.[53] In May, the Party theoretical journal *Red Flag* summed it all up by condemning the democratic movement for promoting bourgeois freedom and individualism, for desiring to eliminate class struggle and Party leadership, and even for violating China's dignity and national sovereignty. In short, the journal questioned the progressiveness and patriotism of any person who deemed civil liberties appropriate for China.[54]

In the face of this challenge, the democratic groups failed to draw together and make a common response. Rather, the pressures opened new fissures among them. Some people were utterly unyielding. Wei Jingsheng saw the issues in Manichean terms: One had to choose between democracy or autocracy, it was as simple as that. Wei accused Deng of manipulating the people by taking advantage of the trust they had placed in him; he saw a danger that Deng might yet become a Mao-style dictator. A political leader, Wei wrote, must not be trusted blindly. He must be judged by his policies and their impact on the people. In short, democracy, while most difficult to achieve, was the only viable way for China (Document 51).

But many took a different view.* In particular, the April Fifth Forum defended Deng and his policies, arguing that both his past history and present attitude showed him not to have been a dictator. Criticism of a leader is everyone's right, the forum acknowledged, but in this case it was misdirected, for it had been middle-level and lower-level cadres who were most responsible for obstructionism and other problems. At any rate, given the serious economic difficulties facing the country, Deng merited support. The people should be patient and avoid doing anything that might damage the national interest (Document 52).

Meanwhile, a series of events had begun which would crush the democratic movement. On March 29, Wei Jingsheng was imprisoned, later to be sentenced to fifteen years as a counterrevolutionary.† In April, police

---

* One first-hand observer maintains that the moderate view was much more popular than Wei's militancy. Wei is said to have been derided in strong, sometimes obscene language.[55] However, when *Exploration* reappeared in the fall of 1979, it was reported to have the largest circulation of any of the alternative publications. Even though no longer edited by Wei Jingsheng, it was still quite militant (Agence France Presse, 2 October 1979; translation: JPRS 74532).

† Wei Jingsheng was also convicted of "supplying a foreigner with Chinese military intelligence" pertaining to the Sino-Vietnam war. In his defense, he reportedly argued that he had obtained the information from published sources. According to one account, the foreign journalist involved had asked the Foreign Ministry about the information, and there was no objection to its being reported. For additional information about the charges, *see Washington Post*, 31 October 1979, and *Far Eastern Economic Review*, 26 October 1979.

An interesting article by Wei which is not included in the present volume is "The Origins of Juvenile Delinquency in Today's China: A Bit of Truth from the Cultural Revolution." The piece was summarized by Meilinda Liu in "Wei and the Fifth Modernization," *Far Eastern Economic Review*, 2 November 1979.

arrested many others, including the deputy chairman of the Human Rights League, Ren Wanding. (Ren was arrested while he and others were in the act of posting a statement at Tian-an-men. The poster maintained that in suppressing the movement the bureaucracy and its "masters" were in fact protecting their vested interests.) Democratic elements were also the objects of various acts of harrassment. Some of the organizations, headquarters were subjected to warrantless searches by police. Individuals were summoned for consultations with their employers. Even the two journals which had been least critical of Deng Xiaoping were forced to suspend publication. Foreign Languages Press denied any further help in the printing of *Beijing Spring*, and *Masses' Reference News* announced that it would stop publishing due to "objective conditions."[56]

On April 1 the new policy concerning wall posters and demonstrations was made known. Among other things, it was stipulated that posters would only be permitted in designated places (where police could observe participants), and that any posters, publications, or rallies deemed anti-government or anti-Party were banned. The public was asked to help the public security apparatus to enforce this, and violators were threatened with detention, supervised labor, or criminal penalties.[57] On the same day, workers were dispatched to remove posters from central Beijing.

The democrats were not easily daunted, as is illustrated by the case of Ren Wanding. Shortly before his arrest, Ren remarked: "If no one utters a word, no one will know. If we don't speak out, we shall not be able to look our readers in the eye. They would not understand."[58] *Exploration* was even more defiant. The Party decision, it declared, "only demonstrates to the whole world that the Chinese government does not want any democratic freedom. The so-called true democracy and freedom they talk about is only [propaganda] to bolster the prestige of the authorities in power. . . . Any criticism is fiercely suppressed as contrary to socialism and to the dictatorship of the proletariat. What brutal hypocrisy!"[59] A Human Rights League poster, in response to claims that the democratic movement was "bourgeois," challenged Party theorists "to analyze the concrete demands of the democratic movement to ascertain whether it represents the interests of the bourgeoisie or those of the people."[60]

From the very beginning of the democratic movement participants had looked ahead to the day in the spring which would mark the third anniversary of the April Fifth demonstrations. The human rights movement would then "explode like a bomb," in the words of one poster writer.[61] But 5 April 1979 came and went with a deafening silence. Although crowds did gather at Tian-an-men, the daring spirit was gone. With many of the movement's leaders jailed, the liberals had been effectively suppressed. Nonetheless, speakers bravely held out hope for the future. The remarks of one young man convey the sense of defiance and hope: "People say that the situation is tense, and that the democratic movement has met with setbacks. But the movement has not died. . . . People have now learned how to think and how to judge; no one can trick them again."[62]

It had evidently been Deng Xiaoping's original conviction that democratization should be very limited and would be merely a tool to get his Four Modernizations off the ground. When and if political stability was threatened, he would always be ready to curtail it. The young men and women in the movement had a different perspective from his. They insisted that economic modernization gains a nation little if the culture and political system remains, as they put it, "feudal." Here they could cite recent developments in Iran (Document 29), but they were also taking a leaf from Mao Zedong's book. Thus, they were determined to see populism rather than bureaucratism prevail. They believed that true popularly-based government could not exist without genuine liberalization. There needed to be a free flow of ideas and information, with individuals permitted to arrive at their own political judgments. Here the democrats were breaking new ground. While private freedom would encourage creativity and thus have economic payoffs, civil liberties were seen as having a validity and legitimacy of their own. They are inalienable, not within any leader's power to grant or deny. The activists also condemned official lawlessness and abuse of power, and demanded a genuine legal system. Government must live up to its constitutional responsibilities and be accountable to the people. It had no higher duty than to protect civil liberties and human dignity.

Deng Xiaoping, on the other hand, was primarily concerned with the Four Modernizations and his own political career. Human rights were ornaments that should deck politics only to the extent that they had the desired effect. There could be no thought of sharing power with elements outside the Party. In demanding a pluralistic society, the democrats were touching Leninism at its core. But some, of course, were more provocative than others.

Wei Jingsheng was certainly the purest of them all. As a Hong Kong observer put it, "If Li-Yi-Zhe had pioneered in dissecting and criticizing the bureaucratic totalitarian system, Wei Jingsheng was the first to break through the ideological confines of that system and declare war on communist theory."[63] Indeed, in refreshingly clear and precise prose, he wrote about remaking the social system so that China could progress both politically and economically. He foresaw a better life for the people, but only when the nation was free of communist ideology and one-party rule. He not only condemned the dictatorship of Mao Zedong, but he rejected all utopianism, which he saw as a vehicle for manipulating and deceiving the public.

But most of the other dissidents probably considered themselves Marxists and revolutionaries. Though pale in comparison with Wei Jingsheng, and willing to meet Deng Xiaoping halfway, they were still more radical than the vice-premier. Furthermore, although there were some philosophical differences between Wei and the majority of democrats, disagreements regarding tactics were even more pronounced. Would the democratic movement have succeeded, at least in a small way, if militants like Wei had not generated the Party's backlash? We cannot know. But even the more moderate among them were proposing ideas that were fundamentally revolutionary, and while revolutions need their pragmatists, they also need their firebrands. The problem was not that this movement had a Patrick Henry, but that it lacked a George Washington.

Still, China's democratic movement of 1978–79 will stand as a monument to the free spirit of mankind. The courage which these men and women exhibited in the face of overwhelming power cannot fail to inspire, and leads us to suspect that, indeed, "the movement has not died."

LAUNCHING THE MOVEMENT

The launching of the democratic movement in China was marked by the creation in late 1978 of numerous organizations concerned with human rights and political reform. Each group usually had its own journal—often poorly printed and irregular in frequency (see Document 61). This section contains inaugural statements of these organizations and publications.

The first two documents are typical statements, both from the Enlightenment Society, embodying the general spirit of the movement. Documents 3 through 9 are specific pronouncements of the purposes of the seven leading groups which were founded at this time. (For a more complete list of organizations and publications, see Appendix, page 291).

Document 10 concerns the Thaw Society, which was not established until February 1979. As the piece makes clear, the Thaw Society was founded by renegades from the Enlightenment Society who found the latter too conservative.

DOCUMENT 1
A CALL TO ARMS
From *Enlightenment*

Arise, Chinese workers, farmers, revolutionary cadres, scientists, writers, artists, poets, professors, editors, university students, and all upright and conscientious people! Step out boldly and fight for truth!

Mass democracy and human rights, which we have long hoped for and pursued, are beginning to appear on the great earth of China. Please support them with the utmost enthusiasm and courage. They must be defended with your lives.

Arise, all who love the motherland! Our ideals can only be realized through action. The words "human rights" cannot be found in China's history—not in two thousand years, nor six thousand years, nor eight thousand years.

Arise, you people of China! Attack all dictators and autocrats! The time has come for the final reckoning, and the final verdict.

Enlightenment Society[1]

Beijing (Peking), 24 November 1978
Guiyang [southern China], 29 November 1978

DOCUMENT 2
WE ARE COMMON WORKERS
From *Enlightenment*

. . . We are a group of common workers. Over a long period of time in the past we came together on our own accord to study social questions under the merciless oppression and cultural despotism of Lin Biao and the Gang of Four. Among these questions are the following: Why have the guidelines adopted at the Eleventh National CCP Congress and the Fifth National People's Congress not been followed in some areas? Why was Yugoslavia, a socialist state like ours, able to develop so quickly, while our great fatherland with such a long history of civilization has remained so backward? What are the basic reasons our nation has made progress so slowly?

In our opinion, the first thing to do is to respect human rights, bring socialist democracy into full play, wipe out fascist dictatorship, feudalism, and fetishism imposed by Lin Biao and the Gang of Four to hoodwink the people, restore the scientific features of Marxism–Leninism–Mao Zedong Thought and, on that basis, continually strive for reform and progress. We hold that to realize the Four Modernizations it is of primary importance to bring about ideological modernization. We have already started this program in the fields of science and philosophy. "Pull a hair and the whole body is alerted," as the saying goes. We should explore new fields and achieve a breakthrough in literature and the arts, including their theories. If the development of our science and technology has already enabled us to gain access to outer space, why should we not push our literature and arts into new ideological areas? We workers, farmers, and soldiers of the new era have new cultural needs and have developed new interests in esthetics. We want enlightenment, enlightenment, and enlightenment! We should start a great enlightenment movement in the fields of ideology and culture. "As soon as a new socialist enlightenment movement is started, it will most assuredly raise the socialist enthusiasm of our hundreds of millions of people to a new, unprecedented level and become a tremendous, immeasurable material force for the fulfillment of the general task in the new era. If you don't believe me, just wait and see." ("Enlightened Philosophy and Philosophical Enlightenment," published in *People's Daily*, 22 July 1978.[2])

Beijing, 11 October 1978

DOCUMENT 3
HUMAN RIGHTS LEAGUE
From *China Human Rights*

China Human Rights is a journal of opinion published by the China Human Rights League at irregular intervals. Its goals are as follows:

To publicize the league's principles, purposes, and directions; to provide guidance for the activities [of the membership].

To study the legal theories centering around the Nineteen Points [see Document 16] and propose amendments to the Constitution.

To promote reforms in our social structure and the management of the nation's political and economic life by the laboring masses.

To publicize the results of our studies in the social sciences and other areas of inquiry.

To introduce new achievements of recent and modern democratic civilization and of the social sciences.

To report on the national and international democratic and human rights movements.

To expose crimes against democracy and human rights, and those violating the Constitution.

In order to accomplish these goals, we solicit articles from people in all walks of life. Please send manuscripts to Ren Wanding, Anzhuang Company, Guangqu Gate, Beijing.[3]

DOCUMENT 4
MASSES' REFERENCE NEWS
From a Wall Poster

We have launched this small periodical as a supplement to Democracy Wall. For now, it is mimeographed, but it will soon be printed with lead type in the octavo format. Our aim in publishing it is set forth below.

We are dedicated to promoting China's Four Modernizations, stable unity, and democracy (the Three Promotions). We will seek the trust of the public and of the [Communist Party] Central Committee. While we intend to faithfully reflect the public's views, we will also explain from the sidelines the strategies and aims of the Central Committee.

This periodical will appear biweekly for the time being. Each issue will have eighteen thousand characters. The second issue will appear on 8 January 1979 and will commemorate the third anniversary of the death of Zhou Enlai.

Our first issues contain these items:

1. "Promote Democracy Not Merely Where Minor Matters are Concerned"
2. "Chairman Mao Should Be Correctly Evaluated"
3. "Three Urgent Questions for the Central Committee"
4. "Protest False 'Rightist' Accusations"
5. "Judging the People's Words and Conduct" . . .[4]
7. Short essays
8. Articles and poems from Democracy Wall
9. Suggestions for the peaceful liberation of Taiwan

The price is six *fen* [U.S. four cents] per issue, plus three *fen* for postage. One may subscribe for five or ten issues. Cash only, no stamps.

We would welcome such manuscripts as:

1. Articles and poems from Democracy Wall
2. Political articles (in general, no longer than three thousand characters, six pages)
3. Essays and commentaries on major policy matters
4. Exposures, disclosures, criticisms, suggestions—articles that express and reflect the people's feelings
5. Poems and songs, cartoons, short stories (including true ones), jokes about politics, etc.
6. Materials and articles about new developments in science
7. Articles on methods of study, work, and management
8. New and old quotations from famous people; proverbs from all over the world
9. Short news items from home and abroad

After we become a regular printed publication, we will pay our contributors. Articles can appear under the author's real name or a pen name.

The publication will be sent to the Beijing Library for its archives.

Subscription fees and articles may be sent to Xia Sunjian, Beijing University, 102 Hongsan Building.

We can keep secret the names and addresses of subscribers and authors who are worried about their safety.

DOCUMENT 5
EXPLORATION MAGAZINE
From *Exploration*

In order to bring the material and spiritual life of the Chinese people to the world's most advanced level through rapid modernization, and in order to bring about, within reasonable limits, the most rational social environment for the Chinese people, the comrades who are participating in the writing and editing of this magazine have pledged to abide by these principles:

1. Our basic guiding premises are freedom of speech, publication, and association as provided by the Constitution.

2. Our discussions shall be based upon the historical facts of China and the world. We shall not consider any theory as absolutely correct, nor any individual as absolutely correct. All theories—including those now in existence and those soon to come about—will be the subjects of our discussions and could become our tools for analysis and study.

3. We intend to become the voice of the suffering masses and to investigate the reasons for the backwardness of the Chinese society. We believe that only when the great majority of the powerless and suffering people speak out will it be possible to establish the reasons for the backwardness as well as the means to overcome it. This is the only way through which we can discover the truth.

4. Our magazine shall become a forum for people to discuss social problems without any restrictions. We are against any vulgar or abusive language. Our movement has developed out of the antibureaucracy movement of the Cultural Revolution and the antidictatorship movement centered around Xidan Democracy Wall. We oppose any statements and theories which support bureaucratism and fascism. As for those who are not prepared to allow freedom to other people, we shall deny their right to publish in our magazine.

Contact person: Wei Jingsheng, 118 Lane Four North, Fuwai, Beijing.[5]

DOCUMENT 6
DEMOCRACY AND MODERNITY
From *Democracy and Modernity*

Today, *Democracy and Modernity** comes into being.

In the past half-century or more, China went through the First Democratic Revolution [1911] and the May Fourth Movement. Such revolutionary democratic movements helped advance social history and plunged
our country from a semifeudal, semicolonial state into the socialist era.

History is developing; society is progressing. Under the new historical
conditions people want democracy. The demand for democratic reform
has become an irresistable historical tide. Without democracy and human
rights it will never be possible to construct a prosperous nation. For the
average citizen, the purpose of demanding democracy and rights is to promote national construction and prosperity for the whole nation. There
should be no other purposes.

Socialism is the lower stage of communism. According to our socialist
system, China is a people's democratic dictatorship based upon the coalition of the working class and farmers, with the working class taking the
lead. But for twenty years autocratic feudalists like Kang Sheng, Lin Biao,
and the Gang of Four staged the restoration of feudal dictatorship here.

Consequently, the strange phenomenon of no democracy, no protection for people's power, and no law has prevailed in our country even
though our country is a people's democratic dictatorship. Since the Gang
of Four was destroyed, the Central Committee, under the leadership of
Chairman Hua, has restored and developed the fine traditions and styles
of the Party, proposed the slogan of an all-out effort for the Four Modernizations, and shifted the emphasis of the work of the Party to the area of
socialistic construction. But, judging from the present situation, there are
in our society many things that are not compatible with an all-out effort
for the Four Modernizations, and they are hindering the successful completion of the Four Modernizations program. These things, therefore,
must be quickly eliminated. At present, the cries for social development,
for democracy, and for the Four Modernizations are becoming louder and
louder. In order to reflect what is on people's minds, to raise the level of
people's understanding, to promote social development, and to speed up
the process of the Four Modernizations, we publish this magazine.

---

* The name of this organ is literally translated "Democracy and Time." However,
"time" (*shidai*) is often used in its articles in the sense of "timely" or "modern." Sometimes it appears in the somewhat old-fashioned form *shidai-hua*, meaning "modernization." Hence our rendering.

For a strong and prosperous Chinese nation, we, together with the people of the whole country, shall struggle hard and forever advance.

Democracy and Modernity will carry articles to publicize new socialist culture, new ideas about the law, and other thoughts on democracy. There will be a "Suggestion Column" to publish studies and comments on proposals and practices related to the speed-up of the Four Modernizations. Articles can be in the form of commentary, essays, fiction, poetry, and so on.[6]

DOCUMENT 7
TODAY
From *Today*

At last history provides us with an opportunity to sing (however cautiously) a song that has been in our hearts for a decade. We could hardly wait any longer, for to delay would be to retrogress; history would have overtaken us.

After the May Fourth Movement [1919], writers shed their blood and also provided us with magnificent literature. But in our generation, these writings are out of date. It is our burden to express the spirit of our own times. The April Fifth Movement marks a new era, one which should give us all reason to live. It deepens our certainty that individuals [in our society] have the spirit of freedom. Our country has an ancient civilization, but its modernization must reestablish China among the nations of the world. And it is within this essential framework that our literature and art must come about.

Today, as we open our eyes once again, we must not stop short and just look at the cultural heritage of a past millenium; we must also begin to scrutinize the horizons around us. It is only by so doing that we will be able to recognize our own true value and avoid being ridiculously pretentious or sinking into despair.

Our movement has its roots in the old, fertile land and in the conviction that we would live and die for it. The past is past, the future not yet here. For our generation, just living for today is not enough.[7]

DOCUMENT 8
BEIJING SPRING
From *Beijing Spring*

It was once predicted that the China giant would shake the world the moment it rose. In 1949 it rose, but over a long period of thirty years it has not yielded proper influence. It not only has failed to surpass the imperialist powers but has staggered along behind, hesitant and wavering. Finally, we realize that this great nation wears two tight shoes—obscurantism and despotism. This is why China fails to keep pace with the times and lacks the ability to stand in the front ranks of the nations in the world. Is it conceivable that the Chinese people truly lack such ability?

To be rich and powerful China must be built into a modern socialist power. This has long been the dream of the Chinese people. However, to stride toward this great ideal we must break down modern feudalism and modern superstition and gradually acquire socialist democracy and modern science.

On the basis of Marxism-Leninism, this publication supports the Chinese Communist Party, adheres to the socialist path, and follows Comrade Mao Zedong's policy of "a hundred flowers blossoming and a hundred schools of thought contending." As a comprehensive mass periodical, it fully exercises the democratic rights of speech and publication as provided by the Constitution. It will publish the appeals of the people and all kinds of articles of an exploratory nature.

The road of progress is arduous and tortuous, but the historical current of the people's desire for democracy and the nation's desire for wealth and power is irresistible. The fresh flowers of socialist democracy and science will brave the flying snow and the chilly spring weather and will bloom forth proudly. Baptized by the great and powerful April Fifth Movement, the Chinese people will, with an indomitable fighting spirit, welcome Beijing spring's hundred flowers.[8]

DOCUMENT 9
ENLIGHTENMENT SOCIETY
From *Enlightenment*

In practical fufillment of .the Constitution, we hereby formally announce the founding of the Enlightenment Society[9] in Beijing at noon,
24 November 1978.
Our emblem: A flaming torch.

> Huang Xiang
> Li Jiahua
> Mo Jiangang
> Fang Jiahua
> Yang Zaixing
> Liang Fuching
> Huang Jie
> Zheng Jilian

*   *   *

1. The Enlightenment Society resolutely supports the Chinese Communist Party and the socialist system.

2. Marxism is the fundamental guiding thought of this society. Marxism must be continuously replenished, enriched, and developed. We oppose the vulgarization and dogmatization of Marxism.

3. We resolutely support the Constitution of the People's Republic of
China (PRC) and actively implement the obligatory duties of citizens.

4. To enable the Chinese nation to become strong, prosperous, and
progressive, and to realize the Four Modernizations, we plead for socialist
democracy and human rights.

5. We encourage and advocate new literature, new arts, a new philosophy, and a new civilized way of life. We will also seek new ideas and
rules of ethics and morality. (As time goes on, and in accordance with the
needs of the situation, we will gradually try to make new explorations
into other fields of social science.)

6. We admit that practice is the sole criterion for testing truth and
that practice is also the sole criterion for testing literary and artistic works.

7. Mental labor and physical labor should be equally respected in
society. We hold that man's creation of science and culture is the common
wealth of all humanity.

8. We will truly promote the "double hundred" policy and revolution in ideology and in feeling. We dare to break through all "forbidden

zones" in the realm of ideology which fetter the development of productive forces.

9. In socialist political life we do not recognize the status of idols nor any kind of privilege. We hold that all people are equal before the truth and that all people are equal before the law.

10. We oppose bureaucracy and will actively assist the government in safeguarding Party discipline and state law and will be a champion of justice. We dare to struggle against all kinds of evil forces.

11. Safeguarding science and culture, and all achievements in science and culture, is our obligatory and lofty duty.

12. In our social activities we accept the leadership and guidance of the Party as well as the surveillance and criticism of various democratic parties, various mass organizations, people in every quarter, and all the people.[10]

DOCUMENT 10
THE THAW SOCIETY
From a Wall Poster

1. Owing to the serious internal split and the growing conservative trend of the Enlightenment Society, Li Jiahua (one of the founders of the Enlightenment Society and the author of the commentary on "The God of Fire" symphonic poem), Lu Mang (author of "Enlightenment Society" and "On Human Rights"), and Wang Yinfeng (who went to Beijing to sell *Enlightenment,* nos. 1 and 2, and to post no. 3) have announced their withdrawal from the Enlightenment Society in Guiyang and have organized the Thaw Society.

2. We now have no connection with the editorial committee of the Enlightenment Society nor with the two factions of their editorial department.

3. We are counting the commentary on "The God of Fire" symphonic poem [Document 68], originally published as the second issue of *Enlightenment,* as our first issue, and "On Human Rights" [Document 27], originally published as the third issue of *Enlightenment,* as our second issue. We take full responsibility for their contents.

4. The Thaw Society is a newborn organization emerging from the Enlightenment Society. It takes up the historical mission which the Enlightenment Society cannot or will not shoulder.

Communications should be sent to: Li Jiahua, 275 Wei Qing Road, Guiyang, Guizhou.[11]

SECTION TWO
ON DEMOCRATIC REFORMS

Movement writers called for wide-ranging political reforms. This section contains five essays which are representative of the demands made. Document 11 is from the relatively moderate Enlightenment Society. The author argues that China's "socialism" is heavily weighted with remnants from the nation's feudal past.

Document 12 is one of the most remarkable essays in this volume. In it, Wei Jingsheng coins the term "fifth modernization," from which we have derived the title of this collection.* It marked Wei, and Exploration, as relatively militant and was doubtless a factor in the author's ultimate imprisonment.

Documents 13, 14, and 15 elaborate on concepts of democracy as held by the Enlightenment Society, Beijing Spring, and the Thaw Society.

It should be pointed out that the "democratic movement," narrowly defined, did not monopolize discussions on how to democratize China's political system. During this same period, more than a few cadres and officials were pondering the issue. People's Daily, Workers' Daily, and China Youth carried numerous articles on the subject. Issues such as secret ballot, permitting choice among candidates, and the right to recall corrupt officials were widely discussed.[1]

But it was of course the dissidents who made the more shrill demands.

---

* Wei's conception of human rights can be compared with that of Luo Longji, who was a leader of the Democratic League both before and after the revolution. In an article written in 1929, Luo defines human rights as "a precondition for living life as a human being." Although Luo later collaborated with the Communists, he was severely attacked in 1957. *See* Mab Huang, "The Four Modernizations and Human Rights" (in Chinese), *Hsintu* (New Ground), no. 11, June 1979; and James D. Seymour, "Communist China's Bourgeois Democratic Parties" (M.A. essay, Columbia University, 1961).

DOCUMENT 11
IS THIS DEMOCRATIC SOCIALISM?
By Zhang Wei

In the past we were suspended upside down and running with a big bag over us. We are now firmly standing on our feet with our heads to the sky and solving our problems scientifically. We were cheated for years, the victims of those who coveted power.

Why could several hundred million Chinese people not do anything about the handful in the Gang of Four, and why could Mao Zedong, who was praised by the people as the Great Savior, not use his monopolistic power to control the Gang of Four? Why was democracy in reputedly most democratic socialist China so limited, not even up to the level of moribund capitalist countries? Why did the economic development of the People's Republic fall behind Taiwan? Everyone concerned about the destiny and future of the motherland wants to find answers to these questions, because our country's antifeudal democratic revolution and the old and new democratic revolutions have not been properly completed. The remnant influence of feudalism has infiltrated not only into our country's system and into various aspects of social life, but has also infiltrated into the Communist Party. This was why Mao Zedong over the past few decades warned the Party and the whole country more than once and adopted a series of measures included in the Cultural Revolution to prevent the restoration of capitalism. However, the restoration was not of capitalism but of feudalism.

When we comment on the national leaders we commit the "crime" of "counterrevolution." What is the difference between this and the feudalist crime of falsely accusing the emperor? When a person has been in trouble, his family, relatives, and even comrades have also been in trouble. What is the difference between this and the feudal practice of involving all of an accused person's relatives?

If a country's leader, not to mention a supreme leader, has a feudal mentality, the evil consequences he can cause will not be trivial. This was the case with Chairman Mao. In many respects our country has followed the methods of feudalism. Quite a few people still hold to orthodox feudal concepts.

The explanation for this is to be found in history. China has not gone through a thorough bourgeois revolution or a democratic revolution as did Europe and the United States. Philosophers believe this is a missed lesson in democracy we must make up for. In particular, the people, who have suffered enough hardship from dictatorship, ought to know more about the precious value of democracy and the necessity for the birth of the Xidan Democracy Wall in the struggle between the Chinese people and feudalism. The cries of this newborn child have openly proclaimed that feudal despotism is bound to collapse under the onslaught of democracy. The banners of democracy and science will flutter over the picturesque land of China and in the hearts of all its citizens. Therefore, to brighten our motherland, improve her appearance, and enable her to stand up together with other nations, and to eliminate the sufferings of future generations, we must struggle to realize the thorough transformation of our country's system, struggle to have the people truly take hold of the power to run the country, and struggle for democratic human rights. This is the mission which history has assigned to red-blooded youth. This is the mission which our era has assigned to every democratic fighter. This is the task which history has handed to the people. Anyone who attempts to obstruct this democratic movement commits a crime against history and is an enemy of the nation. The wheel of history is turned by the people. Due to the people's strength, displayed through Democracy Wall, the deified Mao Zedong has been made human again. In the past we could be condemned and convicted for uttering one sentence. Today we can discuss Chairman Mao's merits and failures not only at home and with our closest relatives but also in our units, at Democracy Wall, and even on the public streets. Through the strength displayed on Democracy Wall, the verdict on the Tian-an-men Incident, miscarriage of justice, has been reversed.

We must understand our own strength. Let us firmly embrace the democratic movement in the same way that we embrace our spouses. When a person loses a spouse, one person suffers. When a nation loses democracy, a whole nation suffers disaster.[2]

DOCUMENT 12
THE FIFTH MODERNIZATION
By Wei Jingsheng

I

At present, the media no longer play up the themes of dictatorship of the proletariat and class struggle. One reason is that this line of propaganda was used as sort of magical potion by the Gang of Four, who have now been overthrown. Another reason, which is even more important, is that the people have had enough of all that and can no longer be deceived.

According to the laws of history, the new will not come about until the old is gone. Now that the old is gone, the people are rubbing their eyes in eager anticipation. Finally, with God's blessing, there is a new promise—the Four Modernizations. Chairman Hua, the wise leader, and Vice-Chairman Deng (who the people consider even wiser and greater) have defeated the Gang of Four. Now democracy and prosperity, so earnestly sought by those who shed their blood at Tian-an-men, seem soon to be realized.

After the arrest of the Gang of Four, people eagerly hoped that Vice-Chairman Deng, the so-called "restorer of capitalism," would once again appear as a great towering banner. Finally, Vice-Chairman Deng did return to his post on the Central Committee. The people were indeed excited, inspired, and . . . [sic]. However, to the people's regret, the hated old political system has not changed, and even any talk about the much hoped for democracy and freedom is forbidden. People's living conditions remain the same and the "increased wages" are far behind the soaring commodity prices.

There has been some talk about the restoration of "capitalism" and the bonus system. After some investigation it was confirmed that the "invisible whip" for "the maximum exploitation of workers," which had been cursed by the Marxist ancestors, could not be used to fool the people anymore. Although without the leadership of the Great Helmsman, people can still be led by the "wise leader" to catch up with and surpass England, the United States, Japan, and Yugoslavia (?), or the advanced world level. Taking part in revolution is no longer "in vogue." Since entering a university will greatly enhance a person's prestige, people no longer need to hear the deafening noise of "class struggle" slogans. The Four Modernizations stand for everything that is good. Of course, it is still necessary to act according to the spirit of the Central Committee, as relayed to us by the

April Fifth Academy. The beautiful vision can materialize only under unified leadership and guidance.

In ancient China there were such maxims as "A cake in the picture can appease hunger" and "Watching the plums can quench the thirst." These witty and ironic remarks were quite popular in ancient times, but today, after a long and continuous development of history, people should never take such stupid remarks seriously. Yet some people not only believe in them but also carry them out in practice.

For several decades, Chinese people have closely followed the Great Helmsman. Communist ideology has provided "the cake in the picture," and the Great Leap Forward and Three Red Banners have served as "plums for quenching thirst." People tightened their belts and bravely forged ahead. Thirty years soon passed and they have learned a lesson from experience. For thirty years people were like "monkeys reaching out for the moon and feeling only emptiness." Therefore, when Vice-Chairman Deng put forward the slogan "Be practical," people's enthusiasm was like surging waves. Time and again he was helped by the people to come to power. The people expected him to review the past and lead them to a realistic future with a "seeking truth from facts" approach.

However, some people have warned us: Marxism–Leninism–Mao Zedong Thought is the foundation of all foundations; Chairman Mao was the Great Savior of the people; "Without the Communist Party, there would be no new China"; "Without Chairman Mao there would be no new China"; and anyone disagreeing with these will come to no good end. "Some people" even warned us: Chinese people need dictatorship. His superiority over feudal emperors precisely shows his greatness. Chinese people need no democracy unless it is "democracy under collective leadership," without which democracy is not worth a dime. It is up to you to believe or to doubt it, but the prisons (from which so many have recently been released) were convincing "proof."

However, someone has now given you a way out. Take the Four Modernizations as the key link and follow the principle of stability and unity and be brave (?) to serve the revolution (?) as an old ox does. Then you will find your way to paradise, namely, the prosperity of communism and the Four Modernizations. Some well-intentioned people have given us this advice. "When you cannot think straight, try hard to study Marxism–Leninism–Mao Zedong Thought!" The reason why you cannot think straight is your lack of understanding which reflects on the level of your ideological accomplishment. You should be obedient, otherwise the leadership of your unit cannot forgive you! And on and on.

I advise everyone not to believe such political swindlers anymore. Knowing that we are being deceived, we should implicitly believe in ourselves. We have been tempered in the Cultural Revolution and cannot be that ignorant now. Let us find out for ourselves what should be done.

(1) Why Democracy?

This question has been discussed by many people for centuries. Others have conducted careful analyses and indicated on the Democracy Wall how much better is democracy than autocracy.

"People are the masters of history." Is this a fact or just empty talk? Well, it can be both. How can there be history without the people's strength and their participation in making it? No Great Helmsman or Wise leader can even exist, not to speak of creating history. From this, we can see that without new Chinese people there would be no new China; but it is not true that "without Chairman Mao, there would be no new China." Vice-Chairman Deng is grateful to Chairman Mao for saving his life. This is understandable. But is it not reasonable too that he should be grateful to the "outcries" that pushed him to the seat of power? Would it be reasonable for him to respond to the outcries by saying, "You must not denigrate Chairman Mao, because he saved my life"? This makes "The people are the masters of history" an empty slogan. It is empty talk because people cannot master their own destiny according to the majority will; because their achievements have been credited to other people's accounts; and because their rights have been used to make somebody's royal crown. What kind of master is this? It may be more correct to call them slaves. In our history books the people are the masters who create everything, but in real life they are lackeys, always standing at attention and waiting to be "led" by leaders who swell like dough under the effect of yeast.

People should have democracy. When they ask for democracy, they are only demanding what is rightfully theirs. Anyone refusing to give it to them is a shameless bandit no better than a capitalist who robs workers of their money earned with their sweat and blood. Do the people have democracy now? No. Do they want to be masters of their own destiny? Definitely yes. This was the reason for the Communist Party's victory over Kuomintang. But what then happened to the promise of democracy? The slogan "people's democratic dictatorship" was replaced by "the dictatorship of the proletariat." Even the "democracy" enjoyed by the infinitesimal portion—one among tens of millions—was abolished and replaced by the autocracy of the "Great Leader." Thus, Peng Dehuai was overthrown because, instead of following the Great Leader's instruction, he had the audacity to show his temper in the Party. Then a new promise was held out: Because the leader is great, implicit faith in such a leader, rather than democracy, will bring more happiness to the people. People have believed in this promise, half reluctantly and half willingly, until today. But are they any happier? Are they richer or more prosperous? Unconcealable facts show that they are poorer, more miserable, and more backward. Why? This is the first question to be considered. And what to do now? This is the second question.

There is no need now to determine the ratio of Mao Zedong's merits and shortcomings. He first spoke about this as a self-defense. People should now think for a while and see if, without Mao Zedong's autocracy, China could be in its present backward state. Are Chinese people stupid, or lazy, or unwilling to enjoy wealth? Are they expecting too much? Quite the opposite. Then why? The answer is quite obvious. Chinese people should not have taken this road. Then why did they take it? Only because they were led by that self-exalting autocrat. If they did not take this road, he would exercise dictatorship over them. The people could see no other road and therefore had no choice. Is this not deception? Can there be any merit in deception?

What road is this? It is called the "socialist road." According to the definition of the Marxist ancestors, socialism means that the people, or the proletariat, are their own masters. Let me ask the Chinese workers and peasants: With the meager wages you get every month, whose master and what kind of master can you be? Sad to relate, you are "mastered" by somebody else even in the matter of matrimony. Socialism guarantees the producers' rights to the surplus production from their labor over what is needed as a service to the society. But this service is limitless. So are you not getting only that miserable little wage "necessary for maintaining the labor force for production"? Socialism guarantees many rights, such as the right of a citizen to receive education, to use his ability to the best advantage, and so forth. But none of these rights can be seen in our daily life. What we can see is only "the dictatorship of the proletariat" and "a variation of Russian autocracy"—Chinese socialist autocracy. Is this kind of socialist road what people want? Can it be claimed that autocracy means the people's happiness? Is this the socialist road depicted by Marx and hoped for by the people? Obviously not. Then what is it? Funny as it may sound, it is like the feudal socialism mentioned in the "Manifesto," or a feudal monarchy disguised as socialism. We have heard that Soviet Russia has been promoted from social feudalism to social imperialism. Must Chinese people take the same road? Some people have proposed that we should charge everything to fascist autocracy under feudal socialism. To this, I entirely agree, because the question of merits or shortcomings does not exist here.

Let me say a word about the "National Socialism," the real name of the notorious German fascism. These fascists, also under an autocrat tyrant, called on the people to tighten their belts and deceived the people by telling them that they belonged to a great nation. Their main purpose was to suppress the most rudimentary form of democracy, because they clearly knew that democracy was the most formidable and irresistable enemy. On this basis, Stalin and Hitler shook hands and signed the German-Soviet Pact, whereby a socialist state and a National Socialist State toasted the partition of Poland while the peoples of both countries suffered enslavement and poverty. Must we continue to suffer the same enslavement and poverty? If we do not want democracy as our only choice or, in other words, if we want modernized economics, science, military science, and so forth, then there must be modernization of the people and of the social system.

(2)   The Fifth Modernization—What Kind of Democracy?

I would like to ask everyone: What do we want modernization for? After all, some men feel that the age of *The Dream of the Red Chamber** must have been perfectly all right, because men were then free to read, write poetry, and fool around with women. One needed only to open his mouth and food would be provided, only raise an arm to be dressed. Well, today's privileged class get to see foreign movies and live like gods. Such a life-style is quite inaccessible to ordinary folk. What the people want are the happy days which they can truly enjoy and which are not worse than those enjoyed by foreigners. All want prosperity, the kind of prosperity which is universal and which can only result from increased social productive forces. This is obvious to everyone. However, there is still something overlooked by somebody. Can people enjoy good living when social productive forces have been increased? Now the questions of authority, of domination, of distribution, and of exploitation arise.

People have tightened their belts for decades since liberation. They have worked as hard as they could and actually produced much wealth. But where has all the wealth gone? Some say that it has gone to fatten some comparatively small autocratic regimes like Vietnam. Others say it has fattened those "new bourgeois elements" like Lin Biao and Jiang Qing. They are all correct. Anyway, it can never get into the hands of the laboring people. If the wealth was not directly squandered by the big and small "political swindlers" who held power, it was bestowed by them to those scoundrels like Vietnam and Albania who cherished the same ideal and followed the same path. Shortly before his death, Mao Zedong had trouble

---

* Famous eighteenth-century novel about a large family that was rich and powerful, but in decline.

with his wife when she asked him for nine thousand *yuan*; but has anyone ever witnessed any qualm on his part when he simply threw away tens of billions of *yuan* earned with the people's sweat and blood? Yet, while people are building socialism by tightening their belts and begging in the streets, there are still some people going to Democracy Wall to flatter Mao Zedong. Since they have eyes, why can't they see all this misery? Have they deliberately closed their eyes? If they really could not see, I would ask them to go to Beijing Station, to Yongdingmen, or just into the streets instead of writing posters. There they can observe the foreign visitors and ask them if in foreign lands the desire for food is considered something rare. I think those who desire to have food are not, as a rule, willing to give away their snow-white rice to aid the "friends" in the Third World! But these people's opinion does not count. The sad thing is that in our People's Republic there are still some people who, after eating a full meal, have nothing to do except read books or write poems. They live like gods and hold dominant power. In such case, are not the people justified in seizing power from these overlords?

What is democracy? True democracy means the holding of power by the laboring masses. Are laborers unqualified to hold power? Yugoslavia has taken this road and proved to us that even without dictatorial rulers, big or small, the people can work even better.

What is true democracy? It means the right of the people to choose their own representatives to work according to their will and in their interests. Only this can be called democracy. Furthermore, the people must also have the power to replace their representatives anytime so that these representatives cannot go on deceiving others in the name of the people. This is the kind of democracy enjoyed by people in European and American countries. In accordance with their will, they could run such people as Nixon, de Gaulle, and Tanaka out of office. They can reinstate them if they want, and nobody can interfere with their democratic rights. In China, however, if a person even comments on the already dead Great Helmsman Mao Zedong or the Great Man without peers in history, jail will be ready for him with open door and various unpredictable calamities may befall him. What a vast difference will it be if we compare the socialist system of centralized democracy with the system of capitalist "exploiting class!"

Will there be great disorder across the land and defiance of laws human and divine once people enjoy democracy? Do not recent periodicals show that just because of the absence of democracy, dictators big and small were defying laws human and divine? How to maintain democratic order is a domestic problem requiring solution by the people themselves, and there is no need for the privileged overlords to worry about it. However, what they are worrying about is not the people's democracy but the difficulty of finding an excuse for destroying the people's democratic rights. Domestic problems cannot be solved all at once. Their solution takes time, during which mistakes and defects will be unavoidable. However, all these consequences, which concern us alone, should be far better than oppressions from the overlords which leave us no way to appeal for justice. Those who worry about the defiance of human and divine laws as a result of democracy are like those who had the same worry when the emperor was dethroned in the 1911 revolution. They are reconciled to this line of reasoning: Be at ease and submit to oppression. Without oppression, the roof of your house will fly sky high!

Let me respectfully remind these gentlemen: We want to be masters of our own destiny. We need no gods or emperors. We do not believe in the existence of any savior. We want to be masters of the world and not instruments used by autocrats to carry out their wild ambitions. We want a modern lifestyle and democracy for the people. Freedom and happiness are our sole objectives in accomplishing modernization. Without this fifth modernization all others are merely another promise.

Let me call on our comrades: Rally under the banner of democracy and do not trust the autocrats' talk about "stability and unity." Fascist totalitarianism can only bring us disaster. Have no more illusion. Democracy is our only hope. Abandon our democratic rights and we will be shackled once again. Let us believe in our own strength! Human history was created by us. Let all self-styled leaders and teachers go. They have for decades cheated the people of their most valuable possession. I firmly believe that production will be faster under the people's own management. Because the laborers will produce for their own benefit, their living conditions will be better. Society will thus be more rational, because under democracy all social authority is exercised by the people with a view to improving their livelihood.

I can never believe that the people can have anything from a savior without their own efforts. I also refuse to believe that China will abandon its goal because of difficulties. As long as people can clearly identify their goal and the obstacles on the way, they can surely trample on that mantis which bars the way.

(3)   March Toward Modernization—Practice Democracy

To accomplish modernization, Chinese people should first practice democracy and modernize China's social system. Democracy is by no means the *result* of social development as claimed by Lenin. Aside from being the inevitable outcome of the development of productive forces and the relations of production up to a certain stage, it is also the *condition* for the existence of productive forces and the relations of production, not only up to that certain stage but also at much higher stages of development. Without this condition, the society will become stagnant and economic growth will encounter insurmountable obstacles. Therefore, judging from past history, a democratic social system is the major premise or the prerequisite for all developments—or modernizations. Without this major premise or prerequisite, it would be impossible not only to continue further development but also to preserve the fruits of the present stage of development. The experiences of our great motherland over the past thirty years have provided the best evidence.

Why must human history take the road toward prosperity and modernization? The reason is that people need prosperity so that real goods are available, and so that there is a full opportunity to pursue their first goal of happiness, namely freedom. Democracy means the maximum attainable freedom so far known by human beings. It is quite obvious that democracy has become the goal in contemporary human struggles.

Why are all reactionaries in contemporary history united under a common banner against democracy? The answer is that democracy provides everything for their enemy—the masses of people—but nothing for them —the oppressors—to oppose the people with. The biggest reactionary is always the biggest opponent of democracy. As clearly shown in the history of Germany, the Soviet Union, and "New China," the strongest opponent of democracy has been the biggest and most dangerous enemy of social peace and prosperity. From the history of these countries, we can also clearly see that the spearheads of all struggles by people for happiness and by societies for prosperity were directed against the enemies of democracy —the autocratic fascists. From the history of the same countries again, we can see that victory for democracy has always brought along with it the most favorable conditions and the greatest speed for social development. On this point, American history has supplied the most forceful evidence.

All struggles involving the people's pursuit of happiness and prosperity are based on the quest for democracy. Therefore, the result of all struggles involving the people's resistance to oppression and exploitation are determined by their success or failure in obtaining democracy. So let us dedicate all our strength to the struggle for democracy! People can get all they want only through democratic channels. They cannot get anything by undemocratic or illusory means, because all forms of autocracy and autocratic totalitarianism are the most open and dangerous enemies of the people.

Would the enemies be willing to let us practice democracy? Certainly not. They will stop at nothing to hinder the progress of democracy, to deceive and hoodwink the people. The most effective method they, like all autocratic fascists, can count on is to tell the people that their present conditions are practically the best in the world. Has democracy really reached the stage it naturally should? Not at all! Any minor victory for democracy has been paid for at a high price, and democracy can be truly learned at the cost of bloodshed and other sacrifices. The enemies of democracy have always deceived the people by saying that democracy, even though achieved, will inevitably perish; so why should any energy be expended in striving for it?

However, let us look at the real history and not the history written by the hired scholars of the "socialist government." Every minute portion of democracy of real value was stained with the blood of martyrs and tyrants, and every step forward was met with strong attacks from the reactionary forces. Democracy has been able to surmount all these obstacles because it is highly valued and eagerly sought by the people. Therefore, this torrent is irresistible. Chinese people have never feared anything. As long as the people have a clear orientation, the forces of tyranny are no longer undefeatable.

Is the struggle for democracy what the Chinese people really want? The Cultural Revolution was the first occasion for them to demonstrate their strength, and all reactionary forces trembled before them. Because the people had then no clear orientation and the democratic forces did not play the main role in the struggle, the majority of them were brought over by the autocratic tyrant, led astray, divided, slandered, and finally violently suppressed. Thus these forces came to an end. The people then had a blind faith in their leaders who were autocrats and careerists; therefore, they became a tool and a sacrificial lamb for the tyrants or potential tyrants.

Today, twelve years later, the people have finally learned where their goal lies. They have a clear orientation, and they have a real leader. This leader is the democratic banner, which has now taken on a new signficance. Xidan Democracy Wall has become the first battlefield in the people's fight against reactionaries. The struggle will certainly be victorious, though there will still be bloodshed and suffering. Liberation (about which there has been so much talk) will surely be attained. However much we may be covertly plotted against, the democratic banner cannot be obscured by the miasmal mists. Let us unite under this great and real banner and march toward modernization for the sake of the people's peace, happiness, rights, and freedom!

II

Since Part I of "The Fifth Modernization" was put up, many small posters have appeared around it. Among them is one signed "Jiao Da" [the same name as that of a character in *The Dream of the Red Chamber*]. This cannot help but bring to mind the "lackey" who, as some spectators commented, wants to be pitied. In modern Chinese, people are fond of using the term "amateur." So let us for the time being call him an "amateur" lackey!

Lackeys are of two kinds: the professional and the amateur. For example, those who brandished their clubs at Tian-an-men several years ago on behalf of "the people's government" can be called professional lackeys. Their duty is to serve their masters, either willingly or unwillingly, in order to earn a living. Then, provided nobody directed his action from behind the scenes, can it be wrong to call "Jiao Da" an "amateur" lackey? I cannot positively say whether or not he could gain any benefit in so doing; but why should he have chosen the same name used by a perfect lackey in *The Dream of the Red Chamber*? Had he chosen to follow the example of the "Young Worker" of the Second Machine-Tool Plant who posted a list of his former occupations, his master would be more sure of his real identity.

To be a lackey is understandable, provided he works for gain. If there are still "amateur lackeys" in a country dominated by overlords of *The Dream of the Red Chamber* type, isn't it clear that autocratic tyranny can stand so firm not because of certain personal charms but because of its strong feudalist social foundation? This is no joke, but is a serious matter for all patriots who do not like to see China going backward until it perishes, and for all who do not like to see Chinese people suffer.

Can the Four Modernizations be accomplished in a society under an overlord-lackey (amateur) type of domination? Stark realities in China tell us that this is impossible! For some time even discussions were forbidden. Now that discussions are permitted, does this not mean some relaxation on the part of the authorities as a favor to us? Should we not be grateful and moved to tears? If you do not show your gratitude, you had better be careful. Some people may note down the registration number of your bicycle. The professional lackeys are not all in uniform.

Our young men are not "sick men of the East." They have sufficient courage to put up and to read posters, and to discuss different views even though some of them are taboo. They are not yet sure what is "truth" because the "truth" before them is no longer trustworthy. They want a new way to a new life. If anyone wants to deceive the "simple-minded youths" with old tricks, he is doomed to fail. They are by no means simple-minded.

Even though you impose a blockade on the materials required to inspire their thinking, you still cannot prevent them from hoping. Through your "bamboo curtain" they can see a beam of light which, like a whip, urges them to explore for the loopholes in your "truth" and for the road to a new life—democracy. Even though you may have the power to block the progress of Democracy Wall once again, you cannot help but tremble before the explorers.

The opinions which I offer here are intended for the eyes of my fellow explorers, not for overlords and their lackeys.

(1) Totalitarianism and Democracy

Despite differences in vocabulary, autocratic rulers of all ages have invariably taught the people that since men are social beings, social interest should predominate; that since social interests are common to all people, a centralized management, or administration, is necessary; that since rule by a minority, or even by a single person, is more centralized, autocracy is the most ideal form; that for this reason, "people's democratic dictatorship" means the autocracy of a Great Helmsman; and that for the same reason, the Great Helmsman is a savior without peers in "centuries of human history and thousands of years of Chinese history."

From the above, we can clearly see the tendency of the autocratic dictatorship and easily guess the type of people served by this system. This is "truth" only to the autocrats or to totalitarianism, but not to the people. So is that the only truth? Or can it be called "truth"? A study of this question must begin from the first logical step.

Since human beings exist in a society, they are all social beings. However, the following factors should be considered: (a) Society is composed of different individuals and, according to natural instincts, each individual exists independently; (b) People's sociality is formed of the common character and common interests of many different individuals. The different social units—individuals—form different societies. Therefore, people's sociality depends on individuality just as human societies necessarily depend on the existence of individuals; (c) Therefore, we conclude that people's individuality enjoys priority over their sociality, although both are important constituents of human nature. In our daily life, we usually see only one part of human nature, namely, that part under suppression, but not the other part which retains different natural individual characteristics. It is the sum total of the latter type that forms human essence.

Human essence changes according to changing conditions of human existence. Some of the conditions affecting the changes in the innate essence of human beings undergo rapid changes, while other remain relatively stable. For example, the condition that man eats is stable, but the conditions concerning the kind of food he eats and the quality of food required change according to changing time, places, and other conditions. People's individuality—just like human individuals—is, without doubt, always present. But since society, formed of individuals, can frequently change without any strict limitation, people's sociality can also change in the same way. The type of sociality [words illegible] which harmoniously follows the changes in the conditions of the social members' existence becomes relatively stable because of its flexibility. The difference between totalitarianism and democracy is not the difference between individuality and sociality, but rather between two forms of sociality.

Totalitarianism regards suppression of individuality as its basic condition of survival; essentially, this is a form of enslavement. Democracy regards harmony with individuality as its basic condition of existence; essentially, this is a form of cooperation. Nobody can find any form of totalitarianism without suppression of individuality and enslavement of people. Similarly, nobody can find any form of democracy without a foundation of harmony of the individuality of the majority of citizens. Totalitarianism is distinguished by its suppression of individuality, while a special feature of democracy is the preservaton of the harmony of individuality. The main difference between totalitarianism and democracy, therefore, lies in the two different and exactly opposite forms of existence for human individuals as well as two vastly different living conditions for people. Do you like freedom or enslavement? This question is unnecessary for most people, except, of course, the lackeys.

However, the amateur lackey has called on us to pay attention to realities instead of relying entirely on subjective will in choosing a road, or, as he claimed, it will not be realistic. If so, then let us take a look at realities!

Under Western "capitalist democracy," people can express their will through election and can determine the nation's destiny on the basis of their will. Even though their will may not be entirely correct, people still have the right to make mistakes and to correct them quickly. Therefore, no "bourgeois politicians" would in any way dare to ignore public opinion on any issue; otherwise people can ask them to get out. However, all "proletarian politicians" can, with or without due process of resolution, decide on the use of a big club to force "proletarian masses" into submission. Even though they are entirely worthless, people can only watch them being promoted, enjoying pleasures, and taking concubines.

Western people can fully enjoy the fruits of social prosperity, while people of socialist countries have to work like donkeys for a bare living.

Moreover, they have to live in a tense and austere atmosphere as though in an army camp. Western people have the right to strike and to demonstrate. Recently, they can even vote through their delegates in board of directors' meetings on arrangements concerning their living and working conditions.

Apart from getting the "Marxist" wages from funds intended for meeting the " most essential needs for keeping a labor force for production," Chinese workers and peasants can only personify the "superiority of socialism" by accepting any arrangements worked out by their leadership regardless of the difference of sexes.

Western people are not satisfied even though they already have many freedoms; Chinese people are already laboring under too many disciplines and yet some people still want to add more. Western governments regard the safeguarding of the citizen's human rights as one of their main duties; citizens of "socialist countries" can only be submissive to a small group of rulers.

Enough! In such a society, who is subject to rule of law? Law is in the hands of a small group defying all laws, while those who are ruled, enslaved, and deprived of all rights are the citizens.

Enough! The propaganda machine of the dictatorship of the proletariat claims that "in our society, at least the problem of food is solved."

Is this true? The question can best be answered after taking a look at the seamy side of socialism, as shown by beggars along the streets of large and small towns, or by workers and peasants driven to almost the same fate. I do not think that Mao Zedong's flatterers fared any better [i.e., Mao's propagandists were unable to persuade the people]. Such propaganda should have been saved for foreigners who are ignorant of the real situation, for no Chinese will ever believe it. Foreigners, however, may think that Chinese people are all like pigs and dogs that wag their tails when they are given any food. However, during the three years of "natural disasters" [1959-61], tens of thousands of compatriots died of starvation. Even if they were pigs and dogs, can they still be expected to wag their tails in the face of starvation?

Liu Shaoqi was honest when he said that "30 percent of the disasters were natural and 70 percent were man-made." Man-made disasters? Yes, they were disasters caused by the autocratic rulers, by fascism under a Marxist-Leninist signboard, by totalitarianism, and by those who toyed with hundreds of millions of human lives according to the vagaries of a small number of persons.

The followers of Stalin and Mao Zedong still said: "However, there are slum areas in capitalist countries too!" Enough! People can easily see the true picture. They need only look at the workers' dormitories behind Chongwen Hotel in Beijing and see if the slum areas in the United States can be any dirtier or more crowded.

Enough!

Those who have benefited from flattery have said: "There is inequality of sexes in capitalist countries!" These flatterers probably believe that men and women should suffer the same oppression and exploitation, live under subhuman standards, and toil to the point of exhaustion in the same way to "increase socialist accumulations" in order to be equal. No wonder their Marxist ancestors proved that equality is infeasible.

Enough!

The amateur lackeys still insisted: "There are prostitutes in capitalist countries!" In this connection, they should get some information from their own people—in the public security bureau—about the number of private brothels throughout China and the Soviet Union. Furthermore, many girls are at all times available to "wait on" the leading cadres, and many others, unwilling to do so, have been assigned jobs in faraway places. We do not have the required statistics and dare not make arbitrary comments. We, rather, leave this job to foreign visitors and those who have made their earnings in foreign currencies.

Is this the ideal society for which numerous martyrs have shed their blood? Is this the kind of socialism ardently hoped for by millions of laboring people? Is this in accordance with the laws of historical development? All this can only show how ideological ignorance and blind faith in the wrong road can bring serious calamity to people in human history.

(2)   Socialism and Democracy

At present, there are two different interpretations of the term "socialism": One of them holds that socialist society is the most rational one as a transition to an even more ideal society—communist society. People holding such a view have mostly been seriously poisoned by propaganda. This poisoning should be entirely attributed to Marx and to his offsprings who are carrying out his theories in practice. Another interpretation holds that socialism is a synonym of modern totalitarianism, because it is in reality totalitarianism. In my opinion, neither explanation is completely correct.

The first interpretation ignores this point: All forms of totalitarianism use a perfect ideal for the future as a compensation to the victims for their misery under tyranny. This compensation is used as an opiate to satisfy people's yearning for good living. Like the "cake in the picture," it spiritually pacifies people but actually deprives them of their rights to enjoy good living. Acceptance and practice of this type of utopianism are heavily counted on by totalitarianism as a support. Socialist movements were started before the time of Marx. At that time, these movements were linked with democratic movements and directly concerned with people's quest for happiness. Later, socialist movements were confined within the orbit of utopianism, meaning totalitarianism. For this "scientific" achievement, Marx has to be thanked, because this type of socialism, namely, totalitarianism, exactly suited the taste of the people whose ideological and moral concepts had not yet been freed from the shackles of feudalist social concepts and, therefore, could not fit into the capitalist social system. Yet, like all human beings, they wanted to live well, and this type of socialism, while pointing out the evils of democracy, offered explanations and held out promises as follows: Because democracy can only be beneficial to a small number of people, dictatorship is necessary; because real democracy cannot fully meet your lofty aspirations, help from dictatorship must be sought; because you are not accustomed to mastering your own destiny, entrust it to dictatorship; because only limited satisfaction could be derived from democracy no matter how hard you work for it, better dedicate all your energy to the "struggle for a beautiful future." This "most beautiful future," as now we well know, is autocratic tyranny.

Why do contemporary socialist countries appear in the most backward societies? This is a thought-provoking question. Up to now, this type of socialism has followed the line which leads democratic revolutions to utopianism. It relies on a feudal culture and traditional customs to destroy the tender shoots of democratic culture, and it invariably uses feudalist social philosophy to encourage blind faith in a small group regarded as saviors and leaders. Therefore, its inevitable trend is toward totalitarianism or autocratic fascism. Such an outcome is not coincidental, but follows a universal pattern. This type of socialism is a direct inheritance from feudal philosophy at its pinnacle—classical German philosophy. This is again not coincidental, but inevitable because of its very nature. Therefore, if we continue to uphold this type of utopian socialism, we are actually supporting totalitarianism or autocratic fascism.

The second interpretation is an attempt, based on observations of conditions in contemporary socialist countries, to judge socialism as a whole without analyzing the entire process of its development or noting its significance. Therefore, it provides only a narrow view. The significance of real socialism originally lies in the socialization of production and consumption. Based on this socialization, the tools on which the material existence of the entire mankind depends, namely the means of production, are managed by the user and beneficiaries. In other words, all individuals should have equal opportunities to enjoy the economic amenities of mankind as well as equal rights and duties in the use of the means of production. Therefore, socialism in its original sense should first insure equal rights for individuals in their livelihood. These rights can be realized only through free organization and coordination with democratic politics. Therefore, socialism is essentially inclined toward democracy. All autocratic fascist rulers, after coming to power, have wantonly suppressed any democratic movement from within the socialist ranks. . . . Unless blind faith in autocrats is eliminated and utopian embellishments are replaced by realism, democratic tendencies will not be strong enough to overthrow autocratic fascism.

People have a dual character. In both typical bourgeois society and contemporary socialist society—a bourgeois society of autocratic monopoly —people have to, on the one hand, create with their labor all forms of wealth including consumer goods and the means of continuing production, namely capital. On the other hand, they have no control over their production and distribution, and have to be satisfied with the minimum means of subsistence provided out of this capital. In a democratic socialist society, people can, through democratic process, control the means of production. As producers, they need to fulfill their social obligations, but, as laborers, they can share the material and spiritual benefits. Then, as consumers, they can make demands. "People" stands for a large number of individuals as well as for each individual. This is my definition of the term "people." Individualism and collectivism are two components of people's ideology. At present, in a social system where there is no room for the independent existence of individualism, there can be no collectivism to speak of. What actually exist are autocratic individualism and small group mentality. Out of their nature, autocrats like to suppress democratic individualism with small group mentality and submerge people's collectivism with autocratic individualism.

(3)   Modernized Production and Democracy

All Marxist theorists have told us that democracy is only some trick practiced on people by bourgeois windbags, and that dictatorship provides the only way to people's equal rights and freedom in daily life. However, from what we can witness, the human rights of Western people, who are "deceived by social windbags," are safeguarded; their thinking is free; and their material life far surpasses what is possible under our "advanced socialist" productive system.

On the other hand, in the East, all of the people's human rights are unprotected. They can only enjoy "Marxist freedom." Even their material life is far below that of our comrade workers who are "victims of currency inflation," exploitation, and oppression. Furthermore, if we compare the peoples of the East with those comrades under bourgeois democracy thirty, fifty, or one hundred years ago, we can see the gap widening with the passing of time. The classics published in the West a century ago could perfectly well have drawn upon our present situation for their examples; it is almost as though history had stood still.

Is democracy empty talk by people divorced from production? Or is it some political means to enrich society; a social condition to develop the economy? Even Marxism can no longer supply the answer. As long as the disciples and successors do not distort facts, this question can be studied with an open mind. . . .

From the standpoint of modern history, we can see that the economies of all well-run democracies have developed fast and with increasing momentum until a very high level has been reached. The United States and Japan are good examples. Japan has been able to develop its economy despite a shortage of national resources.

Autocrats[3] have to use conspiracy and violence in their struggle for power. Such conspiracy and violence, even when on a small scale, usually cause great social upheaval and bring irremediable damage to production and living conditions. For example, in "socialist countries," every change of personnel at the top level has been accompanied by an earthquake, bringing tremendous losses to national production and the people's livelihood. Even lesser struggles at the lower levels, where people plot against one another, can still cause incalculable damage. If, however, these lower-level struggles become merged with a top-level one, the result is catastrophic to the economy of the "socialist country." This is one of the important reasons why socialist accumulation [of capital], though greater than that in democratic countries, fails to sustain the development of production.

Therefore, we are fully justified in asserting that democracy is a prerequisite for rapid economic modernization. Without this precondition modernization of production and livelihood is impossible, all pledges by any Great Man to the contrary notwithstanding.

Human society, like the universe, is pluralistic and not monistic. Why, then, has the philosophical basis of totalitarianism always been monistic? This is an important question to be studied by our explorers. Monism, the core of autocracy, recognizes only one most basic motive force. Does the universe depend on a most basic motive force for its development? Does mankind depend on a most basic motive force for its progress? The theory of the autocrats is self-contradictory, and we must not trust them anymore. Let us set our minds in motion and explore! The hallmark of all lackeys is a willingness to be deceived. Under existing conditions, our task is not an easy one. Unless, of course, we are willing to be deceived.

III

People everywhere are talking about human rights. But successive generations of rulers have never been willing to protect human rights, even though they claim their government is "democratic." At best they say they do not agree with the popular interpretations of human rights. How can this forgotten subject suddenly evoke such divergent points of view? I have been pondering this for a long time and now propose to share my views on the subject.

(1)   Human Rights and Democracy

Human rights is a term used to denote the rights of an individual as a human being. What rights does a person have? He has the rights to live, to live a meaningful life. The reason one must have these rights is that life will not be worth fighting for without such rights, and that he will be able to win for himself some station in life through these rights. We all know that every human being occupies some position in life. If he cannot establish an independent and autonomous position through his own strength and inherent rights, he will be forced by virtue of the power of others to occupy a subservient position. We call such a position servitude. In other words, once one loses his human rights, he loses his rights as a human being, and what is left to him is nothing but enslavement. Viewed from a different angle, this means that when a man wants to make others subservient to him and enslave them, he must deprive others of their rights, and this is what the oppressors of all ages strive to achieve. The oppressed, however, must oppose this in order to win their rights.

There is a widely accepted concept in traditional Chinese culture that making life impossible for the people is a prelude to rebellion and the basic cause of political instability. But it is too simple to equate hunger with making life impossible for the people. The *Water Margin** heroes did not revolt because they were starving. The standard of living of the Chinese on the eve of the Taiping Rebellion was no doubt much higher than that at the time when Tayu launched his flood-control operations.†

---

* A popular old novel (also known in English as *All Men are Brothers*) about eleventh-century rebels.

† This presumably is a reference to the mythical ancient figure who is credited with taming China's rivers. ("Were it not for Yu," remarks the c. 300 B.C. classic *Zuojuan*, "would we not all be fishes?")

Why did poverty contribute to political stability while relative prosperity became the major cause of political instability? Why did the well-fed and warmly clothed heroes of the *Water Margin* revolt? The Marxist theory of "economic determinism" does not seem to answer this question satisfactorily. The Confucian saying that "an oppressive government is worse than a tiger," now so widely rejected, actually seems more telling than the more fashionable Marxism-Leninism.

What do the phrases "oppressive governments" and "making life impossible for the people" imply? Hunger and lack of clothing represent only one of the consequences of "oppressive governments" and "making life impossible for the people." Making life impossible for the people means that people are denied the conditions to lead a normal life. An oppressive government denotes the deprivation of man's position and rights which he has won through his own effort in order to be free of subservience and servitude. If we think carefully, we will see a striking similarity between the struggles of the past to oppose oppressive governments and the current struggles for human rights. We can even say that the history of mankind represents not only man's struggle against *nature* for conditions to live normally, but also his struggle against his *fellow men*. The latter struggle is commonly known as politics.

When a given form of political struggle is widely accepted by people and exists in an established form, it becomes a political system. The political systems of the human race, divergent and numerous as they are, can be grouped into two categories: (1) Autocracy, such as the aforesaid system of servitude, protects the special rights of the few, but denies everyone else his rights as a human being, and (2) Democracy, a cooperative system, recognizes the equal rights of all human beings and resolves all social problems on the basis of cooperation. These two systems, or these two kinds of struggles, are the mainspring of contemporary political struggles. One of the most important aspects of these struggles relates directly to the struggle for human rights. While the high level of productivity achieved in modern times has made it basically possible to provide conditions for human subsistence, the question of the conditions of man's life—a political question—has become the focal point of contention. The struggles launched by the *Water Margin* heroes were exactly the kind of struggle aimed at winning equality of rights for man as a human being. But they did not realize that the struggle for human rights must be continuous and cannot be achieved in one stroke. As a result, they focused their attention on those *individuals* who destroy human rights—corrupt officials and emperors—instead of uprooting the *underlying conditions*—autocratic social institutions—which are the real detriments to human rights. Consequently, the Chinese common people have come to accept the idea that the result of any political struggle is nothing more than the replacement of rulers. Now we must see to it that this idea is changed. Two millennia of Chinese history demonstrate that we cannot rely on a few individuals to win happiness for everybody. Judging by the history of many European and American countries, the struggle to achieve democratic social conditions is the most dependable vehicle to achieve happiness for the greatest majority. Why do we continue to waste our efforts on the power struggle of a few? Why do we rest our hopes on a few saviors? We must dedicate ourselves to the proposition that the outcome of political struggles should secure for all the right to live as equals. We must trust any political group which struggles to achieve this objective because they work for us. Any group or individuals who obstruct us from achieving this objective are our enemies because they stand in the way of our happiness.

(2)   Equality and Democracy

Karl Marx once pointed out that absolute, complete, and final equality cannot possibly exist. I wish this were not Marx's prediction. The struggle for equality in human rights would be meaningless unless man can realize fully all his wishes after reaching the stage of an ideal society. Marx's prediction was arbitrary, and just a little too clever. It shakes up ideologues, but it also provides crafty schemers with a handy justification for cheating the people of backward countries. Let us think carefully. Can there ever be a time when everyone could realize all his wishes? That is impossible because man's wishes increase faster than there are conditions to satisfy them. As soon as man's wishes, once regarded as fantasies, are satisfied, new wishes beyond existing means of fulfillment will grow on top of those already realized. This has been told in great detail by the Russian writer Pushkin in his epic poem called "the Story of a Fisherman and the Goldfish." The development of conditions for the fulfillment of man's wishes can never keep pace with the increase of man's wishes even if we could invoke the power of the Almighty and the power of imagination. Will our physical and human resources develop at a rate faster than the increase of man's appetite? There is no need to answer this question, because Marx said: "Do not take the human will for the changing rules of the objective world."

Is there an answer to this question in the most complete, most inclusive, most correct Marxist philosophy? Naturally, there is. The problem of equal rights can be resolved only in actual struggle. In fact, such solutions have been found one after another in the development of human history, though no ultimate solution can be arrived at in one stroke. To achieve an ultimate solution in one stroke has been the habitual fantasy of German philosophy as well as Marxist philosophy.

A solution to this problem requires continuous struggle to achieve the social conditions which provide the real solution—democracy. Founded on the recognition of everyone's right to live, democracy therefore will provide all with an equal opportunity to realize this right. When there is an opportunity in a democracy for everyone to enjoy equal rights, and if the results show that in the process of realizing one's equal rights one does not infringe upon the rights of others, nor are one's rights infringed upon by others, we must say one's equal rights are already a reality. Whether or not precise equality results is not so important; the essential equality is there.

Is it possible to achieve equality without obtaining equal rights? Of course not. The ideals of communism are obviously as deceptive as "drawing a cake to satisfy one's hunger." Can anyone dream of realizing equality under a system of servitude, or autocracy, where equal rights do not exist? It would be a big lie to say that is possible. Can the people's lives be modernized under conditions of deception and servitude, led by a government which does not recognize the equal rights of man? Of course not. So, the modernization of the people's lives requires the modernization of the social system—democracy. As long as there is democracy, there is a possibility as well as opportunity to realize equal rights. The highly developed economy of the Soviet Union is used first as a powerful tool by the privileged few to destroy the happiness of their own people and the people of other countries. What go to feed the people who produce the tool are but the leftovers of the privileged. Will the modernization we look forward to be as pitiful as this modernized servitude? I hope not.

(3)   The Rule of Law and Democracy

There are people who argue that the rule of law and autocracy are diametrically opposed and that the law means democracy. But that is not true. Law is the permanent part of a political system. Since law is needed all the time, it is reduced to writing to form the basis of a system, which is normally not subject to change. The rule of law backed up by criminal sanctions is a vital political vehicle to sustain society. It is used by democracies as well as by autocracies. It all depends on the actual nature of the political system concerned.

We had law in antiquity. Qin Shi Huang [third century B.C.] used it. But it was neither beneficial to the people nor conducive to democracy. I do not think anything beneficial will come out of it if it is used by a contemporary Qin Shi Huang. As a matter of fact, history shows us that an autocracy backed up by the rule of law is simply tyranny. This has been attested beyond doubt by the history of China. Do you still want a tyrannical rule of law, a replica of the rule of law practiced by the Gang of Four? I am sure you do not want that. That is why the teachings of Confucius about "benevolent government" and that "an oppressive government is worse than a tiger" have been more favorably received by the people for several thousand years than the tyranny of Qin Shi Huang which they have all detested. But the "benevolent government" of Confucius was never put into practice either. Why? Because Confucius and his disciples counted on autocratic governments to realize equal rights. As a result, his disciples became either the accomplices of tyrants or they naively advocated struggling against tyrants (often themselves winding up as the victims of their own fantasies). We must reject the dregs of Confucianism, that is, the fantasy that tyrants can ever be persuaded to practice benevolent government. But the *essence* of Confucianism, which we do want to keep, is the concept that people are born with equal rights.

In traditional Chinese culture, the term "benevolent government" was used to oppose the "autocratic rule of law." But this was an erroneous distinction. A "benevolent government" is only a means to an end, and that end is the realization of human rights. We know now that this objective can be achieved by the rule of law, and we can even say it can be achieved only by democracy. The Marxist socialist experiment of using dictatorship to achieve equal rights has been going on for decades. Actual facts have demonstrated time and again that it simply will not work. Furthermore, a "dictatorship of the majority" is only a Utopian dream. After all, a dictatorship is a dictatorship; power is bound to fall into the hands of a few. The form of government fit for the protection of the equal rights of all is democracy. But it takes the rule of law to sustain the kind of democracy based on the cooperation of all the people. Presently, there are enemies of democracy who want to replace the rule of law by a fascist regime or adulterate the rule of law to destroy democracy. These two approaches, no matter how different they might be, aim ultimately at the destruction of the people's democratic rights. Sometimes they may even try craftily to introduce a new approach as if attempting to discredit a notorious existing system. For example, the Gang of Four once tried to defraud the people by advocating the rule of law as if they were prepared to jettison the bureaucratic dictatorship. In reality, their rule of law is basically a lawless dictatorship. As long as political power remains in the hands of the dictatorial rulers, it is bound to be used to control the people. But how can the powerless people ever expect to seize power from the dictatorial rulers and place them under control?

We want the rule of law, but we want the kind of rule of law which is conducive to the realization of equal rights. The people must attentively watch the progress of lawmaking and be sure that the law being adopted is the kind of law designed to protect equal rights. Anyone who adulterates the contents of the law is our enemy. Anyone who capitalizes on his past meritorious achievements to infringe on the people's democratic rights will be denounced as an unforgivable defrauder no matter how worthy and impressive his past achievements. We must never connive with such offenders; connivance has taught mankind a lesson of bitterness unprecedented in recent centuries. Indeed, China has experienced something the nation had not seen for thousands of years. Our wise and intelligent people must not fall back into the fraudulent trap set by ruthless adventurers. We must never be enslaved again.

DOCUMENT 13
ON THE PRESENT DEMOCRATIC MOVEMENT
By Shou He

On behalf of the [Enlightenment] Society, I hope I can use my name to provide some important information for those who are interested. To be honest with ourselves, we must first be honest with the people. This is the guiding principle of our society. This is essential for our confidence and strength. The birth of this society is a milestone in the on-going search for freedom. However, those who joined our society have yet to feel the bold spirit of encouragement and glorious ideals. We are not putting forward new ideals, but have confidence in the old ones.

Our conclusion has openly given us a high degree of understanding of the emphatic spiritual factor and the meaning of freedom. Therefore we have a specific attraction. The democratic policy and system that our office exercises rely on the hopes, ideals, intelligence, and selflessness of each member. The combination of this hope and understanding is fully reflected in this journal.

Today the warm feeling for freedom is on the rise. The nation that always respects the human rights of the individual is worthy of our following. History has enabled us to understand that our system cannot remain without change. The influence of history has already weakened its foundation. We all remember our past development. Sometimes it was glorious and brilliant, but sometimes it seemed to be particularly dangerous.

We have experienced both the peaks and the deep valleys. We predict that in the future mankind is bound to progress toward democracy and freedom. At present our country is still in the transitional period from feudal sovereignty to the stage of socialist democracy. The supreme leaders of the state still do not have the courage to be elected by the people. We should follow the example of the United States, which holds a presidential election once every four years. The numerous bureaucratic organs are still obstacles to the Four Modernizations. As leaders they have not shouldered their leadership responsibilities. They do not implement and mobilize the people's activism nor implement and fulfill their tasks. They are only the mouthpiece for conveying documents. The government's various leadership organs should be placed in the hands of the local people. In this way we can appoint those best able to shoulder the most important work. At present our people are still very ignorant. They still know very little about the outside world. This is a result of the permanent closed-door policy of hoodwinking the people. We must liberate the politically suppressed people. Our ultimate objective is to smash all the shackles that bind the ideology of the people, to bring about a new outlook, and to produce a new constitution with binding strength.

Up to now the democratic movement still does not receive effective protection. Those who participate in the democratic movement still encounter very great threats and considerable danger. This is taken for granted. It is very difficult to determine to what extent Democracy Wall will develop. Currently we are advocating neither ultraleftism nor ultrarightism. We must have a clearer understanding so that we can not only see the present but also the future. Otherwise we will go astray. At present we are in an era of unprecedented profound and rapid change. We must fully reflect this politically-awakening reality. The Enlightenment Society is fearlessly taking the lead in this. We must shoulder any important tasks regardless of the costs, welcome any difficulties, oppose all enemies, and support all friends to insure that democracy will not be destroyed and that we will win victory. While exerting such efforts, we are also fully confident of the support of our comrades to push the democratic movement forward. We salute those fighters who selflessly and fearlessly offer themselves to democracy! We salute those who launch a full-scale debate on and challenge of democracy and human rights! We salute those who unremittingly run their associations well! Some people might say, let them fool around with Democracy Wall and go mad. Our reply is that the wheel of history is turned by the people. People want democracy and freedom. Anyone who attempts to obstruct and suppress the democratic movement will come to no good. Justice is bound to triumph over evil. Our cause foretells success, since success foretells life and not death.[4]

DOCUMENT 14
DEMOCRACY OR BUREAUCRACY?
By Lu Min

To speed up realization of the Four Modernizations, it is essential to gradually abolish the "system of appointing cadres" and to establish the democratic system modeled after the Paris Commune. To carry this great struggle through to the end, profoundly understanding Marxist theory on the state will be of important guiding significance. This article will summarily deal with this problem. Comrades are requested to give us criticism and correction where mistakes are found.

I

According to Marxist theory, the state used to derive its strength from its bureaucrats and its standing army. Using the pen and the gun as tools, the ruling class suppressed the people. It was both a tumor and a parasite that gobbled up the society's wealth.

However, to thoroughly eliminate the standing army and officials, it is necessary to thoroughly eliminate the system of the standing army and the bureaucratic system which engenders bureaucrats, because these two systems are the foundation of the standing army and the bureaucrats. If we do not eliminate these two systems, the standing army and the bureaucrats will appear again. Therefore, the political tool that really enslaves the people (that is, the state machinery) is not chiefly the standing army and officials but the system of the standing army and the bureaucratic system. To destroy the old state machinery, we must therefore not only topple the standing army and the officials, but also mainly destroy the system of the standing army and the bureaucratic system. We must also replace them with the militia system and with the democratic system which is modeled after the Paris Commune. At that time, Marx did not advocate that the proletariat establish a standing army. He advocated that all systems of a standing army be abolished. He advocated that the standing army be replaced by the whole armed people and that the bourgeois standing army should not be replaced by the proletarian standing army. Of course, he also opposed replacing old bureaucrats with new bureaucrats.

However, to abolish the system of the standing army and the bureaucratic system is not an easy job. First, because imperialism still exists, the proletariat, after its victory, can only destroy the bourgeois standing army, but cannot abolish the standing army system, because it must establish a standing army as defense against imperialist invasion. Practice has proved this point.

Why did Marx advocate that the system of the standing army should be abolished? Why did he not advocate that the proletariat should establish the standing army? Marx lived in an era of free capitalism and could not understand monopoly capitalism and the law of the unbalanced development of its economics and politics. Limited by his era, Marx could not come to the conclusion that the victory of socialism can be won in a country alone. He could only come to the conclusion that the victory of socialism must be won in all countries or in the majority of countries at the same time. Should this situation really appear in the future, the proletariat would not need to build a standing army and could use the armed people to suppress the resistance of the remnant bourgeoisie within the country. On the basis of this situation, Marx therefore advocated that, after winning victory, the proletariat should immediately abolish the standing army and replace it with the armed people. The world situation subsequently underwent a great change. When the victory of socialism was won in a country or in a small number of countries, due to different historical conditions, the proletariat could not mechanically apply the Marxist theory, could not abolish the system of a standing army, and had to build a proletarian standing army. Although preserving the standing army—a "special force"—can under certain conditions become a tool for careerists to restore the old system and enslave the people again, the proletariat cannot but build a standing army. This does not run counter to Marxism. Had Marx lived, he would have held that it would be necessary and correct for the proletariat to build a standing army under the new historical conditions.

II

If the bureaucrats are not abolished, this will fundamentally run counter to Marxism. This is theoretically incontrovertible. Due to the existence of imperialism, the standing army cannot be abolished. However, it is incorrect to say that, due to the existence of imperialism, bureaucrats cannot be abolished. The fatal problem now is that we have superficially abolished the bureaucrats but have not intrinsically abolished them. We cannot abolish the bureaucrats, because at present the bureaucratic system which engenders the bureaucrats has not been abolished.

Although the "system of appointing cadres," which we now use, and the "system of conferring ranks" are different in class nature, the forms that they take are the same. These two systems provide that responsible persons at all levels are appointed by their respective upper levels and are not elected by the people, and can be discharged or changed at any time. Therefore, the "system of appointing cadres" is also antagonistic to the democratic system in which elections are conducted from the bottom up and which is modeled after the Paris Commune. The "system of appointing cadres" is the "system of conferring ranks" in disguised form. We must therefore gradually abolish it; otherwise, the camouflaged new bureaucratic elements will be engendered again.

We must clearly understand the relationship between bureaucrats and the bureaucratic system. We cannot treat them both the same way. The former is "hair," while the latter is "skin." If the "skin" is not destroyed, how can the hair be eliminated? If we regard toppling all old bureaucrats as destroying the old state machinery, we shall run counter to Marxist theory on the state and commit the biggest mistake.

It must be clear that toppling a group of old bureaucrats will destroy a portion of the structure of the state machinery but will not destroy its foundation which is the "system of conferring ranks." Only by destroying the structure and foundation of the old state machinery, that is, destroying the bureaucrats and the "system of conferring ranks," can it be said that the state machinery is completely destroyed.

The proletariat should treat the "system of conferring ranks" as it treats the system of private ownership because they are originally twin brothers. Basically speaking, the proletariat cannot regard the political tool that previously enslaved them as the political tool that liberated them. Therefore, Marx advocated that, after winning political power, the proletariat should immediately abrogate the "system of conferring ranks," or the "system of conferring ranks" in disguised form.

Marx maintained that it would only be possible to abrogate this system after the victory of socialism had been won in all countries or in the great majority of countries. Since victory cannot be won at the same time in all countries or in the great majority of countries, the "system of appointing cadres" cannot be abrogated. Practice has shown that, immediately after a victory is won in a country or a small number of countries, due to the extremely chaotic and complicated situation of the class struggle within the country and the extremely low level of the people's culture and management, the "system of appointing cadres" cannot be immediately abolished and the democratic system modeled after the Paris Commune cannot be carried out. If this were done, the whole country would be in an anarchic condition and go to ruin, and the proletariat would lose the political power which it had just seized. However, following the gradual stability within the country and the gradual promotion of the people's cultural level, management, and skills, the "system of appointing cadres" must be gradually abolished.

Therefore, under the conditions in which the victory of socialism is won in a small number of backward countries, it is impossible to immediately abrogate the "system of appointing cadres." When the conditions are ripe, the system must be abolished. Following the gradual maturity of the objective conditions, it can gradually be abolished. This is the only correct way.

III

Historical lessons merit attention. The Soviet Union ruined its proletarian revolutionary cause mainly because it did not abolish in time the "system of posting according to grades." Lenin firmly pressed for the abolition of this system even before the October Revolution. He pointed out in his famous "April Theses" and in a number of other articles: "All officials are to be elected and subject to recall at any time" (*Collected Works of Lenin,* vol. 24, p. 3). However, this goal could not be immediately attained when the October Revolution was just under way, and the "system of posting according to grades" was retained for the time being. In spite of this, a number of outstanding representatives of the working class were appointed as responsible persons of administrative organs at all levels. This tremendously helped consolidate the newly established regime. Lenin pointed out at the Tenth Congress of the Soviet Communist Party (CPSU): If we opposed leadership by the party immediately after the introduction of universal suffrage, we would be moving in the direction of syndicalism and anarchism because this was "totally at variance with the practical experience of all semiproletarian revolutions and the present proletarian revolution" (*Selected Works of Lenin,* vol. [?], p. 508). Lenin did not want to keep the "system of posting according to grades" forever but simply took it as a stopgap measure, and the system was to be gradually abolished when objective conditions matured. This wish could not be materialized because Lenin died too soon.

China was to a large extent influenced by the Soviet Union and traversed nearly the same course as the Soviet Union did before restoration took place there. We nearly ruined our revolutionary cause because we had not gradually abolished the "system of posting according to grades" following the gradual maturing of objective conditions. Because of this, our revolutionary government was at one time on the brink of collapse.

If this "system of posting according to grades," which has basically become a fixed practice, did not exist and if leading cadres at all levels were elected by the people and subject to recall at any time, could the hateful Gang of Four have risen to power? Even if they had managed to rise to power, could they have avoided being overthrown? Was it not precisely by using this "system of posting according to grades" that the disguised "empress" and "male bureaucrats" could topple a large number of long-tested and beloved revolutionary veteran cadres, strike down a large number of meritorious scientists, technical cadres, and labor models, and promote a large number of careerists, conspirators, hooligans, and villains to important positions? Should not this painful historical lesson make us sit up and think? We must resolutely eradicate the factional network of the Gang of Four and must not be fainthearted and hesitant in action and give up halfway. However, we must clearly perceive that this is merely for "cutting weeds" and not for "removing the roots." If we stop at this struggle and do not go on to eliminate the soil and hotbed for breeding the Gang of Four, that is, the "system of posting according to grades," a "gang of seven" and a "gang of eight" will emerge in the future, the stability of our political and production situation, which has not been won easily, will be upset, and the Four Modernizations will end in failure.

While negative lessons make us sober, Yugoslavia's experience is a source of inspiration. In compliance with Marx's great teachings and in light of the concrete conditions in their country, Yugoslavia gradually abolished the "system of posting according to grades" and step-by-step established a democratic system modeled after the Paris Commune. Because of this, they not only quickly recovered from war losses but in no time achieved economic prosperity and built a socialist society in which there is political liberty, democracy, stability, and unity. They have set an example for us.

At the same time as we are learning from the experience of Yugoslavia, we must clearly recognize the imperfection of their democratic system, which stems from the fact that objective conditions have not yet fully matured. Even if we have basically abolished the "system of posting according to grades," we should not think that everything will go off without a hitch. So long as the standing army is not disbanded, restoration can still take place under special conditions.

Only by gradually abolishing the "system of posting according to grades" and establishing a democratic system can the proletariat secure its foothold and gradually consolidate its revolutionary regime. This is precisely why the revolutionary regime in Yugoslavia is more consolidated. Abolishing the "system of posting according to grades" has a vital bearing, not only on consolidating the socialist superstructure but also on consolidating the socialist economic base.

In our country, the means of production are not directly controlled by the people but are entrusted to people's representatives—administrative cadres at all levels. For this reason, the people cannot control the means of production unless they have control over the cadres. Since the "system of posting according to grades" has rendered the people unable to supervise and control the cadres, the socialist economic base will be threatened if this old system is not gradually abolished. And, sooner or later, people's ownership will be turned into ownership by bureaucrats and emperors, and people will be exploited and enslaved again. Therefore, abolishing the "system of posting according to grades" is a matter of importance which will affect China's destiny and future and is a crucial political issue.

At present, the Party Central Committee headed by Hua Guofeng is leading the people of the whole country to carry out this great and arduous struggle. The revolution will meet with great resistance because it will shake feudal and traditional ideas of the past thousands of years and offend the diehard and conservative elements. It is a lot more difficult to overthrow the old system than to topple the old bureaucrats. We must not only break through resistance from the right, that is, from the people who try hard to obstruct democratic reforms, but also overcome interference from the "left," that is, from the ultrademocracy practiced by the petty bourgeoisie. Whatever the resistance, the historical current of people's demand for democracy is irresistible. Under the leadership of the Party Central Committe headed by Comrade Hua Guofeng, the Chinese people will certainly be able to firmly carry out the correct line, abolish the "system of posting according to grades" and establish a democratic system modeled after the Paris Commune in a planned and systematic way, and win final victory in this great struggle.

Inspired by the heroic April Fifth Movement, the Chinese nation has entered into an era of hard struggle to win genuine socialist democracy.

Long live the people.[5]

DOCUMENT 15
THAW MANIFESTO
From *Thaw*

All things go from hot to cool. Passivity and action alternate endlessly.

In the real world, people are disgusted with struggle and need peace. They are opposed to hatred and need rational and responsible guidance.

All the artificial divisions in the world are temporary.

Everyone seeks light and happiness. Everyone fears darkness and suffering. People cannot long live in a cruel world. They need friendship, harmony, freedom, creativity, and progress.

Under today's glittering sun, China, which has been cut off from the world for many thousands of years, is now facing a great and historically unprecedented thaw in politics, thought, philosophy, economics, theory, and spirit.

In order to hasten the thaw of ice-bound China, to welcome the advent of the first spring, and to realize the long-cherished dreams of the Chinese people, this [Thaw] Society publishes the following manifesto as a working program:

1. Progressive thought of all kinds should be propagated, concentrating for the present on Rousseau's ideas about human rights and Sun Yatsen's principle of democracy.

2. To democratize politics, the study of culture and civilization should be promoted on the basis of the New Testament's teachings of forgiveness, understanding, and universal love.

3. We demand variety in politics, thought, art, and life. We shall oppose all monarchical systems cloaked in republican garb and all "democratic" dictators.

4. We demand that certain impractical elements of Marxism be revised. We must be rid of class struggle and violent revolution because they divide mankind.

5. We demand that the outdated elements in Mao Zedong's thought be discarded, along with Shaoshan-type indigenous policies[6] which were formulated according to certain mistaken and counterproductive principles. We suggest that every kind of idol and tablet which the Gang of Four set up everywhere for Mao be torn down immediately.

6. We demand that old thought and old ethics, which run contrary to the common consciousness and suppress individualism, be eliminated along with the odious minister-prince, father-son feudal ranking system which we have inherited from thousands of years of feudal society.

7. We demand that the country get rid of ancient formulas and be-

gin to explore afresh new philosophies, new political organizations, new economic theories, and new moral principles which are suitable for today and the future. Sun Yat-sen's theories can well serve as the basis for a new national philosophy suited to contemporary life and people's emotional needs.

8. We demand that Mao Zedong's one-man Party quickly revert to being a Party for all its members and for the whole country, on the basis of democratic collective leadership within the Party. We oppose all superstitions and the worshiping of individuals and all dogmatic cliques which are contrary to the people's interests.

9. The Party cannot replace the government. We demand the re-establishment of the position of Chairman of the Republic [held by Liu Shaoqi until 1966, after which the position was abolished]. Mao Zedong was wrong to forbid this. His individual wishes cannot represent the collective will of thirty million Party members, nor of hundreds of millions of citizens.

10. We demand a comprehensive constitution and the formation of a decent, complete, national legal system. According to this constitution, government and Party leaders must be elected by secret ballot, and those elected should serve for four years. The honest and capable may stand for reelection, but they should not serve for more than two terms. We oppose anyone's staying in power for life. The appointment of a "representative" by an official with no endorsement by the people violates the will of the people.

11. We demand modern science and modern cultural life that are suitable for law and democratic government. On this basis, the country can gradually advance toward what Liu Shaoqi called "the peaceful democratic stage."

12. The courageous revolutionary spirit of initiative and self-criticism promoted by the Chinese Communist Party during this new period should be firmly upheld. The policy of ridding the Chinese people of poverty and backwardness, and the wise measures to realize the Four Modernizations, should likewise be supported.

13. Long live Chairman Liu Shaoqi and Marshal Peng Dehuai, who advocated peace and democracy and were sacrificed under Mao Zedong's obscene one-man dictatorship. They are banners of Chinese democracy and live forever in the hearts of the people.

14. We call upon the Chinese Communist Party and the Chinese Nationalist Party to put aside their long-held prejudice and hostility and begin a new cooperation under new historical conditions, thus making a great contribution to the unification of China, the growth of democracy for the Chinese race, and peace and progress for the world.

15. After the two parties have begun cooperating, we suggest that both publicly declare their administrative programs and then carry out a democratic election, letting the people freely choose the government they trust.

16. A thaw is the common hope of both China and the world. Every person who loves truth can shoulder this banner in order to achieve a great thaw. They can struggle for the ideas, politics, theories, spirit, and life of the Chinese people.

This manifesto shall never be retracted! It is in accordance with the trends of world civilization. We are fighting to achieve genuine human rights and genuine democracy for China and to sweep away the ideological barriers obstructing the realization of the Four Modernizations. We are struggling to contribute to peace and progress for China and for the world.

All those who approve of this manifesto may freely join this society, regardless of social, political, or economic position, race, creed, or nationality. We heartily welcome any suggestions.

SECTION THREE
ON CIVIL LIBERTIES

The centerpiece of the democratic movement was the call for human rights. Although this included a demand that citizens' economic rights be honored, it merely underlined official hypocrisy; the dissidents were not fundamentally out of line with official orthodoxy on the point. Rather, it was in calling upon the government to respect citizens' civil liberties that new ground was broken.

On this issue, the Human Rights League's "Nineteen Points" (Document 16) stands as the definitive statement. From there it was left to others to elaborate on the various rights sought. In Document 17 the need for freedom of speech is underscored. The next two documents deal with the right to publish.

A word of background is in order regarding Document 19. Citizens in China are encouraged to write letters of complaint to officials and to newspapers; in fact, selected letters are published. But here a writer in April Fifth Forum *warns that such communications often do not get past the post office from which they are sent and that writers run the risk of reprisals.*

The final essay in this section is from Exploration *and is predictably the most militant. Underlying all of the demands seems to be the author's insistence that the people have a right to a government of their choosing. To the present leaders the author declares: "No one has entrusted you with the authority to rule."*

DOCUMENT 16
NINETEEN POINTS
From Human Rights League

The China Human Rights League was officially established in Beijing on 1 January 1979. The league discussed and approved this human rights declaration.

In the final analysis, the 1976 Tian-an-men Incident was a human rights movement. The significance of human rights is more far-reaching, profound, and enduring than anything else. This is a new mark of the political consciousness of the Chinese people and the natural trend of contemporary history. With a new content and a unique spirit, our human rights movement this year has again won the support and approval of the whole world. This has hastened and promoted the establishment of relations between the Chinese and U.S. governments. To stimulate the development of our social productive forces and promote world peace and the progressive cause, we put forward the following nineteen points:

1. The citizens demand freedom of thought, freedom of speech, and the release of everyone in the country found guilty of offenses connected with these two freedoms. It is likewise absurd to incorporate individual thinking in the Constitution and have a successor listed in Party regulations and the Constitution. This is against the principle of freedom of speech and against the law of human thought. It is also against the materialistic principle of the "diversified nature of matter," is a manifestation of feudalism, and is regarded with great disgust by the people throughout the country. Nothing is sacred, unchanging, or inviolable. The citizens demand the thorough elimination of superstition, deification, and personality cult, the removal of [Mao's] crystal coffin in favor of a memorial hall, the building of a memorial hall dedicated to Premier Zhou, the commemoration of the May Fourth Movement every year, and the emancipation of faith from the confines of superstition.

2. The citizens demand that there be practical safeguards for their constitutional right to assess and criticize Party and state leaders. To save the present generation and all future generations from suffering, to protect truth and justice, and to develop productive forces, citizens demand that the feudal imperial criterion of equating opposition to an individual with opposition to the revolution (a criterion that is still being applied) be given up forever. They demand that our society be built on the basis of the principles of people's democracy.

3. Give the minority nationalities sufficient autonomy. Our country is not only multinational but also has many political parties and factions.

In our socialist development, we should take the existence of various political parties and factions into due consideration. Various parties and groups should be allowed to join the National People's Congress (NPC). It is most ridiculous that various parties and factions cannot join the NPC, which claims to be an organ with supreme power in the country. This is a manifestation of replacing the government with the Party and not separating the Party from the government. This is incompatible with democratic centralism. It will inevitably result in the continuous development of bureaucratism. Our country's citizens do not want a "showcase" constitution.

4. Citizens demand that a national referendum be held to elect state leaders and the leaders at all levels in various areas. Deputies to the Fourth and Fifth National People's Congresses were not elected in a general election involving all the people. This was a scathing lampoon of our socialist democracy. It made a mockery of the human rights of 970 million citizens. The citizens demand the establishment of a "citizens' committee" or "citizens' court" through a direct vote of all the citizens. It would be a standing organ of the NPC and would be able to participate in discussing and voting on policy matters and to exercise supervision over the government. The citizens demand that the state uphold the law and punish those Party and state leaders who have violated the law.

5. Chinese citizens have the right to demand that the state make the national budget, final financial statements, and the gross national product public.

6. The NPC cannot convene in camera. The citizens demand the right to attend as observers and witness the proceedings of the NPC, its standing committee conferences, and its preparatory meetings.

7. State ownership of the means of production should be gradually abolished in a transition to social ownership.

8. China and the Party have altered their understanding of the theory and practice of Comrade Tito and his Yugoslav version of socialism. Major changes in our domestic and foreign policies and guidelines in recent years have borne full testimony to the bankruptcy of "revisionism" in theory and practice. There is no objective basis for ideological differences and disputes to exist between China and the Soviet Union. The citizens demand detente. The Soviet people are a great people. The people of China and the United States, China and Japan, China and the Soviet Union must be friends for all generations to come.

9. The citizen's demand realization of the Marxist doctrine that a socialist society is one in which everyone can develop freely. Any socialist country's form of government is a continuation of the traditional form of capitalism. Without the material civilization of capitalism, socialist democ-

racy and freedom cannot survive. The basic thinking of this classic doctrine is also an important lesson that the Chinese people have obtained after more than twenty years of groping in the dark. We must not only draw on Western science and technology but also on Western traditions, democracy, and culture. The citizens demand that the state continue to keep closed doors open. Let ideas smash through the confines of prisons. Let freedom spread far and near. Let the wise people of China share the treasure of the whole of mankind. Let the suffering generation enjoy freedom. Let the younger generation be spared suffering. Eliminate class prejudices and ban deceptive propaganda.

10. Citizens must have the freedom to go in and out of foreign embassies to obtain propaganda, the freedom to talk to foreign correspondents, and the freedom to publish works abroad. Make available all "inside reading matter" and "inside movies" and let everyone be equal in enjoying culture. The citizens must have the freedom to subscribe to foreign magazines and newspapers and listen to foreign television and radio stations. Citizens demand that the state grant publishing and printing rights that are true to the Constitution.

11. The system in which a citizen devotes his whole life to a unit where he works must be abolished. Citizens demand the freedom to choose their own vocations, the freedom to express support [for a leader], and freedom of movement. Abolish all regulations and systems that stand in the way of solving problems of husbands and wives being obliged to live in different parts of the country.

12. Citizens demand that the state insure basic food rations for peasants and eliminate [the phenomenon of] beggars.

13. Educated young people on state farms should enjoy reassignment rights. Educated young people in agriculture demand that the state abolish inhuman treatment. They demand political equality, an improved standard of living, and a wage increase.

14. Citizens demand that the state ban the use of deceptive means to recruit various technical workers. Those cadres and units that practice deception should be punished by law. Those who give bribes, and especially those who receive bribes, should be punished.

15. While undivided attention is being paid to promoting modernization, no less attention should be given to the firm implementation of policy. The citizens demand that the state put into action the policy once applied to those Kuomintang officers and soldiers along with their families who came over to our side in the early postliberation period.

16. Secret police and the Party committee of a unit have no right to arrest citizens or investigate them. The secret police system is incompatible with socialist democracy. Citizens demand its abolition.

17. Get rid of slum quarters and crowded living quarters where people of three generations or grown sons and daughters are packed close together in the same room.

18. We are "citizens of the world." Citizens demand that the borders be thrown open, trade be promoted, culture exchanged, and labor exported. They demand the freedom to work and study abroad and the freedom to make a living or travel abroad.

19. This league appeals to the governments of all countries in the world, to human rights organizations, and to the public for support.

China Human Rights League

Prepared 17 January 1979 in Beijing[1]

DOCUMENT 17
ABSOLVE THOSE WHO SPEAK UP
By Huai An

People have often cried that "those who speak up should be absolved from incriminating charges." However, in the reality of Chinese society, there have been frequent cases of "those who spoke up being punished." Moreover, they were regarded as "guilty of a crime deserving ten thousand deaths" for which "even death could not atone." Thus, many people were convicted or even killed simply because they uttered some words or wrote some articles. Such cases were frequent in the past, particularly during the ten years of the Cultural Revolution. This kind of "speech persecution" must come to an end!

We hold that as long as people do not pick up knives and pistols to rebel against the proletariat or give themselves over to the enemy and betray the country, and as long as they are not embezzlers, thieves, arsonists, murderers, robbers, or looters, then they should not be arrested or convicted. We should allow differing views on political issues. That which is correct can be defended; the truth cannot be overturned by false words. So, we must not be afraid of false assertions, and we certainly need not fear correct ones.

We must thoroughly implement the principle of "those who speak up should be absolved from incriminating charges" both inside and outside the Party and from top to bottom. Only in this way will it be possible to encourage extensive and free discussions. In this way we can gain the benefit of all useful opinions, and our prosperity will thus be promoted. Otherwise, the consequences will be quite dangerous.[2]

DOCUMENT 18
FREEDOM OF THE PRESS
By Zhang Wei

While human society is continuously surging ahead, a new professional "occupation," journalism, has appeared. Its task is to give the people a few more eyes to let them see still further and know what is going on in a village, city, country, and even in the whole world. News should be true and complete. Otherwise people will not be able to find out anything and will not know the true situation. How then can we correctly judge or make the correct moves to realize the fundamental spirit stipulated in the Constitution of having the people run the country? When Lin Biao and the Gang of Four were in power, the newspapers lavished praise on them. When they were overthrown, people also knew of all their crimes from the newspapers. All these crimes were discovered through later investigations. This should cause everyone to think. Most of these crimes concerned things they had said and done openly, yet the news was not released at the time. Why? If the facts had been directly and quickly announced to the people, I think the people's ability to draw distinctions would not have been inferior to that of the "Great Helmsman"! In the aftermath, we can put forward a series of questions:

Why were all the newspapers at that time fooling the people? What were their objectives? Was it not true that the news the New China News Agency announced to the people had been "filtered" or "screened"? What are the benefits to the people of this type of news? Could this possibly have been managing the press according to the "proletarian line"? Actually, the people were being fooled. The ideological foundation of this way of running newspapers betrays a lack of trust in the people. They do not welcome this kind of newspaper. We invite the editors of the official publications to go to Xidan Democracy Wall to see how the people enthusiastically buy "folk" publications. Only when a newspaper is rooted among the people can it possess vitality. When a newspaper represents only a person or a certain level of publication, it is always dull and weak. Freedom of the press would be a weapon in the hands of the people. We must strive to obtain it. Freedom of the press should be effectively protected by the Constitution. The government should provide material assistance for publications run by the people. News reporters (including "reporters of the folk publications") should have the freedom to report all news including the proceedings of government conferences at all levels, accompanying the head of state on travel outside the country to report news, report on political prisoners, investigate the daily life and property of the head of state, exchange news material with foreign reporters, comment on the government's various policies on all kinds of publications (including publications run by the people), and so forth. Article 17 of the Constitution of the People's Republic of China stipulates that "the state adheres to the principle of socialist democracy and ensures to the people the right to participate in the management of state affairs and of all economic and cultural undertakings, and the right to supervise the organs of state and their personnel."[3]

DOCUMENT 19
DEMOCRACY WALL
From *Beijing Spring*

Shortly after 10:00 a.m. on 13 December 1978, four young people came to Beijing's Democracy Wall and began to put up posters. A plainclothesman surreptitiously copied the license numbers of their vehicles. He was discovered by the masses and arrested on the spot. Under severe questioning by the masses, he was forced to produce his work permit for all to see. It turned out that he was Guo Zhenghong, a cadre of the Political Protection Section, West City Branch of the Municipal Public Security Bureau.

*   *   *

In early December 1978, a reporter from the Central Newsreel Studio, who had been filming the big events at Democracy Wall, was secretly followed by plainclothesmen and illegally interrogated.[4]

DOCUMENT 20
FREEDOM OF POSTAL COMMUNICATION
From *April Fifth Forum*

It is said that in every local post office of the nation there still exists a group of people who, though considered employees of the postal service, are under the command of a certain department of the Public Security Bureau. They do nothing except inspect "questionable" letters. Besides regular wages, these letter inspectors get a "secret-keeping allowance" for not disclosing the nature of their work.

Because of the existence of these letter inspectors, any letter thought to be "doubtful" can be inspected secretly. Therefore, many [kinds of] complaints should not be sent to the central authorities from one's local post office. Letters exposing local leaders, [for example,] are immediately removed by the letter inspectors. You can imagine what the fate of the complainer might be!

When letters are subject to letter inspection, how can we talk about the "freedom of communications"? Is it not a direct violation of the Constitution?

Thus, we appeal to the Control Commission of the Chinese Communist Party, and to the Supreme People's Court, to look into this matter and to end letter inspection in order to truly guarantee freedom of communication. No inspection should be permitted on any letter so long as it does not contain a bomb or other dangerous materials. There should be suitable laws enacted to govern the inspection of letters, and if these are violated, there should be punishment in accordance to law.

As to the question of whether letter inspection should exist at all, and whether there is any theoretical or legal basis for its existence, we shall not delve any further here.[5]

DOCUMENT 21
NONVIOLATION OF PRIVATE DWELLINGS
By Yan Fa

In the article "Truly Carrying Out the Constitution, Resolutely Returning Private Dwellings" published in *People's Daily*, 3 November 1978, page 3, there was the following paragraph:

> A short commentary of *People's Daily* has pointed out that since liberation, our Constitution has always clearly stated that the government should protect citizen's ownership of his lawful income, savings, home, and other life-supporting materials, and "nonviolation of private dwellings."

Whether or not the constitutional right of "nonviolation of private dwellings" should be interpreted to mean that no private property should be taken away from its owner is a question for the Central Standing Committee to decide. Here, I wish to express my personal opinion and talk about my own understanding of the phrase "nonviolation of private dwellings."

I believe that it should mean the following: No matter whether the property is publicly or privately owned, if there is someone living in it, then the property as well as a certain area outside the property should be protected by law. Without the permission of the dweller, no one should be allowed to enter the dwelling by any means, much less remove anything from the dwelling. In addition, no one should be permitted to use any means or any instruments or gadgets to spy on the activities of the occupant. Anyone who violates the above is committing a crime. If the dweller considers it necessary, he may file suit against the violator. The court should, following the due process, punish the violator according to the seriousness of the violator's action.

Whether or not nonviolation of private dwellings means only no occupation of private property is a question which I hope that *People's Daily* and *Beijing Daily* will answer. If there is a difference in opinion, we welcome open discussion and debate.[6]

DOCUMENT 22
THE "LIMITS" OF DEMOCRACY?
From *Exploration*

The "spirit" of the Beijing Municipal Communist Party Committee conference, which was recently convened, criticized the democratic atmosphere that occurred in Beijing after last year's November 25 forum. It also called on "Party members and people to discuss this question: Should we put up big-character posters everywhere?" The new municipal Party committee reached this conclusion: The development of the current tendency is not very good and has "impaired the state system." This is "banding together for creating disturbances," and "enemies have sneaked into our ranks." Therefore, "we must strengthen education" and "take the attitude of drawing a demarcation line between the enemy and ourselves to resolve them!"

We would like to ask these bigwigs a question: Are these the "limits" of democracy you have promised to give the people? A thousand thanks for your kindness. These limits are not lower than the limits set when the Gang of Four ran wild. The charges you have brought against others are not new charges as compared with the Gang of Four's. Are you trying to tell the people that your "revolution" is a continuation of the Gang of Four's "revolution"? Let us examine the charges you have brought against the democratic movement:

First, a few people have attacked Chairman Mao. These people probably are only "a few evil-doers"? Since Deng Xiaoping has said that Chairman Mao had also made mistakes and since the Constitution prescribes that citizens enjoy freedom of speech, why is it impermissible to attack Chairman Mao? You probably hold that Deng Xiaoping outwardly agrees but inwardly disagrees that Chairman Mao made mistakes. You probably hold that Deng Xiaoping has the right to say so and that the common people have no such right; that if Deng Xiaoping says so, he has expressed the style of a revolutionary leader, and that if the common people say so, they can be regarded as committing "counterrevolutionary crimes." You probably also hold that Deng Xiaoping has the right to delay the "evaluation of Chairman Mao's merits and faults" until future generations and that the common people have no right to attack the Great Helmsman at this time. It is said that this attack will create chaos. You probably think that the common people have no right to enjoy freedom of speech and that freedom of speech is a favor bestowed by the leadership. Freedom of speech must mean freedom to criticize anyone. Without such freedom, what is the use of freedom of speech? This is obvious to everybody. It turns out that, in the eyes of the common people, the Constitution is nothing but a scrap of paper.

Second, people are accused of producing underground publications. The existence of different views and the existence of publications of various hues are important characteristics of democracy. The Constitution prescribes that citizens enjoy freedom of assembly, association, and the press. Is it true that your bureaucratic mentality has interpreted this kind of freedom as the freedom to be "counterrevolutionaries"? Is it true that your bureaucratic mentality has interpreted this kind of freedom as the freedom to be imprisoned and shot? If this is not true, then why is it that while you announce freedom of the press you also announce that publishing is illegal? Is this a double-dealing trick or is it just like the proverbial Lord Sheh who claimed to be fond of dragons while in fact he was mortally afraid of them? Or is this just being hypocritical? We are not interested in passing judgments. All we know is that you have turned freedom of the press into an out-and-out veil to cover up the shameless and dirty ambitions in your heart of hearts.

Why do you see these publications as "underground"? This only shows that you have not allowed people to enjoy democracy and that you may suppress them at any time. This also shows that the appearance of democracy you give is nothing but a trick to win over the trust of others.

Third, the charge is that petitioners from other areas have walked in processions to present petitions. Since the Constitution prescribes that citizens enjoy freedom to demonstrate, then why is it that such processions are described as bad? This is probably because such processions were not organized by the government. If freedom must be organized by the government, then is this "freedom" the people's or the authorities'?

Fu Yuehua, a worker in Beijing, was arrested for presenting a petition. This arrest is the same kind of despicable work carried out by the Gang of Four. We demand that the government immediately release this illegally arrested young woman.

Fourth, the charge is that "foreign embassies have frequently carried out activities, that some foreigners have used money to buy big-character posters, that some Chinese have asked for mimeographs from foreigners, that some Chinese have dined in restaurants at the invitation of foreigners, and that all this has impaired the state system." What a solemn appearance the state system has! This face does not look like a face of the 1970s but, rather, like a closed-door face of the Qing dynasty. We would like to ask this face a question: Can we describe Deng Xiaoping's dining with the Japanese emperor at the latter's invitation as a Chinese dining with a foreigner at the latter's invitation? This has probably also "impaired the state system"! Asking for a few mimeographs from foreigners is "impairing the state system" but asking for hundreds of billions of *yuan* in loans and aid from foreigners does not mean "impairing the state system"? What kind of logic is this? Your teachers Marx, Engels, Stalin, and Mao Zedong surely did not impart this logic to you!

Foreigners and particularly diplomats and correspondents of various democratic countries have paid attention to the Chinese people's democratic movement. This shows that they are worthy of the trust of the people of their countries and that they are carrying out friendly relations between peoples of our countries. The support offered by foreigners to China's mass organizations shows that people of various countries throughout the world have not forgotten the Chinese people and that they care for our destiny. In fact, no one has entrusted you with the task of monopolizing friendly relations and, indeed, no one has entrusted you with the authority to rule at all! You do not represent the people. Some bigwigs in the Beijing Municipal Party Committee fear that the people might be able to truly enjoy democracy. They are currently trying their very best to disrupt this present movement. The measures they have adopted are despicable, many, and varied. The people must carefully watch how much further they may walk on the road of opposing democracy. Come what may, our publications will never be frightened into submission by this. We absolutely will not give up our right of free speech. Arrests and sabotages are not enough to stop us from publishing. We will continue to offer our views to the people.[7]

Section Four
ON THE LEGAL SYSTEM

It would be surprising if our writers demonstrated much of an understanding of law. But the following three documents are crude only in comparison with Western thinking on the subject. When considered against a background of three decades of "politics in command" and the general absence of the rule of law, the authors have a surprising grasp of just what it means for a society to have laws by which the public is protected and the government limited.

The first document is an open letter to various members of the National People's Congress on the subject of legal reform. This is followed by another open letter prompted by the first arrest of a dissident during the democratic movement. In the final document, a writer argues that a defendant should be deemed innocent until proven otherwise.

DOCUMENT 23
OPEN LETTER TO THE NPC
Human Rights League

Members of the Standing Committee and Legal Committee of the
National People's Congress (NPC):

The China Human Rights League acclaims the establishment of the
Legal Committee and the appointment of Comrade Peng Zhen as its
chairman. In our opinion, the establishment of this committee shows that
the Chinese Communist Party (CCP) is trying to end the horrifying era
where there are no laws to follow or where laws are willfully trampled
upon and is trying to change the situation in which people constantly live
in fear. It also shows that the CCP is attempting to develop the country
under its leadership into a modern society and attain democratic socialism as demanded by the people. We believe these attempts will gain inspiration from the people's support and will bear fruit through the
people's participation. We wish the Legal Committee success in these attempts and efforts. The China Human Rights League will give all-out
support to the committee's progressive work and will express opinions regarding the work. The China Human Rights League wishes to put forward a five-point proposal to the NPC Standing Committee and its Legal
Committee. We hope the recently established Legal Committee will
seriously appraise this proposal or debate it before the Sixth NPC is held.

1. We hope the NPC Standing Committee and its Legal Committee
will adopt and fully promulgate as soon as possible the laws, rules, and
regulations that are drafted in line with the existing Constitution. We
think these laws, rules, and regulations and the Constitution on which
they are based will be operative but transitional in character. They will
be fully discussed at the Sixth NPC and at meetings of concerned committees, at which time the suitable ones will be retained and the unsuitable ones discarded. We demand that various laws, rules, and regulations
be adopted and promulgated as soon as possible even though they will still
be transitional because deputies to the Fifth NPC, like those to the Fourth
NPC, were not elected by all Chinese citizens. Although the people favor
many of the deputies, the Fifth NPC does not enjoy due authority because
it is not the direct embodiment of the people's will. That is why we say the
Constitution and transitional laws are necessary for the people. Because of
the violent acts of the Gang of Four and their ilk in the past, the Chinese
nation was at the brink of collapse and the Chinese people lived in the
midst of disasters. These hard facts tell us one thing: People can no longer
live without democracy. Since the legal system alone can insure democ-

racy, people find they can no longer live in a society that does not have a legal system. They understand that the harm of a law which does not fully conform with their will is limited, but that a state of lawlessness knows no limits.

2. The most important part of the work of the NPC Standing Committee and its Legal Committee in leading the drafting of laws, rules, and regulations is to discuss and work out with the people a bill to insure true democratic elections. The China Human Rights League firmly believes that it is impermissible to repeat the procedures followed by the Fourth and Fifth NPC in electing deputies and conducting sessions. Now that attempts are being made to establish a modern society encompassing democracy and the legal system, we must first demonstrate the modern sense of legality in true democratic elections. In this regard, the CCP must show itself to be more progressive than the political parties of Western countries. Otherwise the march toward a modern society, the transition to democratic socialism, and all other efforts will be rendered impossible by the lack of fundamental conditions. We think that starting from now or in the immediate future, the Legal Committee should urge the government to provide sufficient media—broadcast time, newspapers, and magazines—for members of various political parties, social strata, and organizations to campaign for seats to the NPC and its committees. All citizens should be called upon to discuss the procedure for electing deputies and conducting meetings now or in the immediate future.

3. People belonging to various social strata, political parties, and organizations have the right to criticize the laws, rules, and regulations adopted by the NPC Standing Committee and its Legal Committee. The lawmakers are also required to hold debates with them. The Legal Committee should support this popular opinion and give it encouragement. We think that criticism and debate will enable all citizens to gain some understanding about the candidates to the Sixth NPC and help mold popular opinion to adopt the Constitution and laws, rules, and regulations drafted by deputies to the Sixth NPC and its concerned committees. In short, various political parties, social strata, and organizations will make their political outlook public when assessing and debating the work of the Legal Committee.

4. We are aware that there are members of certain political parties and associations in the Legal Committee. In an effort to improve democracy and the legal system, we think the Legal Committee should encourage members of these minority parties and associations to work actively toward modernizing Chinese society and let the people know about the work done inside the committee by these minority parties and associations. The China Human Rights League regards the existence of democratic parties

and their active work as essential. Their existence is of still greater importance in drafting laws. This kind of existence and work is an important precondition if the Chinese society's style of party politics is to free itself from bureaucracy. We hope that members of these political parties and associations who have been elected to the Legal Committee will contribute toward developing democratic socialism in the Chinese society. Your efforts will be vividly demonstrated in your activities in the Legal Committee.

5. The NPC Standing Committee and its Legal Committee should pay full attention to violations of the Constitution which have now become manifest and should strive as far as their functions and powers permit to eliminate these phenomena. The people demand that the NPC Standing Committee and its Legal Committee set up a provisional citizens' oversight committee at an appropriate time to see how well the government and parties are carrying out the law and Constitution. The people's judgment of the extent to which you have followed the Constitution will be based on your actions.

This is our five-point proposal to the NPC Standing Committee and its Legal Committee.

The China Human Rights League will make every effort to fully evaluate the role played by the Legal Committee in bringing about the kind of stability and unity that is necessary for the modernization of Chinese society. We are convinced that only when democracy is resolutely safeguarded and the human rights of citizens are fully respected in the transitional laws, rules, and regulations soon to be adopted, will the Legal Committee be able to play this role. We sincerely hope the Legal Committee will be able to accomplish this glorious historical mission.[1]

DOCUMENT 24
PUBLIC SECURITY
Human Rights League

When Chairman Ye [Jianying] recently spoke to a reporter for the New China News Agency, he discussed the problem of how best to establish a system of justice in our country. We welcome and support his views. In the meantime, however, we would like to point out the fact that the organization handling the Fu Yuehua incident* has gravely violated the spirit of Chairman Ye's statement, has damaged the present stability and solidarity, and has weakened our national defense.

1. If the public security organization felt that it was necessary to detain Fu Yuehua, then the detention, according to the law, should have been for twenty-four hours and no longer than seventy-two hours. We believe that the continued detention of Fu Yuehua is an illegal action in which detention constitutes arrest.

2. If Fu Yuehua did indeed commit a crime, she should have been arrested under the law. According to Article 47 of the Constitution, her arrest should have been determined by the People's Court, or approved by the Office of Public Prosecutor, and carried out by the Department of Public Security, which should have presented a warrant before making the arrest. Since the legal procedures were apparently not followed, the arrest must be considered an open violation of a citizen's personal freedom and of one's right to the privacy of one's home, both rights being established by the Constitution. An illegal arrest such as this is in fact an outrageous kidnapping, and anyone involved in committing such a serious crime should be prosecuted.

3. If Fu Yuehua had committed a crime, established by undeniable evidence, she should have been arrested according to the law, interrogated within twenty-four hours after the arrest, and promptly brought to a public trial for which the time and place would be announced in advance. Similarly, her crime should have been announced to the public, and she should have had the opportunity to defend herself.

We believe a "proper system of justice" cannot be achieved with only a single effort; it must pass a historical test. Chairman Ye has said that the purposes of having a proper system of justice are: that there be a law that can be and must be obeyed by everyone; the law must be strictly enforced; and any violation of the law must be punished. These requirements apply not only to the future but to the present time. The term "proper" is rela-

---

* Fu Yuehua organized a demonstration of poor farmers in January 1979 and was subsequently arrested. *See* Introduction and Documents 64 and 65.

tive. The present law is neither absolutely proper nor absolutely improper. Since the law passed by the People's Congress has not yet been abolished by the People's Congress, that law must be considered still in effect, and we must therefore make sure that it is obeyed and enforced. The law not only tests whether the responsible government organizations have the sincerity and resolution to perfect the law of our country but also creates necessary conditions under which our system of justice can be further improved in the future.

Although the main effects of the Fu incident are felt in Beijing, the case is also having national and international repercussions. It is our hope that the organization responsible for the incident understands the true meaning of what Chairman Ye has said:

* The law and the legal system must have both stability and continuity. Legislated by the people, the law represents the prime interest of socialism and proletarian dictatorship. Everyone must obey the law.

* The law has great authority. It can be revised only by an established legal procedure and not by the wishes of any individual leader.

* The investigative organization and the court must be faithful to the interests of the people, loyal to the law and the system of justice, dedicated to the truth and to the maintenance of functional independence.

* There must be attorneys and judges who are devoted enough to die if necessary in maintaining the dignity of the socialist system of justice.

* There must be a guarantee of equality for all people under the law. No one may be given any special privileges above the law.

We believe that the conditions stated above are not only necessary in order to make the justice system of our country perfect, but are also necessary in order to maintain the stability and solidarity required in order to carry out the Four Modernizations. Anything contrary to these conditions would not only destroy our system of justice but would also seriously damage and disrupt the stability and solidarity needed for the Four Modernizations and the national defense.

We watch with close interest the future developments in this case.

*   *   *

Postscript. Even though Minister of Public Security Zhao Cangbi has made a statement to the National People's Congress concerning the revision of the law on detention and arrest, the fact remains that the maximum time of detention is only four days.

According to a joint report issued by various organizations of citizens, the Ministry of Public Security has claimed that what they have done is called "investigation under detention." We do not know what the legal basis is for "investigation under detention." We believe that no one—no government officers, individual, or government agency—has legislative rights except the People's Congress. Certainly no organization of public security has the right of legislation. If there is no provision for "investigation under detention" in the law established by the People's Congress, the use of "investigation under detention" as a basis for breaking into Fu Yuehua's residence is a violation of Fu's personal freedom and a deliberate violation of the law itself. Such activities must be publicly condemned and those officials who violated the law must be punished in order to retain the confidence of the people in our system of justice..

During her present detention, Fu Yuehua's personal dignity must be respected. She must be treated with humanity and must have the right to see her relatives and friends.[2]

DOCUMENT 25
THE ASSUMPTION OF INNOCENCE
By Hong An

On February 17 *People's Daily* carried five articles concerning the legal system. Of these, we believe "An Issue Worth Studying" is the most important. The author put forward the issue of "assumption of innocence," which means that if there is insufficient lawful evidence produced to convict a person, the accused should be pronounced not guilty. That is to say, if there is insufficient legal evidence to prove a person guilty, it is absolutely forbidden to arrest, convict, or imprison him. Only in this way is it possible to insure that the broad masses of innocent people will not suffer injustice. This article should be written into the legal code of China without hesitation.

Facts have demonstrated that whoever opposes this article is a feudal fascist who has inherited "no need for evidence" as his penal code! This is because the "assumption of innocence" is certainly no restraint from producing specific evidence against criminals. As long as specific criminal evidence is in hand, no criminal can deny his crime. However, if the criminal evidence that has been offered can be overruled (or denied), then "criminal evidence" is still not specific enough! If we do not have specific criminal evidence, why must we insist on convicting people?[3]

SECTION FIVE
PHILOSOPHY OF HISTORY

Most of the essays that sprung from the democratic movement of 1978–79 were fairly short, but there were two exceptions: The Enlightenment Society was responsible for a pair of extensive opuses in which the current struggle for human rights and democracy is placed in historical perspective. The first, of which Document 26 is only a brief summary, appeared in the fall of 1978 in Guiyang as a two-hundred-meter poster. The second, which we reproduce almost in its entirety, portrays history as the evolution from exploitative, manipulative dictatorship to democracy based upon respect for human rights (Document 27).

DOCUMENT 26
THE CHARIOT OF HISTORY (summary)
Enlightenment Society

1. All Chinese people of conscience—workers, farmers, scientists, writers, poets, artists, teachers, editors, and all those who love the motherland —arise! Fight for the new ideals, for democracy, and for man's rights!

2. Look closely at Chinese history over the past two thousand years, over four thousand years, or over eight or even ten thousand years, and you will seek in vain for two terms—democracy and man's rights. Thus, to realize our dreams, we must take action.

3. People of China, arise! It is time to deal with all tyrants and despots. We must render the final judgment on them and clear them out to the last!

4. We must reassess the Cultural Revolution. Superficially, it is said that Mao Zedong's deeds were "30 percent wrong and 70 percent right," but this formulation still shields Mao. His errors were more numerous than the people know.

5. China's several-thousand-year history produced one empire, but now it has produced a new empire. We will not allow history to repeat itself, nor will we allow the chariot of history to stop here.

6. The new idolatrous worship is more dreadful than the superstition of an earlier time. True "liberation" can come only by exorcising the new worship from the hearts of the people. Why? Because worship is the enemy of democracy and the enemy of science.

7. Change the long black night into a bright day, and change the tragedy into a drama of romance. History must be seen objectively, but a truthful judgment is no simple matter. That is why we must examine the Cultural Revolution in the light of practice, and that is why we must do the same with regard to Mao Zedong.

8. All the elements against science, against truth, against experience, and against the people, and all the historical hangovers of worship have completely demonstrated their wrongfulness, and they have been cast from the pinnacle to the depths.

9. Qin Shi Huang's feudal society and despotic state are gone, never to reappear. Eastern mysticism must be rejected because people are no longer fools, and we must put a complete end to the calamity of despotic fascism.

10. Today there are two Great Walls of China. One is the barrier against barbarian invasion. The other is the spiritual Great Wall erected by Qin Shi Huang's progeny to maintain their tyranny. The spiritual Great Wall is the theoretical structure of feudal despotism, and we must not fail to shatter it.

11. One hundred years ago, Japan was also a feudal nation, but the Meiji Reformation wrought a great transformation. And certainly the United States, established scarcely two hundred years ago, has made flying advances. China must carry out its Four Modernizations if it is to achieve development and find its future.

12. It is to promote and realize these ideals and dreams that we have organized the Enlightenment Society and proclaim this manifesto.[1]

DOCUMENT 27
ON HUMAN RIGHTS
From *Enlightenment*

The history of mankind is a history of striving from darkness toward light, from sorrow toward happiness. All the struggles of man on this lengthy road of history are struggles for human rights. Tens of millions of years have passed, but the bitterness of mankind has not ended and happiness has not yet been found. Man sacrificed his life to exchange old promises for new promises and old lies for new lies. Human rights are strange words in the minds of many people. In the eyes of the ruler, human rights are prohibited and are not to be made public to the world. In the eyes of the people, human rights are a thing to be hoped for but not to be had, a surrealistic object on the other side of the river. In the eyes of the ruler, human rights are rules used to convict people of criminal offenses.

Since human rights are so important, what do they include, what relationship do they have to other things, and how should we fight to obtain and protect them? Let us now explain all of this in broad and general terms.

NATION AND CITIZENS

A nation is the personification of the will of the entire citizenry, the highest ruler, and the public servant of the entire nation's people. But all these do not exist by themselves.

A long time ago there were no nations in the world. At that time people lived in peace and calm. There was no suppression or exploitation. There was no private ownership and no public ownership. The relationship between man and fellow man was very friendly and peaceful, as friendly as brothers and sisters, full of simplistic sympathy, support, and friendship. Later, selfishness emerged. Smarter and stronger people developed a desire to acquire more property and an ambition to exercise control over other people. The first man, when he started to encircle a piece of land, suddenly thought he could own it and found ignorant people to believe what he said. If a person had come along to remove the stakes, fill up the ditches, and call out to his neighbors, saying "you had better not listen to this liar; if you have forgotten that the fruits of the land belong to all and that the land does not belong to any one person, you may just as well die," this person could have saved mankind from sin, war, and massacres and prevented so many catastrophes and so much fear! (Rousseau, *Discours sur l'origine de l'inégalité des hommes.*)

Usurpation of God-given rights and creation of private ownership created the historical condition for the emergence of nations. The result of the usurpation of natural rights is a society divided "by human efforts" into property owners and the proletariat. Later, the rich hoped to consolidate control over the poor and suggested to the poor the idea of forming a nation and government. They used phony theories to confuse them. They said a nation is the fortress of order, peace, and security ([Hegel,] *Philosophy of History* [?], p. 640).

Thus the nation emerged. After the establishment of nations, mankind started down the road of hardship. In the slow and lengthy travels, mankind suffered from all kinds of enslavement and suppression, from all kinds of masters, liars, murderers, tyrants, and maniacs. In order to gain the right of survival, men resisted and rose up in rebellion, but they all failed. To preserve life, their life, they escaped to other lands, but they were all captured and returned. Their feet were chained. Their bodies were full of wounds from whipping. They suffered. Hopelessness masked the whole of mankind. The beautiful and bright world became an ugly and dark hell. In this suffering hell, mankind imagined the beauty and wonder of Heaven. In the days of hopelessness, mankind hoped for the coming of the Savior. To forget this physical and materialistic catastrophe, they placed their genuine hopes and high ideals on the nonexistent future world and the other world of peace and the all-loving God.

Suppression is cruelty. Life is bitter. "Layers and layers of darkness do not make people forget about the dawn but only increase people's desire for brightness" ("Song of the Torch" [Document 68]).

Through labor, struggle, and reflection, reason delivered mankind from mistakes, and people began to face the world and themselves. People realized that the master, king, lawmakers, and emperors were people like themselves. Their authority was obtained from the people, who should have the highest authority. All rights are the public's. If the people find it necessary, they can change their king and even sentence him to death. ([Hegel,] *Philosophy of History* [?], p. 404).

A nation belongs to its people. The individual who serves as the highest ruler is the central figure who regulates the emotions of the citizens. Violence has been the only way to change this center. Through violence a ruler who does not represent the interest of the people is overthrown. Old dynasties are thus destroyed. But the new ruler depends on deception to rule the people. He replaces the old ruler to establish a new dynasty. When the new ruler breaks his promises, and when his deception and lies have been discovered and exposed by the masses, another era of bloodshed and sacrifices takes place. Each violent action taken to overthrow a nation's ruler is begun on beautiful promises and empty words, but ends with new lies and new forms of suppression. Mankind has advanced through the history of deceit and suppression. The history of mankind is full of deceit and bitterness.

In the past thousands of years, man has handed over to his rulers all of his thoughts, the fruits of labor, freedom of movement, and the right to life. It is precisely because man wants to retrieve these rights that revolution after revolution has been launched to overthrow those who have stripped away human rights, the unjust and the incompetent rulers.

Time moves ahead. History develops. Life progresses. One's outlook expands. Thoughts explore. People have come to understand more and more clearly that there is no savior in heaven. There is no omnipotent and highest king on earth. Everything in nature and human society belongs to all. The ruler may have power, but sovereignty derives from the people. A public servant may never legitimately rob them of their authority or suppress them.

TYRANNY AND REPUBLIC

From the time of the emergence of nations to the present, mankind has had many social systems. Feudalism, slavery, and monarchy are all regarded here as dictatorial systems.

These unreasonable systems have existed in our world for many thousands of years, and they have not been completely eradicated. Under the impact of many revolutions, especially the American War of Independence and the French Revolution, these systems are now in their last dying days. It is absolutely impossible for these systems to revive and continue to rule over and suppress the people.

In the Western world, antihuman dictatorship has dwindled and fallen. It does not have any strength to stand against the masses of people now armed with science. In the East this system still occupies a certain sphere of influence. This backward system can still find a place of revival in the East. This shows that the broad masses of the people in the Eastern world have not fully achieved political awareness. They do not understand themselves, do not have confidence in their own strength, and cannot present a scientific argument in defense of their own existence. The masses of people have not been organized and have not acquired the strength to resist the dictator on an equal footing. This is the reason why the dictatorial system can revive itself at any time. Extreme dictatorship is unsuitable to a highly developed society of people who have been influenced by modern political thought and culture, because it is not controlled by the will of those who are being governed, and it reflects the will of the people very slowly. If a dictatorial system is forced onto or implemented in this type of society, then an extremely unfair and extremely tense situation is created. In the twentieth century, this even endangers human existence (John Strachey, *Contemporary Capitalism* [New York: Random House, 1956]).

People despise dictatorships. Therefore, they revolt and establish republics. The birth of the republican form of government marked new progress in political life. Mankind has made new demands in the name of human rights. The West is currently trying to satisfy these demands. The East is avoiding and suppressing them.

Several decades ago, people of Eastern nations believed that the birth of the republican form of government would mark the end of the situation in which people have no human rights and democracy, and that freedom would be protected. Actually, this did not happen. The concept of republicanism cannot be taken as the standard to judge democracy and human rights in today's Eastern nations. The goodness or badness of a nation's politics cannot be judged by appearances. Rather, the nation's internal nature must be observed. In today's world there are more republics than monarchies. But we cannot seek the right answer based upon numerical majority. England and Japan are monarchies, but there the legislative, judicial, and executive powers are separated. These powers are independent of each other and serve as checks and balances overseeing each other to prevent extremism and imbalance. What sustains the relationship between a nation and its people and the relationship between external affairs and the nation is the constitution. This basic law will judge and check by punitive measures and according to its own ironfisted principles any violation of law committed by any person, including the prime minister and the king, who represent the nation at the highest level. These types of monarchies are in fact more democratic, more caring, and more respectful of people's rights than superficial republics. They are republics clothed as monarchies. In many republics in Asia the situation is worse—they are worse than monarchies. In these superficial republics the nation's prime ministers, chairmen, and presidents have become modern emperors and tyrants. Their "words" and their "remarks" are imperial decrees and are above the law. "Bansai" or "The Father" rules over all. The constitution has lost its function. "Documents" and "notices" replace law. The people's representative congress has become a decorative and empty organization adorning the republic. It is a showcase and is devoid of actual functions. One word can abolish the nation's chairman or label him a counterrevolutionary and revisionist.* The law has been to-

---

* This is a reference to Liu Shaoqi, who was chairman of the People's Republic until he fell out of favor with Mao Zedong in the mid-1960s.

tally devastated. Democracy and human rights have become things that are dreamed about but never realized. The will of one individual rules over all. This is a monarchy wearing the clothing of a republic.

Montesquieu pointed out:

> If the legislative and judicial powers are concentrated in one person or in one organ of the government, then there will be no freedom.
>
> If the judicial power is not separated from the legislative and executive powers, then freedom will not exist.
>
> If one person organizes an office to write the law, to exercise public resolutions, to rule in cases involving personal crime, then all will be finished.
>
> In Turkey all three powers were concentrated in the hands of the sultan. Therefore, frightening tyranny ruled over everything.
>
> In the Italian republic, these three powers were centralized. Thus, there was less freedom than in a monarchy.

The citizens of these republics are imprisoned! The same office possesses all legislative powers and also serves as the executive office. It can use its "commonsense" to trample all over the nation. And because it also has judicial power, individual "will" can be used to destroy every citizen. There, all power is combined. Although there is no appearance of dictatorship and tyranny, everyone feels the existence of monarchical dictatorship.

DEMOCRACY AND RULE BY LAW

"The law is the manifestation of public will. All are equal before the law" (France's "Declaration of the Rights of Man and the Citizen").

The cradle of people's democracy is Athens, Greece. In ancient times the right to vote was extended to every citizen in the city-state, winning praise from the rest of the world. The democracy practiced in Athens was the first flash of human rights. Later, human rights were taken away by emperors and feudalism. These are things that have passed. The democracy we want to talk about today is a democracy that is more meaningful and more valuable than the democracy of the past.

The democratic system in the world today has a history of only several hundred years. Before this, between one hundred and two hundred years ago, tumultuous changes occurred in the world. Dictatorial tyrants were sent to the guillotine. Cruel kings were stripped of the thrones they had inherited generation after generation. [words illegible] was destroyed by artillery. Dark and cruel laws were torn up and burned. The revolutionary people shed their blood and sacrificed their lives to realize their just demands. They wanted to establish a republic that was better, more progressive, and more humanitarian. The birth of the republic opened new paths for mankind and expanded new horizons and the ideal realm. When we have the opportunity to discuss and enjoy the fruits of democracy, we must not forget the American War of Independence of 1777, the French Revolution of 1793, and the struggles of other nations for freedom, democracy, and human rights. We must not forget America's Washington and Jefferson and the American people who love freedom. We must thank the people of France, who so nobly originated the theory of democracy for mankind and turned these theories into realities.

The theory of democracy was developed by those who did not have any human rights and who wanted to seek a system of laws. If these theories are to be turned into reality, they must be based upon a strong system of laws. Without this strong legal support, democracy cannot materialize completely. We do not merely mean a set of laws or that democracy is complete set of laws has been written. Democracy must be realized before laws are established. Then a legal system is set up to recognize and protect it. Before the people and the masses have obtained a true democracy, a complete set of laws that recognize democracy and a strong system that protects the democratic system will be meaningless. To avoid empty talk, the first thing to do is to allow democratic theory to become reality. If this is not done, any system of laws or democratic stipulations that give recognition to democracy will be meaningless.

The people need democracy. People need to be ruled under law. Democracy allows people to speak out and participate in governing the nation. The rule of law protects and guards the right to speak out and the right to rule. If the former is lost, the law will have nothing to protect. If the latter is lost, democracy will not have any basis. Democracy is the right of the people to be their own master. A system of law protects these rights and counters oppressive materialistic forces that suppress these rights. When democracy is lost, the society will be in darkness. When the rule of law is lost, the people will have no help.

Every country should have a basic, correct, and true constitution to rule over everything based on the principles and spirit of constitutional law. That which opposes or counters the spirit and principles of the constitution must not be allowed to exist. All executive orders, all relationships between supervisors and subordinates, all relationships between the state and associations within the state, and all relationships between people and things should adhere to the constitution and be guided by it. Business should be conducted according to it, never allowing personal dictatorship to forcefully replace the law and the constitution and never allowing personal will to rise above the law and the constitution. It is regrettable that these sacred principles of mankind are abused by dictators in many of Asia's republics. These dictators serve as prime ministers, presidents, and chairmen. In these republics the highest ruler is king and is above the constitution and is not bound by the law. His personal will governs all. Law has completely lost its function. The controlling organs do not have a standard of control. The duty of the law has been completely lost. People's life, property, work, rights, democracy, and movements cannot be protected by law. Without law, life is full of tension and terror, and people are driven to the brink of insanity.

It is fortunate that besides the dark side of mankind there is a bright side of mankind. This bright side of mankind is the United States, which champions democracy. The United States is the banner of mankind's democracy. There the Constitution and the law are above all. Whether a person is a senator or a president, the speaker of the House or a common citizen, all are equal before the law. No matter who has committed a crime, he is tried before the law accordingly. The power of the law applies not only to the common citizen but also to the president, who does not exercise public justice. In the United States, the Constitution and law are above all.

Thinking about the good makes people hate the bad even more. The undemocratic ways of the Soviet Union that cause people to suffer bring only tragedy. Only by depending upon the heightening of the masses' political awareness and their ability to tell right from wrong, and only by sharpening the people's ability to differentiate the true from the false and the good from the bad, can we courageously stand up in support of democracy and fight and resist the undemocratic and antidemocratic elements. Only when their power is sufficient to battle all dictatorial measures and reactionary forces can democracy come true and be forceful.

Until the people and the masses have become completely aware of their power and possess the strength to protect their own rights in these countries, democracy is but an empty word. The present democratic system is being brought into our present life by science and rapidly progressing economic development. This kind of system is visible evidence of a modern republic. But it is disappointing that in these so-called republics people cannot enjoy true democracy. Although this is the case, we are not disappointed or discouraged. We believe that no matter how much interference and suppression now result from Asian paternalism and totalitarianism, in the end democracy will defeat dictatorship and prevail throughout the world.

ON HUMAN RIGHTS

". . . that all men are created equal, that they are endowed by their Creator with certain unalienable Rights, that among these are Life, Liberty and the pursuit of Happiness" (U.S. Declaration of Independence).

1. Voting Rights. In the past the theory of voting to elect the nation's ruler did not exist. All rulers were hereditary. Their power lasted from the time they used armed force to overthrow a dynasty to the time when they or their descendants who inherited their estate were killed. This was the rule of order established according to family rule based on blood relationship. This system of family rule and lifelong dictatorship not only suffocated the advancement of man's wisdom but also prevented social development and scientific and artistic progress. Because this type of social system was unreasonable and could not be tolerated, progressive people gradually overthrew it. After dynastic rule was ended, mankind established the modern republic. Internally, this type of republic requires the separation of legislative, judicial, and executive powers, and checks and balances that are mutually independent and oversee each other. The most important principle of a republican government is that the highest leader and leaders at all other levels must be changed at definite intervals through election by the people. Ballots are cast to elect the head of state, a person most trusted to serve as the nation's spokesperson. This is a great achievement of mankind! The actual exercise of this right will prevent the emergence of dictatorship and all evils associated with a lifelong ruler. Increasing the number of people participating in the election means that power is distributed among the people. This is a recent development of the past several decades. When this sound system of election is expanded, propagated, popularized, and recognized by the Constitution, the people will acquire a balanced sense of good and bad, and conflicts between the ruler and the people will be reduced. Since the people have the right to vote, they can change their ruler and no longer fear him. The ruler, fearing impeachment and accusation by the people, does not dare cheat and suppress the people.

The right to vote is a sacred right of the people. It is certain that with the passing of time man's cultural advancement and increase in knowledge will enable the ruler and the people to regard voting as the most just and rational course. Voting is the way to popularize power. We must overcome the legacy of history. The people must start regaining the rights of which they have been deprived for thousands of years. Highly centralized power leads to social regression and catastrophe. Power in the hands of the people means social progress, happiness, and well-being for all. If everyone possesses equal wealth, there will be no millionaires. If all citizens have equal rights, dictatorships and dictatorial tyrants will not emerge. For thousands of years, people have been plagued by disasters and whipped, chained, subjugated, and enslaved like animals because too much power was concentrated in the hands of a few. But now that members of society possess more political awareness and knowledge, they can stand up and protect their rights and use these rights to oversee their nation and government. Thus people will be happier and more secure.

The United States and Great Britain are two model nations that hold elections. In these countries, the constitutions stipulate that the ruler [may be] replaced after serving a definite term, whether he or she likes it or not. A term is no longer than four years. Personal dictatorship and lifelong rule are impossible. People, as stipulated in the constitutions, can exercise, at a certain time and according to their own wishes, the right to change the old government and elect a new government. In those countries, the nation belongs to all citizens. The citizens change the government they dislike according to their will. It is natural and proper. This right is not interfered with or hindered by any means. In many republics in Asia the right to vote is still a major problem that has yet to be solved. These nations appear to possess a complete elected body and a complete electoral system. Their constitutions also stipulate that the president, prime minister, or chairman can only serve a term of four years and that they are elected every four years. But in actuality this is not the case. People cannot act according to constitutional stipulations to elect their nation's leaders. Those who even dare to suggest and point out social wrongs will be labeled as modern counterrevolutionary elements, and those who attack the socialist system are labeled as class enemies. Concerning these police states which rule people's thoughts, John Strachey pointed out: they do have a secret organization to create and measure public opinion. But nothing can replace the competitive process of the democratic system. Unless there are at least two candidates in the election, the opinion of the voters and their feelings cannot be tested and measured. Thus dictators step forward, sometimes vicious and sometimes showing generosity, but always blind to the true feelings of the people. It can be said that dictators exercise dictatorship, cruelty, and suppression because of this blindness rather than because of their sins. Under such high-pressure policies, the masses of people will lose faith in their own nation because they have lost their opportunity to speak out. Because they have lost their right to life, they have to escape to other nations or engage in passive or open resistance. Public opinion is completely raped. It is certain that in this type type of extreme dictatorial nation, the right to vote given to the people by the constitution is only an empty word. As to the numerous rights of being elected, of impeachment, supervision, accusation, movement, and choice of employment, all are empty words. Under such tyranny, feelings cannot be communicated and people's will cannot be expressed.

No matter how Asian and other dictatorships hinder and suppress elections, mankind will enter a world of popular elections. There is no doubt that in the near future all will have the opportunity to express their will and emotions completely. The people will have the opportunity in a democratic atmosphere to elect as leader a person they trust. The nation will no longer be plagued by interference and undercurrents of resistance. Unity of the people is a spiritual condition which is necessary for a nation to be stable and to develop. Without this condition, no ideals can be realized.

All good things must be brought about by active struggles. True right of election can be realized only when democracy undoubtedly and truly exists in our actual life. This can be realized only through real struggle. Today we crave the freedom of ancient Greece and the freedom of thought in the Warring States Period in China, because we do not enjoy as much freedom of speech and thought as the people did then. To fight for more freedom of speech is undoubtedly the popular overall demand of the people. To realize such just wishes and to prevent suppression of these wishes, there must be a true democratic government. . . .

2. **Freedom of Speech.**   One of the most obvious physical indicators of a truly democratic government is that it protects and allows freedom of speech and provides modern facilities for communication and material conditions for such freedom. This kind of country not only does not fear public opinion but also opens up more horizons for freedom of expression to prosper. The constitution stipulates this freedom, and the system of laws protects this freedom in society so that it can be exercised without interference. This is true freedom. Freedom does not mean unprincipled freedom. Exercise of the right of freedom is limited by noninterference in other people's freedom and nondenial of other people's freedom. Language is used to exchange ideas and communicate emotions to the outside world. This is a great thing. Only a dictatorship fears and suppresses these sacred rights to exercise the freedom of speech and thought that unites people. This society is sick. This society is hated by the people because it opposes the people's will. Sick people fear the doctor's words foretelling their death. This society opposes the people's will but still tries in every way to close people's mouths. To protect this irrational rule, the two shameful methods of armed suppression and spiritual threats against the people's freedom of speech are employed.

Where there is freedom for the people there will not be any freedom for individual dictatorship. Where there is freedom for the people the dictator's power and ambitions will be exposed in time and will be greatly limited. This is the most basic reason why the dictatorial nation's dictators fear and suppress people's freedom of speech. In today's world people's freedom and thoughts are still being suppressed, but the spark of freedom will not die out. The banner of freedom will not fail.

Long live freedom!

They who have fallen in the name of freedom shall live forever!

3.   Freedom to Demonstrate.   Demonstration is a form of expression by a group of people. Through this direct form of expression the people can voice their views and opinions. The people can express their indignation against unreasonable policies, dishonest decisions, and unsound systems, and express support for and recognition of all actions that benefit mankind. This is the most active expression of the freedom of speech. This is freedom that is more direct, freer, more concrete, and more ardent. When this right is exercised by the people and the masses, the people can take concerted action at any time to resist and counter mistaken policies which may have serious consequences and to prevent undesirable government decisions and unreasonable, dangerous economic measures. Opposition is awesome, for it can force a government to see the light and remain within the law. When there is a right to dissent, a government is less inclined toward wrongdoing and corruption, and is more apt to stand with and serve the majority of people.

Spontaneous demonstrations are an indication that the people are their own masters. Such events are limited to certain Western nations. Only when the people are the masters is their right to demonstrate protected by law. In these countries, citizens can gather freely and use this freedom as the sharpest and most effective method to express opposition to dereliction of duty and atrocities on the part of the rulers and overly harsh economic measures. This form of concerted and open expression of people's outcries can condemn the tyranny of the dictator and expose the hidden crimes and darkness in society. It can be used to fight for freedom, democracy, and all other rights. In a dictatorial nation these actions are criminal. In a true democratic nation these actions are protected and recognized by law. In dictatorial nations of the East the people's right to demonstrate exists only in the constitution. It does not exist in actual life. The constitution and the law are seriously out of touch with reality. This explains the existence of serious problems. This type of nation not only fears the people's freedom of speech but is more fearful of self-initiated and concerted action by the people—demonstration.

Demonstrations that are organized, planned, and ordered by the government are meaningless. They cannot truly reflect public opinion and are not proof of true human rights and democracy. Planned demonstrations will only arouse the opposition, disgust, and anger of the people.

The government that promotes and supports this freedom is more stable and secure. The more the government suppresses this freedom, the more endangered the future of the government will be.

4.   Freedom of Publication.   Freedom of publication is an important mark of a modern democratic society. When individuals have the courage to explore and then are able to commit their thoughts to paper, they naturally want to publish them. Whether or not this is possible is the standard against which the truth or falsity of a nation's law and constitution should be tested. In a truly democratic nation, the masses are free to choose among published ideas about nature and society. The lack of freedom of publication is the most obvious characteristic of dictatorship.

To truly carry out the policy of "letting one hundred flowers bloom and one hundred schools of thought contend," let people's thoughts break out from the imprisonment and forbidden areas so that life may be lively, rich, and full of adventure. The publications media must serve to bring the producers of ideas and art to the consumers of ideas and art in the most natural way, encourage production of different art forms and different ideas, and stimulate public expression of different opinions. The strength of such opinions will push social development forward and stimulate spiritual life. The law should protect and recognize the rights that benefit the cultural enrichment and prevent external interference and sabotage by the will of an individual.

Society must develop and progress. Social development and progress need material production as well as a variety of ideas to enrich them. The[2] expansion of ideas is not harmful. It helps to advance the nation and its people, science, culture, and business. The people themselves must strive for perfection through great human effort, hard work, and correct thoughts and ideas. Sometimes in a particular historical era thoughts and ideas may be regarded as wrong or mistaken. There is no comparison, and truth cannot show its strength. Uniformity of ideas causes society to stagnate and brings disaster. Although a few people may [take advantage of freedom and] engage in evil schemes, most people acquire clearer vision and more rational wisdom. They do not expand upon mistakes.

People should be proud of our rich store of wisdom and knowledge. They should be proud of their multifaceted ideas. Only those shortsighted politicians who cannot completely satisfy their own selfish desires despise others' wisdom and talents. They employ base means to attack those who are ideologically better than themselves and who oppose them. The dictator who suppresses freedom of expression is a criminal who has committed crimes against history and ideology and freedom of publication. The time of his overthrow by the people is not far away.

Until thoughts are tested in practice, nobody can prove which ones are right and which are wrong. Conclusions must be drawn by the people, and history must judge whether the thoughts are good or bad. The basis upon which history makes its judgment is precisely the written and published material left to posterity. If we do not have Greek philosophy beside us, if we do not have the Bible and other classics of Christianity, if we do not have the ideas of the European Enlightenment, if we do not have the philosophies of all schools left to us from the Warring States Period and the history of each of the dynasties, if we do not have records of the dynasties, their laws, and customs, how can we judge today whether the past thousands of years of history were right or wrong? The fact that we can read the history of the past thousand years and correctly evaluate the people and their thoughts is something to be thankful for. We must thank those who have hand-copied the documents and those who have printed them and left them to posterity. It is because these documents have been preserved completely intact that the history of our nation is continuous. In fact, philosophies, science, and art that were opposed in the past still enrich our lives today, guide our action, and give us enjoyment. The life of man should be rich and adventuresome. Uniformity of opinion, ideas, art, and esthetics will not satisfy all the needs of progressive and developing mankind. A great statesman who thinks he possesses unique viewpoints and understands himself will not suppress these rightful demands for freedom. If he is smart, he will see that the great ideas and thoughts that he and his contemporaries believe to be great are but a drop in the great river of history and a small drop in the great ocean.

In the West, there is freedom of publication. This situation, in which a hundred schools can contend via publication, is the basic reason underlying the Western world's rapid development and high cultural achievements.

In the East, publication is not free. This ideological and emotional singularity is the reason for the stagnation and lack of progress in Oriental society! It is a vicious circle that shuns all active elements and negates all alien thoughts. This is the characteristic of a dictatorial society.

Without freedom of publication, mankind's ideological flowers will not blossom in its ideological garden.

Only those who cannot face Heaven will suppress and negate this sacred right of mankind and sacred duty to one's self, to society, and to others.

5. Freedom of Belief. Faith is mankind's higher spiritual life. It is the product of everyone's ideological exploration and social practice. When a special concept is formed in one's mind or is wholeheartedly accepted, it is very difficult to change it by external force. This concept which is so difficult to shake off and which cannot be changed is belief. A person likes a particular way of expression or a particular philosophy because he believes in it. The ideas thus expressed coincide with those of the spiritual world within his mind. The ideas, conscious knowledge, and suggestive knowledge thus expressed are the same as those he keeps in his mind. People's thoughts, like man himself, are the result of personal contacts and experiences. People have experienced the bitterness and suffering of human life. The painful human life, ceaseless struggles, and massacres have made man choose goodness and peace as ideals. This is the inception and beginning of belief. Later, knowledge about human life, nature, the future, and the past causes the seeds of belief to germinate, settle in the mind, grow and mature in the soil of the spiritual realm. This is the great tree of belief. This great tree cannot be shaken by any forced transformation, pressure of terror, or lengthy imprisonment. Faith is a secret within man's heart. It is the highest standard by which man recognizes right and wrong, good and evil. It is the yardstick by which darkness and light can be judged. With its invisible but strong support you will be able to courageously step forward in difficulty, fearing neither danger nor hardship. Without its support, you will feel empty. Your actions will be confused. Your thoughts will be timid. Your spirit will lose support. When faced with difficulty and terror, your physical body will be paralyzed. Belief supports man to live bravely, to courageously explore and discover and be brave in the struggle against hardship and tyranny. It is the pillar of life assuring that life will be fresh, lively, and healthy.

Every nation and every citizen should have a strong faith. Without creed, a nation will have no principles. Without belief, people's spirit will lose balance. To a nation, belief is the wealth of the nation's people. To an individual, faith is personal property.

In a dictatorial nation there is no freedom of belief. In this kind of a society, people can have only one concept. They can only worship one principle and are never allowed to create or believe in another realm or another philosophy. People's material and spiritual life is dull. If each person's highest form of personal life is destroyed and torn down, then he will lose his purpose of existence.

But true belief cannot be taken away by those who are strongest and who possess the most power. Giordano Bruno faced the burning stake and loudly announced his discoveries. Heroine Saint Joan of Arc faced cruel death while singing. Revolutionaries stepped proudly into the enemy's court. Christians marched right into Rome's great inferno . . . .

Faith not only supports your thoughts but also helps you to live bravely. When you are sad, it gives you courage. When you are surrounded by darkness, it gives you light. When the enemy rushes over, it gives you strength. When difficulty falls upon you, it gives you the faith to win. . . .

In this world, only belief will not lie to you. Only faith will enthusiastically support you. The rest are only temporary flashes and appearances. Although in life rulers inevitably will confront you, suppress you, and force you to believe in something you do not believe in, they can only limit your movement, they cannot seize your spirit or expose the forever secret world of your soul.

During the Manchu dynasty, a Christian who lived on an island for twenty years and who wandered across the seas for a long time introduced Christianity to Beijing (Peking). In the seventeenth century, Columbus and Magellan courageously traveled around the world and shocked the West. In China's Tang dynasty Xuanzhang went down to India to receive the sutras of Buddhism, guided by belief. This is the strength of belief. This is the result of belief.

Have faith in your own belief. Do not change your belief because of temporary situations. Do not withdraw your belief because of social pressure. Do not abandon it because of attacks and slander by others. Have faith in what you believe. Whether you believe in the void of Buddhism or the Muslim's fire and sword, whether you believe in Christianity that professes brotherly love and equality or Laozi's metaphysical philosophy, whether you believe in Marxism or the Western world's pragmatism, your belief should not be changed or revised at will. Beliefs that can be revised and changed are not true beliefs.

Like being faithful to your first love, be faithful to your belief. Never abuse her. You must not spoil her. Doubting your lover is being unfaithful to love. Doubting belief is betraying belief. Do not betray belief. Do not be like Judas, who is scorned by all. One must face danger fearlessly, be honest, and like Jesus, risk one's life beyond the call of duty and courageously walk toward the cross of rebirth.

6. Freedom of Association. If a person does not understand the right of association and related things, the importance of what is called working class democracy, then it is like not having entered the gate of modern political thought and emotion (Strachey, *Contemporary Capitalism*).

Association is a social form. It is a necessary physical evidence of a modern democracy. Whether it can function and exist is a test of whether the democracy is true or false. In a true democracy, association is protected. A free country will provide material conveniences for such activity. In a false democracy, association will be suppressed and prohibited. . . .[3]

7. Comparison and Selection. Through thousands of years of history, dictatorships contributed no progressive achievements. They hindered the development of production and delayed social advancement. Under their lengthy control and rule, democracy and human rights were not upheld, developed, or protected, but were negated and suppressed. Dictatorship is the bloody murderer of democracy and human rights. Today we will never move backward to share the same world with dictatorships. . . .

Now is the time for us to make choices. Choosing means deciding our destiny and determining our future. There must be selection to have progress. There must be comparison to make selection.

Should we choose dictatorship or democracy? Should we regress or advance? This is the great issue facing us!

Everyone should make sacrifices for democracy and human rights.

OUTLOOK

Although the sun of democracy and human rights has risen, we in China can still barely see the light. While most of mankind has already awakened from the bad dream of superstition and dictatorship, we are still sound asleep and suffering nightmares. What is our future? What can it give us? Do we have to be exploited and suffer for our entire lives? Will our ideals be mere spirits wandering among the pages of books? No. All this must come to an end.

Today we stand behind the Great Wall looking toward the other side of the sea. We see the blue ocean and a mast that brings peace and friendship. Now it sails with culture and science toward the ancient civilization of the Orient. With nervous excitement, we wait and think. Should we bravely break out of the Great Wall and welcome change, or should we remain dead in our tracks just looking around? Should we forget about the misfortunes of the past and divest ourselves of the heavy burden, or should we hide in the dark corner to cry and let our lives pass by?

This is the demarcation of darkness and dawn. Those who fear brightness and calm can retreat into darkness. Those who welcome the arrival of new days can run forward in big strides toward the light. Those who want to rush ahead cannot be blocked by anyone. Those who want to fall back cannot be brought forward either.

> Tomorrow is beautiful.
> Face the future without despair!
> Let the opposers be forever condemned.
> Let the pioneers be remembered and praised!
> Remember, at the end of the dark night
> There is the colorful rainbow of brightness.
> Behind the enclosed and icy world.

Is life that is prosperous and colorful.
Be quick to rush out of this dark night,
Extend both arms toward the thousand miles of morning glow,
Cross over icy rivers and cold mountains
And step into the first thaw of early spring.

SECTION SIX
ON CLASS STRUGGLE

Until 1977, China's recurrent political campaigns were typically cast in terms of the so-called struggle of the proletariat and poorer farmers against other "classes." Indeed, perhaps none of Mao Zedong's slogans was given more emphasis during his lifetime than "Remember the Class Struggle!" Even from a theoretical point of view this presented difficulties, at least as time went on, because it became less and less satisfactory to define classes in Marxist terms. After all, a class is supposed to be defined in terms of the group's relationship to the means of production, and in China the bourgeoisie and landlords had long been deprived of their property. Thus, in strictly Marxist terms, the classes against which the many "struggles" were being waged did not exist. Inevitably, while no one dared say so, "class struggle" came to be regarded as fiction.

Nonetheless, there was an increasing tendency on the part of whatever group happened to control the government and media at any given time to fall back on "class struggle" arguments to attempt to persuade people of the wisdom of its policies. By definition, anyone who was not persuaded became a "class enemy." The opposition was thus silenced; but papering over the issues in this way did not make the underlying social problems vanish.

Following Mao's death, class struggle came to be de-emphasized as his successors sought to grapple with the nation's problems in a more pragmatic way. But the democratic activists were not content to let the question of class struggle—the mainstay of ideological indoctrination for so many years—be so quietly abandoned. The main article in this section (Document 29) reviews the history of what had been promoted, and what had been neglected, in the name of class struggle, with a view to learning some lessons from history.

For more on the question of class struggle, see Document 39 in Section Eight.

DOCUMENT 28
PICTURES OF CAKES
From a Wall Poster

The nation used to be graced with slogans about the class struggle, but the people became fed up with it all. You do not "suppress hunger by painting a picture of a cake," they would say, seeing right through the deception.

We have not heard much lately about the class struggle.

But there are still some who believe the slogans.[1]

DOCUMENT 29
THE CULTURAL REVOLUTION AND CLASS STRUGGLE
By Xiao Zhu

The earth-shaking Cultural Revolution [1966–75] was ultimately brought to an end with the smashing of the Gang of Four. What have the ten years of cultural revolution left and revealed to the Chinese people? This is obvious to all Chinese people and is something they always think about.

The decade left China in a hopeless mess, so that it now lags farther and farther behind the world.

* The national economy was on the verge of collapse and a loss of several billion *yuan* was reported in the national income.

* A large number of senior and middle-ranking party and government cadres were criticized and struggled against, dismissed from office, expelled from the Party, imprisoned, or even persecuted to death. Their dependents, subordinates, colleagues, and relatives were also victimized.

* Unwelcomed in the countryside and rejected by the cities, the millions of rusticated intellectual youths created instability in society.

* As a result of millions of false and unjust cases, many people lost their families and had to flee their homes. Hundreds of thousands of people have now gone to the authorities to lodge complaints.

* Because of the ten-year hiatus in scientific research, education, literature, and art, a whole generation of people lost their opportunity to study. This produced an age-gap in the contingent of intellectuals and caused scientific research to lag behind.

* National defense was weakened, and the weapons of the armed services remained what they were in the 1950s.

* There was great confusion on the ideological and theoretical fronts, morality was low in society, and the crime rate rose higher and higher.

What was the aim and meaning of a cultural revolution like this one? Mao Zedong said: "The current Great Proletarian Cultural Revolution is absolutely necessary and most timely for consolidating the dictatorship of the proletariat, preventing capitalist restoration, and building socialism." Was it absolutely necessary? No. It was completely unnecessary.

Mao Zedong also said: The current Cultural Revolution "is a continuation of the class struggle between the proletariat and the bourgeoisie." Was it really a class struggle? Le us look at the facts. "Classes struggle, some classes triumph, others are eliminated. Such is history." Which class emerged triumphant and which class was eliminated in the Cultural Revolution after all?

History is merciless. As soon as the Cultural Revolution began, Liu

[Shaoqi], Deng [Xiaoping], and Tao [Zhu] were branded as representatives of the bourgeois headquarters and were "eliminated." Peng [Zhen], Luo [Ruiqing], Lu [Dingyi], and Yang [Shangkun] were branded as counter-revolutionaries and were "eliminated." He Long and Peng Dehuai were eliminated. Yang [Chengwu], Yu [Lijin], and Fu [Chongbi] were "eliminated." Tan Zhenlin was branded as a "renegade." Li [Fuchun], Li [Xiannian], Ye [Jianying], Chen [Yi], Zhu [De], Nie [Rungzhen], and other old generals were branded as rightists' representatives. Scoundrels like Lin Biao, Chen [Boda], Kang [Sheng], Jiang [Qing], Zhang [Chunqiao], Yao [Wenyuan], Wang [Li], Guan [Feng], and Qi [Benyu] became "staunch leftists of the proletariat" and emerged triumphant. In the second stage, Lin Biao died while fleeing the country after an unsuccessful coup; Chen [Boda], Huang [Yungsheng], Wu [Faxian], Ye [Chun], Li [Zuopeng], and Qiu [Huizio] were overthrown one after another; and Deng Xiaoping re-emerged and became the chief of staff of the proletarian headquarters. There were signs of a recovery in China then. In the third stage, Premier Zhou [Enlai] became the target of attack during the anti-Lin Biao, anti-Confucius campaign. When Deng Xiaoping fought back and it seemed that China had hope again, there came the campaign to beat back the wind and reverse correct verdicts, the *Water Margin* criticism, and the criticism of Liu Bing.* After the passing of Premier Zhou, Deng Xiaoping was branded as the source of this wind and was again "eliminated."

In short, this is the cultural history of the Cultural Revolution. Some proletarian revolutionaries of the older generation were branded as bourgeois representatives and "eliminated." Some scoundrels became revolutionary "leftists" and triumphed. Afterward, these scoundrels were toppled one by one and genuine revolutionaries were invited back to office one after another. This process repeated itself many times.

Deng Xiaoping's rise to power after three falls became a legend of all times. This repetition of "class struggle" made us dizzy and confused. In this bewilderment, we suddenly saw a ray of sunlight and everything seemed bright again. If we sort out the history before the Cultural Revolution, we will get a clear picture.

After the land reform, the movement against "the three evils" and "the five evils," and the shift to joint state-private management following the liberation of China, the economic base of the landlord and bourgeois classes ceased to exist. They lost their political influence and some were even physically eliminated. Therefore, Comrade Liu Shaoqi pointed out

---

* Deputy secretary of Qinghua University and author of a report complaining that, as a result of the Cultural Revolution, incoming students were of low quality. Mao Zedong took the report as an attack on the education revolution which he was promoting.

in the political report to the Eighth National Congress of the Chinese Communist Party (CCP): "Class struggle has basically come to an end," and from now on the principal contradiction will be one "between the backward productive forces and the advanced social system." This meant that people should set about developing productive forces. However, after living in happiness for a few days, some people began to feel uneasy and wanted to wage struggle.

The struggle against rightists in 1957 was an outrageous trampling on democracy and human rights. Hundreds of thousands of intellectuals were branded as rightists, made targets of criticism and struggle, insulted, taken prisoners, expelled from the Party, and sentenced to labor reform. Many died as a result. According to a recent investigation, all those who were branded as rightists by the Ministry of Public Security were wronged and 96 percent of those branded by the central Party school were wronged. When central organs make such mistakes, what more can we expect from the local grassroots units? We do not have the necessary statistics right now. However, even the small number of rightists who were correctly labeled had done nothing more than voice their disagreement with a certain policy or a certain responsible person of the Party. This was part of a citizen's freedom of speech provided for in all previously adopted constitutions. The antirightist struggle had far-reaching consequences because it sealed the mouths of intellectuals, party members, and the people of the whole country, allowing them only to sing praises and not to voice their opinions. Tyranny and the trampling of democracy and human rights all stemmed from this.

The first direct outcome of the antirightist struggle was the Great Leap Forward and the conversion to people's communes in 1958. It dealt the first and most serious blow to China's economic base. Countless valuable assets were burned, and the enthusiasm of the cadres and the masses was seriously dampened. People were at a loss about what to do.

Peng Dehuai, a man of high principle, bravely stepped forward in the name of justice and outlined the pros and cons of this policy. As a result, at the Lushan Conference [August 1959] he was branded a member of the antiparty clique. What a singular case of injustice this was! As the struggle against rightist deviation unfolded, the Chinese people's suffering only increased.

Mao Zedong pulled back to play a secondary role,[2] and Liu Shaoqi was elected state chairman and asked to preside over the work of the Central Committee. With the all-out support of Premier Zhou and Comrades Chen Yun, Deng Xiaoping, and Peng Zhen, Liu Shaoqi implemented the correct policy of "readjustment, consolidation, filling out and raising standards." This gave the people and the country a chance to recover.

The air of democracy was somewhat enlivened, and the people gradually straightened their shoulders.

In December 1964 Liu Shaoqi was reelected state chairman. He [re-] published the essay "On the Self-Cultivation of Communists." His prestige rose higher and higher. Despite all this, people could clearly see that he respected Mao Zedong. He told Mao Zedong what he thought and always followed his instructions. This goes for the resolution of the Eighth CCP National Congress, the four clean-ups movement, and the measures adopted before the Cultural Revolution.

However, Mao Zedong thought otherwise and finally started the Cultural Revolution. A new disaster befell the Chinese people. The first ones to bear the brunt were Liu Shaoqi and his supporters. This was very similar to Hong Xiuquan's trick of using Wei Changhui to kill Yang Xiuqing, his family, and his subordinates [in 1856].

In an article entitled "Memorial Oration Marking the 300th Anniversary of the 1644 Incident," written by Guo Moruo thirty-five years ago, there was this passage: "After consolidating his rule, every founding emperor invariably set about slaughtering his meritorious officials." This had been done by Liu Bang, Zhao Kuangyin, and Zhu Yuanzhang [the founders of the Han, Song, and Ming dynasties, respectively]. Li Zicheng came from a peasant family. He also performed this "feat" after he captured Beijing [in 1644] and became Emperor Dashun. In this way, he ruined the achievements of a vigorous and seething peasant revolutionary movement.

In a political struggle, one who has popular support wins a kingdom, and one who loses the hearts of the people loses his kingdom. Mao Zedong understood this simple truth in the first half of his life. Mao won his kingdom because the CCP led by him had the sympathy and support of the people of the whole country. However, he flung this truth to the four winds after he entered the capital. Particularly during the Cultural Revolution he forgot himself and did as he pleased. God knows how many people were killed under the ruling that "anyone who opposes Chairman Mao is a counterrevolutionary." People tolerated his deeds because of his early achievements. It was only when he gave "tacit consent" to Jiang Qing and company to attack Premier Zhou and frame Deng Xiaoping that the people reached the end of their forbearance. The world-shaking April Fifth Movement broke out as a result of this shaped public opinion and prepared organizational grounds for the downfall of the Gang of Four. It also paved the way and provided the necessary experience for the democracy and human rights movement in China. The light of the April Fifth revolution will forever shine on the vast land of China.

Following the death of Mao Zedong, the Gang of Four were smashed.

The Party Central Committee headed by Hua Guofeng negated the "great strategic arrangements" of the Cultural Revolution one by one and restored some of the methods used on the eve of the Cultural Revolution or in even earlier years. Those who had been toppled were reinstated, redressed, and posted to suitable jobs. "Heroes who went against the tide" and "Red Guard leaders" were arrested and penalized. All this is still being done and is firmly supported by the Chinese people.

"One who loses the heart of the people loses his kingdom." Mao Zedong eventually lost his kingdom, but Zhou Enlai's monument will always stand erect in the hearts of millions.

The history of recent decades demonstrates that our problems are not inevitable; it is simply that "stupidity creates trouble." In point of fact, class struggle ceased to exist in China after 1956. China experienced this tragedy because people continued to suppress dissidents under the signboard of class struggle and even stood truth on its head and made no distinction between good and bad. What a serious lesson this was!

People's Daily recently published a number of articles by guest commentators. These articles talked about many things but evaded questions of substance. They might have had something to hide from, but I have nothing to be afraid of. I might as well continue exposing to the end.

After the elimination of the landlord and bourgeois classes, only two classes, the working class and the peasantry, were left in China. (Of course there are also government cadres, intellectuals, and armymen, but they are a part of the working class.) Viewed from the development of things, the peasantry will definitely undergo a change. A small portion of peasants will become agricultural workers and a large portion of them will become industrial workers. The working class and the peasantry should coordinate with each other. There should be no class struggle.

As for hooligans, murderers, and other criminals, these people do not belong to the landlord or bourgeois classes. They do not necessarily have any political, economic, or blood ties with landlords and bourgeois elements, just as criminals in capitalist societies do not belong to the proletariat. They should be dealt with according to law. In terms of political theory, it is ridiculous to call what they do "class struggle," and for us to think this way causes great practical harm.

The so-called "self-interests," "bourgeois ideas," and "bourgeois world outlook" were inhibiting magic phrases for dealing with the masses, particularly with intellectuals. They were also grounds for brazenly waging class struggle among the people. Different classes and different societies have diffeernt moral standards. However, it has been a commonly accepted principle since the formation of society that those who work for and dedicate themselves to the interests of the majority will be respected and those who profit at the expense of others will be despised. Premier Zhou lives in the memory of so many people because he personally carried out this principle. It is impossible to transform people's thinking by wantonly using the big stick of class struggle against them. This will only lead to society's degeneration of morality and give rise to abnormal psychology. Such influence can hardly be eliminated in one generation. Ideological questions can only be solved by employing the democratic method of persuasion and letting people speak for themselves. It is useless to wage class struggle haphazardly.

Now that China is engaged in the campaign to promote the Four Modernizations, what is the principle issue facing us? The conviction of the participants of the current movement for democracy and human rights is that the contradiction between democracy and bureaucratism is now paramount, and that our main struggle has to be to safeguard the Constitution and oppose lawlessness.

China has never gone through the stage of capitalism. The Chinese people have no idea what democracy and human rights are about. They are not accustomed to having democracy and human rights and are inured to acting according to the instructions of officials. The trouble is, many of our officials are uneducated bureaucrats who climbed to high posts by specializing in waging class struggle (but then they would be dismissed if they did not wage class struggle). We can hardly bring about the Four Modernizations under such circumstances.

Modernization requires that every one of us gives full scope to our resourcefulness and wisdom. Without full democracy and fully emancipated minds, modernization is inconceivable. Without democracy, it is also impossible to achieve highly centralized and unified command in modernization. Without a competent and authoritative command and coordination system which is adopted through democratic processes and constantly renovated, modern machines are just a heap of scrap iron. Without democracy, even if we can buy, exchange, or borrow modernization, we cannot keep it. This is what has happened in Iran today.

In short, the Marxist-Leninist teachings on class struggle are no longer applicable in China today. As for Comrade Mao Zedong's teachings on class struggle in the present Chinese society, they are wrong and must be discarded and replaced by genuine socialist democracy and legality.

ON EQUALITY

Both in China and elsewhere, the suspension of civil liberties is sometimes rationalized by the argument that egalitarianism is more important than "bourgeois liberties," and that such liberties inevitably result in social inequities. In the first essay below, Wei Jingsheng tackles this argument head-on.

This is followed by three vignettes relating to the problem of social inequality in China (Documents 31–33).

We conclude this section with a portion of a poignant short story. A young man, by dint of both virtue and luck, has landed a soft office job, but he finds himself alienated by the careerism and social climbing that he sees around him (Document 34).

DOCUMENT 30
HUMAN RIGHTS, EQUALITY, AND DEMOCRACY
By Wei Jingsheng

More people today are discussing the issue of human rights than that of equality. Actually, these issues are two aspects of the same question. We can practically say that the two are inseparable, because without human rights, equality is an empty expression. Because human rights and equality are two aspects of the same issue, I myself use the term "the equal human rights issue" (*pingdeng renquan de wenti*).

Human rights is an ancient concept. It was revived during the European Renaissance when, under the influence of humanist thinking, human rights was given more thought as a social issue. Early socialist trends of thought and socialist movements developed, based on the common desire to build a society that acknowledged equal human rights for all. The ability to respect and protect the equal human rights of every member of society became the premise of socialism. In the eighteenth and nineteenth centuries, when people were unable to satisfy their basic material needs, they naturally thought that the prerequisite of realizing equal human rights for all was for every member of society to have control of economic rights. Thus, at the time when the influence of mechanistic materialist philosophy was very strong, many people went a step further and assumed that the essence of social control was to be found in the economic realm. Socialist trends of thought have developed along these historical lines, with economics as the starting point for achieving equal human rights. Marx's great contribution to this trend of thought was to build a comprehensive ideological system covering both philosophy and economics, and to use his theory to expound economic socialism forcefully and in detail. . . . Socialism became separated from the human rights issue, which was to affect the whole "scientific socialism" movement.

Thus, a hundred years later, we can see that Marxist economics— "scientific socialism"—has led to nothing! All the social systems set up according to Marxist principles—i.e., the present communist countries— almost without exception neither acknowledge nor protect the equal human rights of all the members of their societies. Even if these countries repeatedly and smugly proclaim themselves to be "truly democratic" societies, on what basis can they say that the people are their own masters if universal equal human rights is absent? The living reality is that the basis of these "true democracies" is "the proletariat," that is, the vanguard of the proletariat, the communist parties, the parties' monolithic leadership. To put it simply, we are talking about dictatorships. What an absurd "truth" this is! We must begin to investigate this absurdity, beginning with some theory.

1. *What Are Human Rights?*

The concept of human rights (*renquan*) is basically defined as the rights (*quanli*) that people have. What rights do people have? From the moment one is born, one has the right to live and the right to fight for a better life. These are not bestowed but, rather, are inherent. At the same time human rights only exist in relation to other things, for people do not live in a vacuum but are surrounded by other things and relate, directly or indirectly, to their environment. Thus, human rights are limited and relative rather than unlimited and absolute. This limitation constantly grows and changes with the development of the history of mankind and with man's quest to tame and control his surroundings. This explains why the main points of the concept of human rights constantly change and are constantly being improved. Human rights in everyday life have to be gradually achieved. There is no such thing as "ultimately achieving" human rights.

Man, like all else, exists in relation to things outside himself. Both in terms of time and space, there is a mutual influence between man and his surroundings. Thus, his existence will take the form of mutual struggle and mutual support. This struggle/support phenomenon between man and his environment can be divided into two main categories: the struggle between mankind and nature to obtain the necessities of life (production), including finding out about the natural world (science); and the struggle among people themselves to obtain power (politics), including the activity of finding out about mankind (social science). So we can say that politics is the activity of obtaining or suppressing human rights. Through politics, people's rights to manage their lives are either realized or suppressed.

2. *What is Equality?*

The struggle among people for the right to live involves two basic types of activities. First, there is the question of how to distribute the fruits of material production and culture, commonly referred to as the political economy. Through this struggle, each person receives a rightful share. The second type involves the fight for the right to carry out struggle in the political sphere—commonly referred to as political struggle. The aim of this is to fight for the right to obtain one's share and then to secure this right. In other words, all are rightfully entitled to share the fruits of labor and to carry out political activities as equals. The basic content of the latter right are basic political rights, such as freedom of speech, assembly, association, the press, religion, movement, and the right to strike.

Only when everyone has the above freedoms will political equality and economic equality be protected and become real. These freedoms are the conditions that protect the people when equal rights are endangered and that come to bear at any time to defend equal rights. Thus, basic political rights are the preconditions for equal human rights. It must be acknowledged, in theory at least, that these freedoms should be unrestricted within their various spheres. After all, in an ever-changing world no one can possibly determine what ways and means may be used to deny one's human rights. Therefore, it is impossible to [define] limits that might [legitimately] be placed on rights. One can only determine a few relatively safe and peaceful methods that avoid suppressing rights, relying on legal methods of struggle to protect equal human rights. Inasmuch as there are many people who abuse human rights to gain social power, and since the powerless common people find it relatively easy to use the above freedoms as methods of struggle, these freedoms must be unrestricted in theory and unregulated in reality. In this way, everyone is equal in respect to them.

Equality does not mean that if you eat an apple, I must also eat one. It means that both of us have the right to eat apples, but if I do not feel like eating one, I have the right not to do so. This is called freedom. Equality must encompass these two aspects of freedom to measure up to its name. Thus, equality in reality does not mean "averaging." Equality points to the similarity of opportunity and allows the same possibilities to be used for different purposes. The average points to the similarity of achievement, not to the use of opportunities for dissimilar aims. It restricts opportunities [of people with] dissimilar aims in order to achieve "sameness," and thus does not provide equality of opportunity at all. Equality gives the same opportunities to the various disparate elements that make up an ever-changing world and gives every member of society the same chance to complete his life course. Inasmuch as the starting points are different, the results must necessarily also be different. The important thing is that these different results be obtained by different people under the same conditions, using the same opportunities. Thus, this result will be uniquely satisfying for the people taken as a whole; it is the result from which the people can gain the most satisfaction.

What are rights (quanli)? Rights mean that one can be accommodated (shoudao) by one's [natural and social] environment (waijie). These opportunities are unequal in a class-structured society. In modern times, politics has involved the struggle to achieve equality of opportunity, that is, equal rights. But this is certainly not the struggle for similar, or average, achievement. The absolute average, absolute sameness of achievement, is an unobtainable illusion. The equality of rights, or the similarity of opportunity, on the other hand, can and must be completely attained. Thus, it is realistic to struggle for equal rights; this is a struggle which must be waged because of its social value and significance. To struggle to achieve an intellectual averaging is value-destroying, has no significance, and is to be eschewed.

3. *What Is Democracy?*

Freedom is the right to use one's capabilities to satisfy one's desires, though not the right to satisfy any kind of desire one pleases. When a baby is born, he has the right to go on living; to do so comprises his first struggle. There are two types of struggle. One type does not hinder the rights of others; the other rescinds or partly rescinds the rights of others. We believe the latter to be immoral and exploitative, while the former provides the opportunity for freedom of choice. Only when one's right to choose is not hindered can everyone's activities be protected and accommodated. The freedom we recognize is the kind that provides opportunities for unlimited choices and possibilities; it is not the kind of freedom that results in everyone acting exactly as they wish to satisfy their desires. This would actually deny freedom for the majority, with the inevitable result that a minority would be satisfying their desires [at the expense of the majority]. On the other hand, equal freedom for everyone would surely realize fair opportunities for all. Thus freedom can only be obtained if it is enjoyed by all mankind and can only be realized under conditions of mutual protection. It cannot be realized by some people depriving others of their freedom, nor can it be attained through the willful satisfaction of the desires [of a minority]. . . .

Democracy in its primitive sense means letting people be masters of their own affairs. The concept of democracy covers a wide range. Briefly, it means that people have the right to exercise control over all things in human society, including control over economic, political, cultural, and social affairs. The desires of people are not completely identical. If we only emphasize control and neglect the aim of satisfying the desires of the majority, we will end up in the absurd state of "democratic dictatorship." The Marxist theory of "the dictatorship of the proletariat" was developed on the basis of analyzing and magnifying the aspect of control in democracy. When this theory was fully developed, it fundamentally negated the fact that different members of society have the right to satisfy their different desires. In other words, it denied people's right to live as equals. By the time Marxism developed to the Leninist stage of "ruthless suppression of counterrevolutionaries," it fundamentally negated the fact that each man is free to carry out political activities to satisfy his personal desires in life and to fight for survival. This was an out-and-out negation

of the most fundamental principle of democracy. As a result of this negation, democracy was cut off from reality and only its name was retained
to adorn the ugly features of despotism. This explains why all social systems based on Marxist socialism are without exception undemocratic and
even antidemocratic autocracies.

Democracy is not a goal in actual life. Instead, it is a social condition
insuring that all have equal opportunities to attain their goals in life.
Thus, democracy is a social system. In the first place, it is a political system; in the second place, it is an economic system. It is not a subordinat-
ing or enslaving system designed to do away with people's freedom, but
one which protects people's freedom and consequently provides them with
a chance to work in cooperation with each other. In actual life, different
people have different ideas. If people are not free to live and do things as
they wish, it is impossible to have large-scale cooperation on a voluntary
basis or to establish a cooperative social structure. Hence, to begin with,
democracy must be a social system that protects freedom. On the basis
of freedom, it must encourage voluntary cooperation and achieve unity
of relatively unanimous interests. Democracy is not a means of centralism,
nor is freedom a window dressing for discipline. Democracy is a means of
protecting freedom, and discipline is the pillar of democracy. If we reck-
lessly reverse the means and the end, we will only find ourselves sinking
into the quagmire of Maoist dictatorship. . . .

In a democracy, people work according to their wishes and ideals, and
thus the best conditions and fairest treatment are insured. All ideas and
wants are treated equally. Democracy will not be dictated by any idea and
will not even tolerate [monistic] ideology. The reason for this is that [mo-
nistic] ideology not only rejects the rationality of alternative ideas, but rules
out the right of other ideas to exist. It demands the merger of all ideas and
declares that an ideology will only be realized to the extent that ideas
have been forcefully unified. Hence, ideology is essentially despotic and
undemocratic. Actually, all dictatorships have some kind of ideological
foundation. In the old days, the feudal dynasties used religion to dominate
society ideologically. For modern socialism, it is Marxism that serves as the
ideological prop. The promises given by these ideological props regarding the ideal state are utterly visionary and unverifiable. They may
be a little better than the stuff sold by ordinary swindlers, but in terms of
effect they are not only useless but harmful.

4. *The Realization of Democracy is the Precondition for Winning Human Rights*

Some people say: We do not have human rights. I think what they mean is: We do not have human rights based on equality. Do people living in despotic societies also have the right to live? Yes. Some people have the right to live by enslaving others. The majority of people only have the right to live as slaves. In a despotic society, people do not enjoy equal rights of existence. Any social system which denies the equal rights of existence is despotic and totalitarian. Contrary to despotism, a democratic social system primarily recognizes the equal human rights of all citizens. All social systems which acknowledge that everyone has an equal right to exist are democratic systems. Since, as we have said, democracy gives all an equal right to seek a livelihood, it follows that democracy is a precondition for gaining human rights.

As a result of years of absolutist politics based on Marxism and Mao's thought, the workers, farmers, soldiers, and masses of our country do not enjoy political freedom. They are not in a position to affect their social system or their own lives. Seldom do their hopes and aspirations influence the government. This political powerlessness spells enslavement and economic exploitation. Contrary to what Marx asserted, between politics and economics, the former is not always decisive.[1] Nor will politics invariably determine economics, as Mao Zedong maintained. Politics and economics are two aspects of human society that influence each other while simultaneously governing each other. If either aspect fails to cope with the other, social development will be impeded. In a modern socialist society where the lure of idealism is combined with the coercion of dictatorship to exercise social control, the fact that people are powerless in political affairs and enslaved and exploited will cause economic development to lose its importance in making life easier. This will hamper social development.

If we want to free ourselves from enslavement and live in such a way to keep abreast of the modernization program, we must first secure the preconditions for winning all this; that is, democratic politics. The reform of the political system and the thorough practice of democracy are the first steps toward pushing the Chinese society forward and thoroughly improving the livelihood of the Chinese people. It this is not tackled, all other pending issues will remain pending forever.

DOCUMENT 31
THE PEOPLE LACK HOUSING
Poem by "A Revolutionary Citizen"

While the people in Beijing have a housing shortage,
Mansions are being built in Zhong-nan-hai!*
If the Chairman [Mao Zedong] and the Premier [Zhou Enlai] were still
    alive,
Who would dare to go in for such a blind and haphazard extravagance?
Cultural objects and historical landmarks have all been pulled down;
This is utterly preposterous!
Numerous tower cranes operate daily,
And hundreds of trucks are bustling in and out every evening.
Year in year out,
Half of the city's construction forces have been transferred.
Cases of local unlicensed buildings have been handled with extreme
    severity,
But the wrongdoings of superiors are surely not right.
We should learn from the Premier's spirit of serving the people,
And should never try to build an edifice like the A-fang Palace
Built by Qin Shi Huang [third century B.C.].
Vice-Chairman Wang [Dongxing] should carefully think on this:
A common citizen's home covers an area of two square meters.[2]

---

* Zhong-nan-hai is the section of Beijing where top officials reside.

DOCUMENT 32
BEGGARS
From a Wall Poster

Whoever does not believe the wall posters here should go to the Beijing railroad station and ask the people from the provinces if there are any beggars there. I do not believe that these beggars are particularly happy when rice is exported for friends in the so-called Third World. But is anyone concerned about what these beggars think?

It is a disgrace that in our People's Republic only those who hold power eat well and have nothing to do except read books, write poetry, and lead a happy life. Do the people not have the right, then, to snatch the power from these masters?[3]

DOCUMENT 33
FAMILY BACKGROUND
From *Beijing Spring*

... At 7:00 P.M., on 27 December 1978, a man set fire to himself in Tian-an-men Square. Discovered by the soldiers on duty, he was promptly rescued and taken to the collecting post. Upon investigation, it was found that the man's name was Wang Guohui, a worker of the Dalian Oil and Fat Chemical Plant. Because of the wrong classification of his family, he sought an audience with the authorities many times but got nowhere, and he was even detained. Desperate, he tried to commit suicide by setting fire to himself.[4]

DOCUMENT 34
STORY: ONE BUREAUCRAT
By Yong Cun

I have only been in this organ for two weeks, but these people have found out that I am the commanding officer's son-in-law.

I notice that people's expression has become more friendly; those who ignored me before are now greeting me, and even some chairmen of a superior level also say hello to me.

I have been to two different places, and everywhere it is the same. There are also some who, after learning of my status, become distant. They do not wish to join the ranks of those who are friendly to me. It makes me feel bad. What I need are those comrades, yet they avoid me.

I recall my years in the rural village and in school. In those days, I was only the son of a middle-school teacher, not yet the son-in-law of the commanding officer, nor a staff officer of the Liberation Army. I was one of the common people who must fend for himself.

However, I would rather be one of the common people.

I put my desk in order. It is almost quitting time. Little Ye of the Confidential Room downstairs pushes the door open and enters, and sits down in the soft chair facing me. "Little Jiang, there's going to be a movie in a short while, an American film—*Patton*." Stuffing a filter cigarette between his lips, he continues: "Still more than half hour to go yet. Let's chat for a while. Commander Yu's family has been notified." He smiles humbly, indicating that he was the one who performed this honorable duty. "Little Jiang, a few days ago Political Commissar Hu praised you highly, finding you intelligent and able. You have only been here a few days, yet you have mastered the affairs. It looks like you are considered a good potential to be cultivated. . . ."

"Little Ye, what kind of shoes are those you're wearing?" Thus I interrupt him. I know that my abilities are ordinary, and I also know why Political Commissar Hu praised me, but Little Ye's true skill is playing all kinds of fashionable games, not assessing people.

"Three-jointed shoes. But don't joke. How could you not know this?" While talking, he shakes his feet under the desk where I cannot see them. "My father says that he plans to introduce me to the daughter of X X [*sic*]." He names a person of such a high position that I feel it improper to write it down. "It seems that the girl is quite refined, except that she is somewhat temperamental." He lets an expression of triumph remain on his face, waiting for my reaction.

He has not yet found his prospect, yet the rumor is known to everyone.

When I do not express an opinion, he lowers his voice: "Little Jiang, are your old K [sic] and Commander Yu old comrades-in-arms? Commander Yu has only this one daughter. He would not have given her to you otherwise." Again he smiles mysteriously.

"No," I replied sternly. "My father is a middle-school teacher. He has never joined the revolution, nor is he a Party member."

"Oh? Then how did you?" Little Ye is apparently surprised and begins to look me up and down as if discovering the president of the United States in front of him. My looks are ordinary, without anything outstanding. I am not "smart" or "elegant" by the standards of the young people today.

Looking at this playboy with his fair skin. I imagine that he has never suffered any hardship since leaving his mother's womb. He has never been soaked by the rain, nor frozen stiff by the cold, nor has he worried over survival, nor has he experienced the responsibilities of a son with an aged mother seriously ill. The shoulders under his military uniform most likely are fair and delicate and have never encountered the unreasonable fisticuffs of others. His flighty eyes have probably never become angry from shame and insult. What could he understand?

"Do you want me to tell you my experience?" I laughed grimly and looked at him.

"Do tell me. You have a few tricks up your sleeve." His impudent expression makes one want to hit his face with one's fist.

"There's too much to tell, and I don't have time now. I still have some work to do." Suppressing my anger, I bend over a document which I have already read.

[*The narrator proceeds to recount to the reader his experiences, some of which we reproduce later in this volume as Document 40.*]

I longed to relive the life of those carefree days. It is true that my clothing had been threadbare and my hands dirty. It is true that my wage had only been eight work points a day, with each work point amounting to only 7.6 *fen* (U.S. eleven cents). Nonetheless I had been happy as lark.

But those are bygone days.

I reached for a piece of paper to draft a memorandum. I would request a transfer to a company in the field and serve as a common platoon leader. My men would judge me only by my hard work. And I would win their esteem.[5]

SECTION EIGHT
ON MANAGING THE ECONOMY

The first document in this section discusses political economy in terms of the broad historical perspective. We then move to the central point of contention between the government and the democrats: the relationship between democratization and economic modernization. We have already had a taste of the democrats' view in Wei Jingsheng's "The Fifth Modernization" (Document 12). But Wei's militancy was not shared by all participants in the democratic movement. Some, while urging a degree of liberalization, cautioned against Wei's radicalism. The April Fifth Forum, for example, while acknowledging the continuing shortcomings in the way the economy was being managed, placed primary blame on bureaucrats and refused to go along with the attacks on Deng Xiaoping (Document 36). However, these writers agreed that democratization would stimulate the economy. Document 37 briefly underscores these points and calls for greater reliance upon material incentives.

The final two articles are from Beijing Spring. In Document 38, the standard Marxist contention that achieving socialist economy is a more fundamental need than political democracy is accepted. Nonetheless, it is insisted that democracy is still important, especially democracy within enterprises. The latter point is expanded upon in Document 39.

DOCUMENT 35
DEMOCRACY AND NATIONAL CONSTRUCTION
From *Democracy and Modernity*

Since last year, a nationwide movement for democracy, typified by Xidan Democracy Wall, has risen and flourished. This mass movement, the likes of which we have not seen in two decades, has met with the interest and support of people throughout the country. What path is this movement taking, and to what goal will it lead? These are the points which we wish to discuss below.

The development of the democratic movement.   If one wants to understand the meaning of this movement, one must examine its origins.

For twenty years, various political opportunists, such as Kang Sheng, Lin Biao, and the Gang of Four, plotted and deceived in order to secure high position. They were able to do this because of the profound influence of feudalism in our country, and because of theoretical errors and illusions on the part of certain people in the Party. Constituting themselves as a counterrevolutionary group, they acted out the absurd scenario of restoring feudal despotism. They resorted to oppressive and deceptive practices, insuring that those who supported them prospered and that dissenters vanished. Many true revolutionaries were attacked and jailed simply because they dared to write dissenting (and correct) opinions. They used every conceivable way to suffocate the new emerging forces and revolutionary elements and to destroy the nation's productive power. All this brought China to unprecedented political and economic crisis.

History inevitably moves ahead. Anyone who attempts to forcefully protect his throne will be toppled sooner or later. In April 1976, a movement to defend Premier Zhou and denounce the Gang of Four erupted like a volcano. People were demanding democracy instead of dictatorship. This was the popular will, and it reflected the tide of history and marked the beginning of a new era in China's quest for democracy.

Neither the power of the people nor this historical tide can be blocked by anyone. Since the Gang of Four was crushed, the Party Central Committee has altered its policies and revised the laws and Constitution, all in keeping with a fine tradition and work style. This clearly reflects the people's longing for a democratic China. But is must be pointed out that our society has been built on a foundation of semifeudalism and semicolonialism, and that we have suffered a long period of imperialist invasions and wars. Consequently, our people have been kept at a relatively low cultural level and have been unable to set themselves free from feudalistic thinking. Notwithstanding the steps taken in raising cultural standards after 1949, these gains were erased by the restoration of feudalism in later years. Many [leaders and cadres] forsook their obligations, failed to do their duty, transformed from public servants into masters of the people. They were profiteers, not revolutionaries. At the same time, a group of even greedier nouveau riche emerged. Consciously and unconsciously, they cultivated authoritarianism. They felt that it was simpler to do things themselves than to be democratic about it. It was easier to adhere to the old rules than to reform. Thus, they were the stumbling blocks for democracy. If we want to eliminate the remnants of feudal authoritarianism, restructure our country along democratic lines, and increase productivity, then it is not enough merely to let matters take their course and hope for a gradual reform carried out from above. The people have risen up. They are demanding human rights and democracy. This is the inexorable wave of history.

Increasing production.   The purpose of a movement is to solve a certain problem. What is the substance of this movement, and is the movement necessary? To answer these questions, we must further examine some modern Chinese social history and analyze our origins.

Beginning with the Opium War (1840), foreign powers constantly invaded, plundered, and oppressed our nation politically and economically. Gradually, China became a semifeudal, semicolonial country. The tyrannical Qing rulers, in order to protect their dynasty, kowtowed and surrendered to the foreigners. They suspended the modernization and constitutional reform movements led by Kang Youwei and Liang Qichao and suppressed the Taiping rebels and the Boxers. China was pushed into a political and economic trap set by the imperialists. Although bourgeois democratic revolutionaries led by Sun Yat-sen successfully overthrew the feudal Manchu dynasty in 1911, they were not able to expel the "barbarians" and insure the independence and integrity of China. Opportunities for national growth were also lost because of the warlord chaos fanned by the imperialists. During this lengthy period, our country also lost the opportunity to have the kind of industrial and cultural revolution that Western countries had enjoyed. This left China far behind the West in terms of productivity. Thus, the democratic revolution was not satisfactory and cannot be termed a success.

Even though our country has entered the era of socialism, we still require a double revolution: capitalist and socialist. Capitalist revolution emphasizes raising cultural and ideological standards, thereby liberating people from the confines of feudalism. It also involves an industrial revolution to promote the development of productivity and enrich society's material resources. Socialist revolution, on the other hand, emphasizes both political revolution, which upgrades people's political consciousness and wipes out the old ideology of exploitation, and social revolution, to correct the shortcomings of capitalism and to collectivize the private sector. We must have both revolutions, because without the capitalist foundation socialism cannot be achieved.

With the elimination of oppressive foreign monopolies, an immense market was opened for our national industry, and the future was promising. Businessmen were encouraged, and the result was rapid industrial development and prosperity. In addition, the prompt completion of land reform was a boon to farmers, and thus the nation's economic base was broadened.

With increasing productivity came a certain metamorphosis in the superstructure. Our social system was imperfect, and bureaucratism developed in both the Party and the government. This was a roadblock to the development of productivity that had to be removed. There was a demand for a rapid increase in productivity, and then the movement for democratic reconstruction erupted. This was intended as a meaningful movement, but the real outcome was confinement, oppression, and the destruction of democracy. This was due to theoretical errors and conceptual illusions on the part of some Party people who failed to promote productivity. The meeting at Lushan [1959], and later the Cultural Revolution and the emergence of Kang Sheng, Lin Biao, and the Gang of Four, all restricted the thinking of people both inside and outside the Party. All over the land there was feudalistic authoritarianism. Thus, people's ideological bondage was exacerbated, and the sprouts of democracy were destroyed. Indeed, people are still fearful. Without a broadly based democratic movement the shackles on people's minds cannot be broken; nor will the completion of the dual revolutionary task be possible.

The reason that our people have such a low level of consciousness and such a low cultural standard is that the country entered into socialism while remnants of feudalism still existed. The old culture, old notions, and old concepts lingered on, especially in the countryside. There continued to be a typically feudal absolute obedience, and people continued to respect the authority of, for example, the husband, the clan, the divine, and the royal. And of course, they were always nurturing their successors. In other words, the foundations of socialism were inadequate. This is also why people like Kang Sheng, Lin Biao, and the Gang of Four had their way for so long. This conceptual problem must be solved before there can be a successful socialist revolution and improved productivity. These goals will not be attained through indoctrination and oppression. We have to be practical. This is the time to educate the people in democracy and thereby allow them to liberate themselves.

History teaches us that modern productivity requires a modern society.

Even with the Four Modernizations, it is still necessary to promote democracy. Only thus can society modernize and quickly achieve the Four Modernizations.

The times call for this democratic movement. Prosperity depends upon its success. Without democracy the Four Modernizations will only be a mirage, and we will have failed our duty to history.

The movement's purpose. A true Chinese will never do anything to harm our nation. The purpose of the democratic movement, then, is to promote China's prosperity economically, technically, culturally, and politically. Any other motive would be wrong.

Our movement is a lesson in democratic revolution. But the wheel of history cannot be turned backward. We must be pragmatic materialists and operate on the basis of present realities, not on the basis of conditions sixty years ago. So we must combine the democratic movement with economic modernization, thus fulfilling two great and important revolutionary missions. Failure to take this approach will widen the economic gap between China and the West. Thus, the original meaning of the movement will be lost. It would also demonstrate that "haste makes waste," and the goals of the Four Modernizations would elude us.

Inasmuch as the modernization of society is the foundation of the modernization of production, during this democratic movement we must begin by solving the problem of the modernization of the society. At present, there are still many undesirable phenomena. To wipe out these phenomena is to modernize our society. We need to undertake a fair and comprehensive analysis of China's condition and draw scientific conclusions. In this manner we can work out ways to solve and eliminate the major contradictions [i.e., conflicts, obstacles.]

From the start, we must oppose those who want not democracy but only absolute monarchy. In promoting democracy, we should emphasize the protection of human rights, in order that the people may become the masters of the nation. At the same time, we firmly oppose anarchism and extreme democracy.

Comrades, let us make our country a people's democratic dictatorship. Let us work together for the prosperity of our country.[1]

DOCUMENT 36
THE STATE OF THE ECONOMY
From April Fifth Forum

. . . From what we know, our national economic development leaves much to be desired. The large bonuses which were paid last year proved to have very little effect. Billions [of *yuan*] invested in large-scale enterprises produced irrecoverable crises due to the inevitable deficiency of government-run enterprise. A big factory at Wugang, constructed according to the economic plan, failed to include electric power in the planning; thus, a factory built at high cost produced nothing. As for foreign loans and technologies, our "businessmen"—who can do nothing but shout slogans—have caused more losses for the Chinese people. As a result, it is reported that even though production was up by several trillion [*yuan*] last year, the balance sheet still showed a loss. With such great losses, and the fact that production is not increasing much, the economy of China today is in considerable difficulty.

Apparently, Comrade Chen Yun's opinion that an economic "adjustment" is most urgent has won the support of a majority of the Communist Party's Central Committee. So a leap backward is to aim at two leaps forward. But how can we make the two leaps forward? Rapid and steady development can only be achieved through a well-planned, comprehensive policy of modernization. Such a policy should be formulated through the full utilization of our work force and with the collective wisdom of our people. The final decision should be made by a vote of all the people in order to fill the political vacuum produced by the deaths of Mao Zedong, Zhou Enlai, and Zhu De. As it is, the power of the people is the most uneconomically utilized resource of all.

Many problems have been caused by the long reigns of Lin Biao, the Gang of Four, and bureaucrats who have severely harmed the basic rights and benefits owed to the people. Those who had been injured the most severely are still engaged in a life-and-death struggle. Because of these left-over problems, there have been numerous strikes by workers, farmers, and students around the country, as well as demonstrations, interference with trains and buses, and sit-ins at government offices. In addition, some tumult has been stirred up by a small number of opportunists. These incidents have aggravated our difficulties somewhat.

Whether we are talking about low productivity or strikes, the primary problem lies in a series of flaws rooted in our political and economic system. We have departed from scientific socialism in many fundamental aspects. The country's ownership system is hampering the development of production. Therefore, the democratic movement is aimed at transforming the country's ownership system.

If a small number of nonproducers in our country control the production workers with regard to their personal files, wages, and transfers, it will be impossible to expect the workers to surpass the productivity of labor attained under the capitalist system. It is precisely those who dislike others airing independent political views that are suppressing production workers from expressing their views on production, distribution, and exchange. If this is so, laborers under socialism will only be expected to mind their own business as handicraft workers traditionally did in the past. Naturally, it will be impossible for them to compete with their counterparts in other countries.

We must understand that these problems did not arise in a few days but have evolved over two or three decades. There are no quick solutions. The people have the right to demand prompt solutions, but they should not expect the government to solve everything at once. This would be asking too much. The issue is whether the government is sincere about solving problems, and whether it will take concrete steps to do so. If so, more time should be allowed. But if not, the people naturally have the right to exercise their power to force the government to work out solutions.

Today the Central Committee and the State Council are not without sincerity about solving our problems. However, the speed of execution appears to be too slow, due to the inefficiency of the middle-level and lower-level bureaucrats. Under these circumstances, although it is proper for people to express their opinions, violent actions are counterproductive. . . . In general, we are convinced that a set of concrete laws and regulations is necessary to safeguard production and social order. Otherwise, if everyone acts according to his own wishes, society will not survive. . . .[2]

DOCUMENT 37
WHO SHOULD BE THE MASTERS?
From a Wall Poster

According to the concepts of Marxism-Leninism, the people should control the means of production. But ask yourselves, Chinese workers and peasants: Apart from the small wage which you receive each month, what do you control? What belongs to you? The answer is shameful: Others are your masters. In a socialist society, the product of labor should belong to the worker. But what do you get? Just enough so that you can continue to work! Higher salaries have not sufficed to compensate for soaring prices, and our standard of living has not improved.

Marx may have called them the worst scourge for oppressing the proletariat, but material incentives are inevitable.[3]

DOCUMENT 38
DEMOCRACY IN ECONOMIC MANAGEMENT
By Han Zhixiong

. . . For more than a decade our national economy deteriorated day by day, and a general collapse appeared imminent. The people's livelihood went from bad to worse. All of this was due to the absence of democracy.

We must move quickly to establish democracy. We must also waste no time in achieving the Four Modernizations. These desirable goals have been dreamed about and sought by everyone for a long time. The decision of the Third Plenum of the Central Committee [December 1978] to place emphasis on the Four Modernizations has received a warm welcome from the people. I firmly support this Party decision.

Ours is a socialist country, and the state belongs to the people. But to really have it this way, we must have democracy. In the old China there was political suppression of laborers, farmers, and other working people. The fundamental reason for this was that the means of production belonged to the landlords and capitalists. The people had no rights to land or factories. For the very reason that they had no economic rights, they suffered oppression and exploitation which then led to political suppression. It follows that people can attain their political liberation only when they become economically liberated.

Chairman Mao led us in the construction of a new China and of a socialist society which brought liberation for workers and peasants, and also political liberation. However, bureaucratism is a serious problem in our economy. It stands in the way of the rapid development of production and prevents the people from exercising control over production. In many units, production is controlled by a small group of people. Orders have had to be carried out as given, with work performed according to the will of the superior and not according to the laws of economics. The lack of democratic ways in economic management leads to a lack of democracy in politics. So if we want to have a system of democracy in politics, we must insist on a system of people's democracy in economic management. Yugoslavia has already achieved excellent results in testing such a system. We shall learn from Yugoslavia's example; this will encourage our workers to exert great efforts for the realization of the Four Modernizations. . . .

We are determined to fight for the realization of democracy in both economic management and in politics.[4]

DOCUMENT 39
HOW TO RUN A FACTORY
By Lu Min

Under the "dictatorial rule" of basic-level party organizations in factories, mines, and other enterprises, workers have very limited democratic rights. Although leaders of shifts and groups, sections and workshops are elected by the workers in a democratic way, they cannot do much because the party organizations in basic-level units have the final say in crucial matters and matters of concern to the workers. These elected section and workshop leaders do not have much actual power. Therefore, this incomplete democratic election cannot fundamentally arouse workers' enthusiasm in production. The workers also treat this minor reform coldly.

To truly arouse workers' enthusiasm in production, it is necessary to give the workers genuine democratic rights and do away with the power of the administration leadership of basic-level party organization in factories, mines, and other enterprises. I will briefly discuss this question in this article. Would comrades please kindly give me criticism and point out my mistakes.

Anyone with an elementary knowledge of Marxism-Leninism knows that a political party is a class concept. It is the child of class struggle and at the same time a tool of class struggle. It grows strong with the strengthening of class struggle and withers with the withering of it. Its strengthening and withering are decided by the situation of class struggle. Since class struggle is withering now, the party should also gradually wither. This should first take place in the basic-level units of the factories and mines.

According to the Marxist-Leninist class theory, classes are based on the relation of different social groups to the means of production. Lenin firmly established this point in his classic definition of classes. He said: "Classes are large groups of people which differ from each other by the place they occupy in a historically determined system of social production, by their relation (in most cases fixed and formulated by law) to the means of production, by their role in the social organization of labor, and, consequently, by the dimensions and mode of acquiring the share of social wealth of which they dispose" (*Selected Works of Lenin,* vol. 4, p. 10). Hence, classes are social groups with different status in specific relations of production. Classes are determined by the system of ownership and are therefore engendered by it. Engels incisively pointed out in his thesis on the emergence of classes: "With slavery, which attained its fullest development under civilization, came the first great split of society into an exploiting class and an exploited class" (*Selected Works of Marx and Engels,* vol. 4, p. 172). This means that without private ownership there will not be any class antagonism. Only when there is private ownership will there be exploiting classes, because public ownership will not engender them. If a particular system of ownership can engender an exploting class, it can only be private ownership and not public ownership. For example, the slave-owning class did not emerge from the system of public ownership in primitive communities but, rather, after the emergence of private ownership following the development of the productive forces. For another example, the state bourgeoisie in the Soviet Union is also not the child of public ownership in Stalin's days. It is a new bourgeoisie which eventually takes shape after the handful of Party capitalist roaders (still this is not a class) usurped supreme leadership and turned public ownership into a new form of state-planned capitalist ownership. Therefore, as long as public ownership does not turn into private ownership, exploiting classes will not emerge.

If private ownership is basically eliminated, and if the system of public ownership is established and has not degenerated, the number of old exploiting classes will diminish and new exploiting classes will not emerge. Facts also show that, at present, the few old exploiting class elements left behind by the old society cannot form an exploiting class, and the small number of bad elements engendered by the new society are also insufficient to form such a class. These facts tell us that our class enemies are diminishing in number and class struggle is weakening. The assertions made by Lin Biao and the Gang of Four that we would have more and more class enemies in socialist society, and their so-called "all-round dictatorship," were all reactionary fallacies that went against the Marxist-Leninist class theory and objective reality. They not only tampered with the sole Marxist criterion of determining class status according to people's relations to the means of production, but they arbitrarily classified the millions and millions of cadres, experts, technicians, and innocent people as bourgeois elements, and exercised ruthless fascist dictatorship. Millions of cadres and masses died in this "class struggle." This brought a great disaster to the Chinese revolution and dealt a punitive blow to the historical idealists inside the Party. We should learn this painful lesson and take it to heart.

Practice is the sole criterion for testing truth. Facts have eloquently shown that turbulent class struggles have already come to an end, and, although class struggles still exist, they are gradually withering. At present, the emphasis of our work is shifting from large-scale class struggle to socialist construction.

Political parties, as tools of class struggle, should wither with the withering of class struggle to suit the needs of the new historical situation. This is the same as wearing clothes. Now that the weather is getting warm and spring has already arrived, we should take off the heavy and thick cotton-padded clothes. Otherwise we will get sick. Those who defy objective conditions and indiscriminately emphasize the need to strengthen Party leadership are going against the law of class struggle. When we announce that we are shifting the emphasis of work to production and construction, we are also announcing the withering of class struggle. When we do this, we must also announce the gradual withering of the Party in order to live up to the realities of the day and the laws of historical development.

If the Party does not wither with the withering of class struggle, it is possible that a new large-scale class struggle will take place again. The reason is that what the Party enforces is the strictest "system of assigning duties according to grades." Not only are cadres appointed by Party organizations from the highest levels down to the grass roots, but the titles of Party members are also bestowed by Party organizations in the same manner. For this reason, the proletariat is not in a position to supervise the Party members and to dismiss those Party cadres who go against the interests of the people. Thus, careerists like the Gang of Four can break away from people's control, stir up trouble inside the Party, and spurn and attack the revolutionaries. Some revolutionary cadres estrange themselves from the masses and degenerate as a result of the lack of supervision from the masses. If this goes on, the careerists and bureaucrats could form the majority of the upper strata inside the Party and eventually usurp supreme leadership and turn public ownership into private ownership. A new class could then emerge, followed by acute class struggles; and the tragedy of the Soviet Union becoming revisionist would repeat itself.

As proven by numerous historical facts, anything which ought to withdraw from the arena of history (no matter what a progressive role it had played) will be detested by the people and become a historical stumbling block if it persists in this arena. This holds true for the power of the administrative leadership of basic-level Party organizations. Due to the gradual withering of class struggle, it is losing its progressive role and prestige. Instead of supporting it, people are now avoiding, "fearing," and even detesting it. This is common knowledge. People have felt more and more strongly that the power of the administrative leadership of basic-level Party organizations has now become an obstacle to the development of production.

Yugoslavia's experience deserves our attention. In conformity with the law of class struggle, they have abolished the power of the administrative and production leadership of party organizations at the grass-roots units of factories and mines in the nick of time, and they have set up "workers' committees" in their place. Thus, they can give full play to the workers' enthusiasm in production and expedite the development of production.

For this reason, we should also gradually diminish the Party's leadership power to meet the needs of the situation in which class struggle is withering. We do not advocate the total abolition of Party leadership at this stage, because that is wrong and adventurist. Only when classes and class struggle have been completely wiped out can we do away with the Party. Nevertheless, we must gradually do away with it. We should start from the grass-roots units of factories, mines, and other enterprises. The abolition of the power of the administrative leadership of basic-level Party organizations spells the withering of the Party. By letting "workers' committees"—which are democratically elected by the workers—exercise leadership in administration and production, outstanding workers and competent technicians can assume leading posts and give free rein to their initiative. Party members and cadres should strive to be elected into "workers' committees" because of their exemplary deeds and, hence, lead these committees. We should not indefinitely expand the Party's leadership power in the middle-level and upper-level administrative organs. Instead, we should strengthen the power of the National People's Congress and create the necessary conditions for gradually abolishing the Party's leadership at these two levels. It is the great historic mission of the proletariat and Communists to abolish classes, the Party and the state. We must fight hard for the gradual fulfillment of this task.

We should take note of another problem. The Gang of Four's reactionary slogan, "Kick aside the Party committees to make revolution," incited many people largely because the power of the administrative leadership of basic-level Party organizations had, in an objective sense, hampered the development of production. The question is, did the Gang of Four really want to kick aside the Party? No. What they really wanted was to kick aside the erstwhile Party organizations and replace them with their own party. They did not intend to let the "workers' committees" exercise power. Hence, their practice was reactionary and had nothing in common with "self-government by workers" as practiced in Yugoslavia. Furthermore, because class struggle is only withering and has not died out completely, we should not at this point do away with the leadership power of middle-level and upper-level Party organizations. For this reason, it is a violation of the law of class struggle to kick aside all Party organizations.

Some people said we are antiparty and antisocialist because we put forward the call to do away with the power of the administrative leadership of basic-level Party organizations. Our advice to these people is that they should show a little more respect for the law of class struggle and should make a more in-depth study of the changed situation before drawing any conclusion. Furthermore, in Yugoslavia, where the power of the administrative leadership of party organizations in factories, mines, and other enterprises has been done away with long ago, socialism not only has not collapsed but is prospering daily. The Party Central Committee and Chairman Hua called the people of Yugoslavia comrades and comrades-in-arms. Does it not seem rather unfair for us to be branded antiparty and antisocialist just because we raised this question theoretically?

The question of "Party leadership" is the focal point of arguments in the current movement for democracy. We must break through this "forbidden area."[5]

SECTION NINE
GLIMPSES OF CHINESE LIFE

Much of the material published during the winter of 1978-79 was a reaction to the official media's glorification of the human condition in China. Thus, many of the dissident writers insisted on describing the darker side of life. We reproduce here three examples: an extract from a short story and two brief news items. The short story (Document 40) is a flashback by the narrator of a longer work which was also excerpted in Document 34. He is one of the millions of "educated youth" who were sent from the cities to work in the farm villages.

DOCUMENT 40
STORY: A HUNDRED METERS
By Yong Cun

In 1972 I went to work in an agricultural village called Taoyuan. Some say that the village was named after Tao Yuanming,* but I doubt it. The place consists of only two bare hills. Very little water is available. A single road leads off to the provincial capital.

At the edge of the village was an army post. Even now I do not understand what the post's function was. Inside were several rows of buildings in which a battalion was quartered. In addition to the soldiers, there were cadres and some other people who wore spectacles. The unit did reclaim several hundred *mou* of land which had been flooded by the river. Members also performed weekly labor in aid of the civilians, and their relations with the local people were cordial.

Because I was responsible for irrigation, I often had dealings with the soldiers. As time went by, I got to know them well. Several of them often came to visit the compound where we "young intellectuals" from the cities lived.

One day I discovered an old man laboring among the soldiers. His hair was grey, and he appeared to be about sixty years old. He wore an old collarless uniform, and there was no insignia on his hat. It was evident that he had not been a manual laborer, for his hands were white and soft, and his face, although now roughened by the wind, had obviously once been well cared for. The skin now hung loosely from his cheeks.

The old man often stopped working to rest, but he never said a word. I surmised that he had been a target of investigations, resulting in his having been labeled a "capitalist roader" and a "demon monster." The soldiers always called him "Old Man" or "Fatty" and never addressed him by his name. When the soldiers rested, he was told to rest, but he always sat by himself away from the others.

[In response to my question about the old man,[1] a soldier said,] "I don't know. Seems he was a high official."

"I hear he's a commander," interrupted another.

A soldier who better understood the spirit of the era responded, " 'Commander!' So what? Wasn't Yang Chengwu dragged down?"†

"What was this old man's mistake?" I inquired.

"Who knows? Probably following the wrong line."

---

* Tao Yuanming (365–427) was a poet and magistrate in Jiangxi Province.

† Yang Chengwu was a military hero during World War II. He rose to the position of acting chief of staff in 1966, but was subsequently purged.

I looked at the form of the panting old man, the wind fluffing his grey hair, his weak chest rising and falling. He squinted and gazed into the distance. There was no knowing his thoughts.

Strong sympathy for him overcame me. Perhaps in his youth he had tended a landowner's sheep. Maybe he had endured a lonely and painful infancy and was rescued by the Red Army. Or, he might have left his footprints on the snowy mountains and grassy plains, or he might even have led a unit to capture Chiang Kai-shek's palace in Nanjing (Nanking). Yet here he is, toiling on land liberated by his blood, giving his life to the people's army. And he is working under a bunch of kids! What could I do for him?

One day, finding an opportunity to approach him, I said in a low voice: "If there is anything you want me to do for you, I shall do it."

He stared at me suspiciously and then shook his head. "Thank you. Nothing."

I could only imagine how he was being treated.

One day I wrapped a piece of cooked pork and stuffed it into his pocket when he was not looking, He turned, felt it, and without a word, averted his head and rubbed his eye pretending that there was something in it. Then I noticed that he was weeping.

The next day I borrowed a light from his cigarette and, while returning his cigarette, I stuffed a package of roasted peanuts into his pocket. In a very low voice, he said: "Child, be careful!"

This time it was not he, but I who could not hold back the tears.

[*During the Cultural Revolution it was not uncommon for intellectuals to be locked up near their place of employment and compelled to engage in manual labor.*]

My father, a teacher at our high school, was imprisoned for four years in the "cow shed." The reason, I am told, was that he had gone to school with [former Chairman of the Republic] Liu Shaoqi. I saw my father every day. I did not enjoy doing so, but I had to go to school. It pained me to see him there, with his *yin-yang* haircut, sweeping floors. In my heart, I felt (was it hatred or humiliation?) as though I was being boiled.

My father would write us letters which he would roll up into a ball and throw into a dark corner near the toilet, where I would collect them. In the evening, my mother, sister, and I would read the letters and cry on each other's shoulders. The replies to Father I would throw into the same corner, where he would soon come along with his broom and pretend to sweep them away. On those rare occasions when he could speak to me, he would whisper: "Child, be careful!"

And now I heard these same words again.

That day after work I noticed the old man picking up the jacket he had taken off during work. He pointed to a stone slab on the ground, looked at me, and then walked off.

When they were all far enough away, I went over and lifted the stone, and there next to a colony of busy black ants I found a neatly folded paper. I opened it, and a slip fell out. It read: "Little Jiang, help me send these letters. The address is indicated."

There were two letters, one addressed to his wife, with another to his daughter Yanyan. He wrote of his present condition, comforting them, telling them not to worry. Of course, he mentioned me, telling them to trust me.

I immediately dispatched the letters.

After a few days I received a reply. One letter was for me, thanking me a thousand times. Another letter was for him, telling of their condition and asking him not to worry. (I knew quite well that none of them were telling the truth. My own family had written such letters to my father.) The next day I put the letter to the old man under the same stone. To avoid error, I marked the stone with a small chalk cross.

After a time the group came. I waited until he had seen me and then pointedly glanced at the stone before going to exchange greetings with the soldiers. He took off his jacket and put it on that stone.

The next day I took from under the stone his reply.

A few days later I put another letter from his wife and daughter under the stone.

Is this not strange? Not knowing of one's own family's true condition, and even being uncertain of one's own fate? Feeling most concerned for one's family and writing letters that sound like there is peace and prosperity everywhere and that one's own condition is splendid—I understand this to reflect one of the noblest of human sentiments: unselfish love.

A third letter came from the family, and it raised a question which frightened me. They wanted to come to see him. I quickly put the letter under the stone.

The old man replied that they could not come, for it would be taking too great a risk. There were some people who would recognize them. If something went wrong, the only channel for communications would be cut.

I, too, wrote them a letter. I said that there were only a few people who might recognize them and if, after giving the matter careful thought, the family still wanted to come, they could say that they were my relatives. This way, they would not necessarily be found out.

Three days later, when I had finished work and was returning to the village, a child came to me saying, "Your maternal aunt has come." An aunt?

I had no maternal aunt! Then I understood. It was they who had come. I hastened home and on opening the door saw a stout woman of about fifty and also a young woman of about twenty with small pigtails, who was curiously looking over our messy room. I opened my mouth, but stopped myself because there were two other educated youths in the room looking at us. Then I addressed her as "Auntie." She smiled and pressed my hand, then began to cry, as did the young woman. I don't know why, but I also began to cry. Mystified and stupefied, the two youths left the room.

The next day I led them to a place where the old man was working, having again admonished them to be very careful not to give themselves away. Even from some distance the old man could be identified by his white hair. The "aunt" went forward with an unsteady gait, faster and faster, with the "niece" finally having to almost run. But I kept in front, reminding them in a low voice: "People will notice you! Slow down!"

About a hundred meters away from the place where the soldiers were working there was a long narrow mound of earth. . . .[2] A policeman stopped them: "Sit here; don't cross over there."

"Aunt's" face was bathed in tears. She plumped herself down on the ground, pulled her handkerchief, and vigorously rubbed her face. She seemed almost ready to cry out. "Niece" Yanyan stared blankly and emotionless, gazing at her father's figure. [I am sure that] he had seen them, for he waved his shovel. I don't know why, but [instead of facing our way he just looked at the ground], his face drooping lower and lower.

When rest time came, the soldiers played cards. The old man was sitting by himself, and now he was looking our way. A hundred meters away were the loved ones he had longed for day and night. I espied his quivering lips and two tear-filled eyes. There they all sat as if separated by an unfordable mountain stream, when actually there was nothing between them but a field which could be crossed in half a minute.

They sat and looked. "Aunt" finally stopped crying and was staring with a blank expression, the wind having dried her tears. Yanyan's expression was even more frightening. She stared, biting her lip. She did not blink. Her face was deathly pale.

DOCUMENT 41
QUILT FOR SALE
By Liu Jing

At 10:00 A.M., on 31 Decmber 1978, a cotton padded quilt was seen hanging from a tree on Taiping Street. Pinned to it was a sign which said "22 *yuan.*" Next to it was standing the owner, whom passersby asked why he wanted to sell his quilt in winter. The man told this story:

"My name is Wang Xueren. I came from Anhui Province to seek an audience with the authorities. I wanted to report how our commune and village cadres violate laws, disrupt discipline, deceive their superiors, and suppress their subordinates. I was in Beijing once before to make an appeal, but without result. This time I have been here for more than two weeks, but until now there has been no reply. I have spent all the money I had with me. The reception center provides free lodging but no meals. I have no alternative but to sell my quilt. Not being a resident of the city, the only place I can sell it is on the street."[3]

DOCUMENT 42
BLOOD BANK
From *Beijing Spring*

Our Tianjin (Tientsin) correspondent reports:

Ever since the beginning of this year many people in Tianjin have ex-perienced difficulties in their livelihood, including long periods of unem-ployment. For these and other reasons, they have been driven to sell their blood in order to make a living. In 1977, 1,068 people sold blood; in 1978 the number increased to as many as 1,510. Among these, there were 116 un-employed youths and 48 educated youths; 568 of the people were between twenty and twenty-six years of age. According to law, nobody below the age of twenty is allowed to be a blood donor, but some youths below twenty borrow other people's residence cards and donate blood under their name. The law also prohibits a person from donating blood more than once a year, but during these two years some youths gave blood over fifteen times.[4]

SECTION TEN
ON CHINA'S LEADERS

One craving which many Chinese obviously have is for more objective and balanced news and discussion about the men and women who have been leading the nation. The official media generally carry very little concrete information about even the most publicized luminaries. Democrats have often complained about the phenomenon of these "well-known strangers"; though their names appear daily, "they are strangers because we do not know their life stories."[1] Indeed, considerable cynicism has been generated as a result of the practice by those in control of the media of portraying present leaders as flawless heroes and their opponents (who may have once been similarly "flawless") as villains with no redeeming features whatsoever.

Thus, for example, a writer in April Fifth Forum, *while not defending Lin Biao, complained about the "metaphysical" nature of the current criticism of Mao's former top aid.*

> *Following Lin's collapse, all of his words and actions were considered to have been wrong. He has even been described as a marshal who knew nothing about military affairs. Nobody even dares use the phrase "getting immediate results," because it was once spoken by Lin Biao. A similar thing happened to the term "self-cultivation," which became forbidden immediately following Liu Shaoqi's fall from power. Now that the "Gang of Four" have collapsed, it seems that all vices were committed by them. All evil deeds have been blamed on the Four without any exception! But this may not be the true portrayal of history.*

On the other hand, the writer continued, if a leader is portrayed in the media as good, the implication is that "he cannot possibly improve," and for anyone to criticize him would constitute a "monstrous crime." The writer concludes with the question: "Is there even the slightest trace of historical materialism or historical analysis here, conducted on the basis of seeking truth from facts?"[2]

Thus, during the thaw many writers attempted their own evaluations of China's current and former leaders. One cannot claim that the pieces selected comprise a representative cross section of national opinion, but only that they help establish the range of views that has existed regarding the leaders in question.

DOCUMENT 43
ZHOU ENLAI
From *Enlightenment* and *April Fifth Forum*

I

Heaven and earth are dark and gloomy, mourning the hero.
Suddenly and unexpectedly, he has gone forever.
Looking up at the universe, the heart is broken
By this requiem of the great achievements.
An entire life's energy devoted to the revolution,
At the cost of his life he died heroically.
Wholeheartedly and loyally he created miracles and made history.

After working daily for fifty years,
He was finally overcome by chronic illness;
But still not retiring, he fought and struggled
Against the Four Pests, the arch enemies.[3]
His great and intricate plans are not easily seen and analyzed.
He passionately pushed forward the sacred plan,
Hoping to transform the principles,
Regretting that the prosperous land was not realized in time.
Missing it by a day,
He died in sorrow.

II

How should grief and sorrow be revealed?
To whom should they be expressed,
After being suppressed by layers and layers of black clouds?
They suffocate heaven and earth.
Evil spirits laugh and suck human blood.
Billions and billions of beings died in the catastrophe.
Recalling the tyranny of Zhou and Qin [1122–207 B.C.],
There is still no precedent.
For more than ten years, day and night,
The best years of one's life pass with hidden tears.
He was hopeful that both the dragon and the fish were present.
Under a sword, yet he survived.
He hoped to expose his soul wholeheartedly to the sun and moon.
He launched struggles, but the force of his justice was weak
As he was lacking the strength.
In future years, I shall be ashamed to face the younger generation.

*   *   *

Though he is always deeply admired, people cannot help but ask: Why could not Premier Zhou, with his great prestige and power, avert the national crisis that the country suffered during the period of the Gang of Four? Why could he not prevent even the executions of marshals and vice-premiers?

All of this is thought-provoking and should make people wake up. From this experience we learn that in a feudal nation there cannot be a real socialist revolution until there has been a democratic revolution. In a country where people cannot enjoy even the most rudimentary democratic rights, how can they correct any deviation on the part of the helmsman in time to prevent bureaucratism, the slandering of virtuous leaders, and disasters suffered by ordinary people?

We do not want a repeat of what happened to Comrade Zhou.

DOCUMENT 44
LIU SHAOQI
By Qi Dai

[*Liu Shaoqi was the second most important leader of the Chinese Communist movement from the mid-1940s until the mid-1960s. Thereafter he was the target of repeated vituperative attack in the media, but otherwise he vanished from public view. As we go to press, he appears headed for posthumous rehabilitation.*[4]]

The Third Plenum of the Eleventh CCP Central Committee realistically reappraised the merits and demerits of Peng Dehuai, Tao Zhu, Bo Yibo, Yang Shangkun, and other comrades. This has won the warm support of the people of the whole country. Practice is the sole criterion for testing truth. Based on this principle, we must resolutely correct and overthrow all false charges "no matter when and under what circumstances they were made" in our present nationwide endeavor to reexamine wrong and unjust cases. Comrade [Liu] Shaoqi, who was branded as a "renegade, hidden traitor, and scab" and persecuted to death by Lin Biao and the Gang of Four, was the victim of a big frame-up which ought to be reexamined.

To counter Wang Ming's "ruthless struggle and merciless blows" against Party comrades and Kang Sheng's practice of making false charges against good people and enlarging the scope of attack, Comrade Shaoqi wrote the pamphlet *On the Self-Cultivation of Communists* during the period of the Yanan rectification. In those days, this book was considered as "rectification literature" which all Party cadres had to read. It remained one of the classic writings of our Party for a long time afterward. At the Seventh National Party Congress, convened in 1945, Comrade Shaoqi delivered a report on the revision of the Party constitution and pointed out that Mao Zedong Thought had to be taken as the guiding principle in all work. He was elected first vice-chairman of the Military Commission and secretary of the Party Central Committee Secretariat at this congress. After the Sixth Plenum of the Eighth CCP Central Committee, in December 1958, the central leadership was divided. . . . In April 1959, . . . Comrade Shaoqi was elected chairman of the Republic.

In 1959, the steadfast and upright General Peng [Dehuai] submitted a ten-thousand-word letter to the Central Committee meeting in Lushan, bravely expressing his opinions about the serious problems caused by the Great Leap Forward, the movement to form people's communes, and the "petty-bourgeois fanaticism" displayed by certain comrades. Comrade

Shaoqi was more coolheaded. First, he held that we must seek truth from facts. He stressed at the Fifth Plenum of the Eighth CCP Central Committee: "Leaders must combine revolutionary zeal with the spirit of striving for thoroughness and refrain from idle talk and exaggeration. They should not lightly announce a plan unless they are sure they can handle it." Second, Comrade Shaoqi held that the conversion to people's communes had greatly weakened the vitality of the rural areas, confused the three-level system of ownership, and dampened the enthusiasm of the peasants. He also pointed out: "We have launched quite a few movements in the past few years. Many of these movements started in a rush. Some were initiated on the basis of incorrect information instead of official documents. This is not a good way of doing things." Third, Shaoqi held that the Lushan meeting should combat "left" deviationism and not right deviationism. He said: "Many concrete things mentioned in Comrade Peng Dehuai's letter tally with facts. He should not be considered as having erred." "We made a mistake at the Lushan meeting. We should have continued to combat 'left' deviationism and should not have combated right deviationism then. As it turned out, we combated right deviationism." Because of this, Lin Biao and the Gang of Four accused Shaoqi of "supporting Peng Dehuai in opposing the three red banners, launching an offensive against the Party, and trying his best to reverse correct conclusions" during the Cultural Revolution. Now that Comrade Peng Dehuai has been rehabilitated, can this false charge against Comrade Shaoqi stand?

Our country experienced grave economic difficulties between the years 1960 and 1962 as a result of serious natural disasters and the disruption of Party and state relations with the Soviet Union. This situation was exacerbated by the abnormal "democratic life" within the Party Central Committee. At this moment of tension, Comrades [Liu] Shaoqi, [Zhou] Enlai, [Deng] Xiaoping, and Chen Yun were asked to take charge and save the situation. Liu, Zhou, Chen, and Deng discarded the sham Marxist theories championed by Chen Boda, Kang Sheng, and others, and adopted bold and decisive measures to arouse the enthusiasm of the people of the whole country in production and readjust the national economy. They pulled the country from the brink of starvation and bankruptcy within a short time. Shaoqi said then: "In the period of transition, all methods which can help arouse the production enthusiasm of the peasants are feasible. We should not say which is the sole method." Xiaoping said: "White or black, any cat that catches mice is good cat." As we see it now, these plain and simple words are much more useful than the high-sounding "communist" slogans of Lin and Jiang. As a result of the persistent efforts made by Comrade Shaoqi and others, and under the guidance of the correct line, China's economy again picked up in 1966, its first economic rise since 1957. At this juncture, the Cultural Revolution began. Comrade Shaoqi was overthrown and died a victim of unjust charges.

No doubt Comrade Shaoqi made mistakes in his revolutionary life. Since God also makes mistakes, it is only natural that our Party leaders would err. Those who erred should be criticized. However, after ten years of testing, the "criticism" and handling of Comrade Shaoqi during the Cultural Revolution have been proven to be completely wrong and at variance with the aspirations and interests of the people of the country. The "renegade, hidden traitor, and scab" verdict is not at all convincing. Comrade Shaoqi should not be made solely responsible for disarming the worker pickets in Wuhan. Confessions of Kuomintang criminals kept by Kang Sheng's famous "special case investigation group" also should not be taken as magic weapons to persecute Communists. This historical tragedy of relying on the enemy to destroy one's comrades should not go on any longer. The handling of Comrade Shaoqi set the precedent for the persecution of other proletarian revolutionaries of the older generation. The nonsense about Liu Shaoqi's revisionist line also laid the political and theoretical foundations for toppling leading Party, government, and army cadres at all levels. One by one, members of the so-called "Liu Shaoqi headquarters" have been proven by history to be unbending old revolutionaries. Can it be possible that the Chinese people have no reason to demand the realistic reappraisal of Comrade Shaoqi?

DOCUMENT 45
CHEN YONGGUI
By Jin Zhiqing

[*Chen Yonggui rose to national prominence as Party secretary of the famous Dazhai agricultural brigade, which was much praised by Mao Zedong. In 1973 he was made a member of the Politburo.*]

Those who are over thirty can still clearly remember that during the Great Leap Forward various places throughout the country launched "satellites," not only in the industry and iron and steel production but also in agriculture and animal husbandry. The average per *mou* yield of grain throughout the country at that time was only a few hundred catties. However, the high-yielding "satellites" raised it to several thousand, several scores of thousands, and even a million catties. Without counting what was used for people's rations, the grain produced by our country at that time could only raise one hundred million pigs. However, to reach the quota of "one person one pig, one *mou* one pig," the number of pigs throughout the country had to increase to several hundred million. As a result, the meat yielded from this number was much less than that yielded from one hundred million. Those who launched "satellites" were promoted, became rich, and were cited by newspapers. Those who did not were labeled as "rightists," criticized, and corrected.

The higher the "satellites" were launched, the greater the state's procurement tasks became. Most rural areas throughout the country delivered all their storage grain, rations of commune members, animal feed, and seed stock which they had stored for years. However, they still could not attain the procurement tasks of the high-altitude "satellites." Within a year, the grain, meat, and fruit were used to settle the years of debts with the USSR. Therefore, "natural disasters" which lasted continuously for three years occurred throughout the country in most cities and rural areas. There was unprecedented damage to the development of industrial and agricultural production, and science and technology. The people recall those three years as extremely frightening long years of hunger and cold!

Comrade Chen Yonggui at that time had indeed gained one merit: his "satellite" was launched low. He also had a small piece of land not included in the reported farmland area. As a result, the Dazhai people had rations, the animals had feed, and there was seed stock. Comrade Chen Yonggui naturally could not attend the "National Meeting of Heroes" because of this, but he prevented the foundation of Dazhai's agricultural production from being wrecked. Therefore, the "three years of natural disasters" which spread all over the country did not affect Dazhai's agricultural production; on the contrary, there was development.

Zhang Huaiying, formerly of the Xiyang County[5] Party Committee (and now secretary of the Yuncheng Prefectural CCP Committee and an ultraleftist opposed to Liu and Deng) at that time offered Dazhai's miracle to Lin, Zhang, Jiang, and Yao through Shanxi Provincial CCP Committee Deputy Secretary Wang Qian (now secretary of the Shanxi Party Committee). He also distorted Dazhai's experience as a spiritual victory. The flower of the Dazhai "red banner" had blossomed. Chen Yonggui also began to prosper and smoothly ascended to fame.

It was not enough just to cover up their shame. Lin, Zhang, Jiang, and Yao wanted to have even more clout. They therefore invested large sums— thirteen years of total investment was close to ten million *yuan*—and gave an average of ten thousand *yuan* to each person in Dazhai. In this way, Dazhai became a target on the horizon for others to catch up with. This was a point that could never be reached. As long as you could not reach Dazhai's target, Lin, Zhang, Jiang, Yao, and even Chen Yonggui himself would curse you, saying that your "ideology" was not advanced and that you had not learned the spirit of Dazhai. They further relentlessly accused you of being anti-Dazhai. This was also their true objective in establishing the Dazhai "red banner."

Chen Yonggui directed the Dazhai Party branch to publish, by early 1976, frequent articles criticizing Deng's "hitting back at the rightist wind of reversing verdicts" and criticizing the opposition of Liu and Deng to Dazhai. Under the pretext of criticizing people as being "anti-Dazhai," Zhang, Jiang, and Yao also denounced Comrades Liu Shaoqi and Deng Xiaoping in various major newspapers and journals throughout the country. Even if we only give it casual thought, it will not be difficult for us to distinguish between what is genuine and false in this red banner of Dazhai.

Following a policy of deception, they launched a full-scale persecution of intellectuals and science and technology personnel. Youth work then became the cardinal task of Lin, Zhang, Jiang, and Yao. From 1966, Chen Yonggui himself also made plans to actively drive "educated young people" into the countryside to settle. He also liked to see science and technology personnel and "intellectuals" take part in labor reform in the May Seventh cadre schools. Chen Yonggui forcibly enrolled county-level science and technology personnel in "work teams for learning from Dazhai in agriculture" and "work teams for education in the Party's basic line." In this way the science and technology personnel could not bring their individual specialties into play and thus become genuine members of the labor reform work teams. Dazhai itself also became a labor reform camp where intellectuals from the Chinese Academy of Sciences, various scientific research organs in Shanxi, institutes of higher learning, literature and art groups, and labor reform camps were forced to take part in labor reform. Dazhai sometimes also allowed some science and technology personnel to take part in capital construction and the reform of farming technology. When reported to the outside, all the achievements belonged to the "Dazhai people." Those science and technology personnel were only "talking tools" and talking computers which had been temporarily borrowed. Lin, Zhang, Jiang, and Yao frantically publicized that people at Dazhai got up at 4:00 A.M., finished work when the sun set (did not go home for lunch), did three hours overtime after dinner, went to political evening school to study for three hours after working overtime, and gained spiritual sustenance from politics.

They worked like this 364 days a year, only taking New Year's Eve off, and they were never tired. They then achieved their Dazhai red banner. If necessary, they worked continuously all day and night because the Dazhai people's "ideology was advanced." They were people made of special material. This method was wonderful! No one dared utter a negative word. They followed the example of the robot in continually working for a living. This also prevented the peasants from thinking about forbidden things. Peasants throughout the country all worked continuously in this way!

To "destroy the breeding ground of the bourgeoisie" and to prevent the peasants from having the opportunity to be lazy, Chen Yonggui ordered the "abolition of the capitalist free markets." He even disguised this by saying that "if we do not block the capitalist road, we cannot take socialist steps." What would happen if someone asked questions about food and clothing? "'Poverty belongs to socialism, riches belong to capitalism." Only when everyone lacked food and had no money could a true revolution be proclaimed!

All of Shanxi earnestly followed Chen Yonggui's way. Industrial and agricultural production became very backward. To prevent other provinces from doing better than Shanxi, Chen Yonggui misappropriated funds intended for construction of railway lines. Consequently, three new railway lines between Shanxi, Henan, and Shaanxi [Shensi] are still not open to traffic. It is not even known when construction will begin. "Can any province do better in promoting agriculture, forestry, animal husbandry, sideline occupations, and fishery? I, Chen Yonggui, deliberately block roads, do whatever I want, and unscrupulously give commands. Let us see who dares oppose Dazhai. I order the south to slash mulberry and tea plants, the north to destroy the grassland, the east to eliminate fish ponds, and the west to destroy forests. All this is to enable us to take 'grain as the key link' and 'promote a big and rapid increase in production!' Most of all, I hate the bourgeois ideology of keeping overnight grain at home and of being lazy and afraid to work. To let the peasants get the idea that 'poverty gives rise to the desire for change,' I have issued the order to follow the standard of 'one person one pig, one *mou* one pig.' I have done this to raise pigs on a large scale so pigs can snatch rations away from lazy people and to see if the people are willing to work." (Note: Areas in Shanxi do not distribute pig feed to the peasants.[6]) As a result, many peasants sold pigs every year, pigs died every year, and a society in which pigs snatched grain from men became a society of "pigs eating men." (According to reports, a peasant in Shanxi raises ten pigs, but the meat yield is only equal to that produced by one pig raised in the United States. The cost is extremely high.)

It is time to realize agricultural modernization. Comrade Chen Yonggui should also consider what he is going to do in the future. In case Comrade Chen Yonggui does measure up to the requirements of a vice-premier, he should display his real ability and put forward effective plans. Otherwise the peasants and educated young people throughout the country will tell him: Retire!

The history forged by Lin, Zhang, Jiang, and Yao must be cleared up now!

The Chinese people do not want three years of natural disasters!

We do not want the serious retrogression which has occurred since the Cultural Revolution!

We do not want Hitler and fascism!

We want Tito and Yugoslav-type socialism! The Palestinian refugees must return to Palestine! The Soviet Tartars must return to the Caucasus! We do not want our families to be separated.

"Educated young people" from Beijing want to return to Beijing!

DOCUMENT 46
KANG SHENG
From *Beijing Spring*

[*Kang Sheng rose to power as an intelligence and security official. He was a prime mover and theorist of the Cultural Revolution and became a member of the Politburo's five-man Standing Committee. His political power began to ebb in 1969. He died in 1975.*]

1. On the failure of the first great revolution, who was the first one to turn traitor and confess?

2. Who, from the Trotskyite base in China, colluded with the international Trotskyites to sabotage the Communist International?

3. Who took advantage of the Soviet Union's effort to expand its purge of counterrevolutionaries to make a sudden change and, under the pretext of opposing Trotskyites, murdered many Chinese comrades who had studied in the Soviet Union?

4. Who first smeared Yugoslavia as out-and-out revisionism in the 1960s? And who first said that Yugoslavia was not a socialist country?

5. Who returned to Yanan in 1937, seized the pretext of opposing the line of Wang Ming, deceitfully won the trust of the Party, conspired with and instructed renegade Jiang Qing to marry the Chairman, wormed his way into the core, sought out the secrets of the Party and government, sought senior positions within the Party, and deliberately conspired to usurp Party and state power?

6. Who, when examining the personal records of cadres during the "movement to rectify incorrect work style" in Yanan in 1942, babbled, "those who had any contact with the Kuomintang and those who came from the white areas are all spies," thus harming many good cadres of the Party?

7. Who seized the post of director of the Social Affairs Department of the CCP Central Committee, vigorously embarked on espionage activities within the Party, pushed aside those people who disagreed with him, and deliberately conspired to usurp Party and state power?

8. The Third International announced its own dissolution in 1943. Who, when in charge of the Shandong Bureau, still called himself Standing Committee member of the Communist International, struck grand poses to intimidate people, and vigorously developed his "independent kingdom"?

9. Who first described "A Commentary on the Newly Written Historical Drama 'Hai Rui Resigns from Office,' " conspired and dished up by renegade, spy, and alien class element Jiang Qing, Zhang Chunqiao, and Yao Wenyuan, as a "prelude to the Great Cultural Revolution," thus

laying a foundation for the Gang of Four in their attempt to usurp Party and state power?

10. The February Outline Report of 1966 was a document of the central authorities which proposed to seriously implement the principle of "letting a hundred flowers bloom and a hundred schools of thought contend" during the period when there was confusion on the theoretical front. Who deceived Chairman Mao, saying: "He has not read it himself. That is a sinister outline"?

11. During the initial period when Chairman Mao launched the Great Cultural Revolution, who usurped the great banner of the Cultural Revolution, replaced the Party Central Committee with the "Cultural Revolution Group"—and in partnership with Lin [Biao], Chen [Boda], and the Gang of Four—issued orders, sabotaged the Great Cultural Revolution, and above all sabotaged our great Party?

12. Who first commanded the U.S. and Chiang spies to make a breach in the education departments from within the Party and then charge into the society, sabotaging the Great Cultural Revolution on a large scale?

13. Who commanded Nie Yuanzi[7] of Beijing University to put up the first big-character poster and also had it published in *People's Daily* the same day, thus disrupting the plan of the Great Cultural Revolution?

14. Who maneuvered the people of Qinghua [University] to stir up trouble in various provinces and municipalities, issued orders, disrupted the Party and the army, and sabotaged the Great Cultural Revolution on a large scale?

15. Who controlled the Senior Party School, silenced those cadres who had exposed his criminal history, and leveled false charges?

16. Who advocated using "the form of struggling against feudal landlords" to struggle against those senior intellectuals and against the Party's veteran cadres, causing tens of millions of people to suffer great disgrace?

17. Who first described Chairman Mao's writings as "every single sentence carries a truth" and "every sentence carries more weight than ten thousand ordinary sentences," deified Chairman Mao, dogmatized Mao Zedong Thought, and fabricated Chairman Mao's words?

18. Who insisted that it was necessary to dig deep into the "three sinister lines" in Inner Mongolia and slaughtered tens of millions of Mongol cadres, causing hatred among the nationalities which has still not dissipated?

19. Who suggested that Liu Shaoqi's "sinister" *Self-Cultivation* be reprinted?

20. Who was the one who first said that "democrats are capitalist roaders"?

Who in fact did all these? It was none other than big careerist, big conspirator, big spy, big traitor, and veteran Trotskyite—Kang Sheng!

DOCUMENT 47
JIANG QING
From *Human Rights*

[*Jiang Qing, who had been an actress, married Mao Zedong in 1939. She rose to political power during the Cultural Revolution.*]

It has been learned that Jiang Qing is in Qincheng Prison. The first thing she said after her imprisonment was: "Reprisals have been made and favors extended where due. I will die without regret."

When she found out that her name had been placed third in the Gang of Four, she asked, "Why not put my name first?"

She is still her ambitious self.[8]

DOCUMENT 48
CHEN YUN
By Xue Xi

[*Economist Chen Yun ranked fifth in the Party hierarchy between 1950 and 1962. The article from which the following has been extracted was written just after Chen was restored to office as a Party vice-chairman.*]

When Chen Boda, Kang Sheng, and others dished out the theory of the so-called "class struggle," Comrade Chen Yun was their first target and was brought down by them. Comrade Chen Yun was then removed from the political stage for a long time and lived in semiseclusion. After the Gang of Four had been smashed, Comrade Chen Yun was the only one left of the country's "eight great" vice-chairmen; the whole Party and the whole nation felt an ever increasing respect for him. Comrade Chen Yun first returned to the front and then submitted his opinions and proposals, becoming the CCP Central Committee's high counselor. Although he enjoyed popular confidence, there were still some who opposed Chairman Hua's decision to bring Comrade Chen Yun back out of seclusion. The question of whether he will be called to shoulder the great responsibility is still pending at the presently deliberating Central Committee Plenum. However, Comrade Chen Yun is a tough revolutionary with a clear conscience. On questions of principle he was never ambiguous. The doctor had permitted him to speak at meetings for no longer than half an hour, but he went on speaking for five hours.

Chen Yun acted democratically throughout the meeting, and thus set a very good example. Comrade Chen Yun pointed out: "Comrade Mao Zedong is a man, not a god; Comrade Peng Dehuai is not a ghost, but a man. Kang Sheng is a devil, not a man. If these questions are not clarified, there will be no guarantee for democracy in the Party and he himself will not come out to work." On 12 November 1978, Comrade Chen Yun said at a meeting (in the Northeast China Group) that the righting of judicial mistakes is an essential condition for the establishment of solidarity and for turning the emphasis of our work toward modernization. The Tian-an-men Incident; the injustice inflicted on Bo Yibo and others, numbering sixty-one people; the question of Peng Dehuai, of Tao Zhu, of Yang Shangkun; the question of some mass organizations (such as the one-million-man contingent of Wuhan); all require reversal of judgments. Otherwise we are determined not to give in; the people will not accept it. The firm stand of Comrade Chen Yun deserves the enthusiastic support of the entire Party and entire nation. A small handful of unprincipled people who tried to stop the current of history have been defeated; Comrade

Chen Yun is to shoulder the heavy responsibility of the office of vice-chairman. The people hope that Comrade Chen Yun, who has worked so hard and performed such valuable services, will make new contributions for the realization of the Four Modernizations!

DOCUMENT 49
PENG ZHEN
From *Beijing Spring*

[*Peng Zhen joined the Communist movement in the early 1920s and was a member of the Politburo from 1945 until 1966, when he was arrested. Between 1951 and 1966 he was in charge of the politically-important Beijing area, where there was strong resistance to the Cultural Revolution. He was rehabilitated in December 1978. The following are extracts from three articles that appeared in* Beijing Spring *during the following month.*]

It was 4:45 in the afternoon of December 28 when a gray passenger plane appeared over the capital's airfield. At the terminal building several hundred men and women of all ages had their eyes fixed on it. The plane circled, landed, and taxied to the front of the crowd, which impatiently rushed forward even before the noise of the engines had ceased.

The door of the plane opened and an old man stepped out, smiled, and waved. He was white-haired and pale, but with a hardened mien. His face was full of emotion. There were shouts of sympathy and welcome from the crowd.[10] "Elder Peng, how are you?" "Welcome Comrade Peng Zhen." With firm steps, our comrade descended the stairs. His wrinkled face revealed his mixed emotions of joy and grief as he maintained a kind of forced smile. So many old friends. Comrade Bo Yibo rushed up, and the two old comrades embraced for a long time. They had been comrades through many great changes, fighters for the same cause in troubled times. The two were now speechless as their wrinkled faces touched. Everyone knew that this welcome needed no words or consolation. The close embrace and warm tears said all.

As the long line of cars entered historic Beijing, Comrade Peng's perceptive eyes took in the sights. Oh, this capital city! Though it had been long since he had seen it, he had dreamed of it day and night and had hoped for its rapid development. There were a few new sights—the diplomatic quarter, the still unoccupied apartments in front of the Qian Gates, and the stately, solemn, glorious mausoleum of Mao Zedong standing imposingly in the center of Tian-an-men. Otherwise, but for the growth that twelve years had added to the trees, and the aging of the buildings, the scenery was much as it had been before.

Just because Beijing is like this, our dear Mayor Peng Zhen, the eight million citizens of Beijing have been eagerly waiting, waiting, waiting for you to come back to us at an early date.

Old He [revolutionary hero He Long] once said: If one wants to hang oneself, one can do so by hanging oneself on Peng's big neck! Peng Zhen has a thick neck and the courage to take responsibilities, and there is no problem which he cannot solve. In July 1963, Comrades Deng Xiaoping and Peng Zhen led the Chinese Communist delegation to Moscow to hold talks with the Soviet Union. Upon their successful return, Comrade Deng Xiaoping joked: Khrushchev tried to overwhelm others with his bearing, feeling that his big fat stature could overpower us. Luckily we had big Peng Zhen with us to block him! One can thus see that Comrade Peng Zhen's way of conducting himself, his standpoint, and his ability are outstanding.

Comrade Peng Zhen firmly advocates a sound social democracy and legal system and proposed the famous theory that "the equality of everyone before the truth" is "the equality of everyone before the law." The people do hope that Peng, who has courage to take responsibility and who has been engaged in political and legal work, will concern himself with political and legal affairs. Certainly he has had an ample taste of the suffering caused by the absence of any legal system.

During a pitch-black night in the fall of 1966, a group of faithful and enthusiastic Red Guards charged into Peng Zhen's residence and arrested him. Thereafter, he lived an even more miserable prison life than he had thirty years previously. [During the Republican period, Peng was imprisoned three times for a total of six years.] This time the sixty-four-year-old comrade often lost consciousness as a result of torture. Instead of cold water being thrown on him to bring him around, he was subjected to a violent burst of blows and kicks. But with his indomitability he weathered the excruciating twelve years.

When Lin Biao issued his Circular Order No. 1, Comrade Peng Zhen was moved from Beijing to a place in Shaanxi [Shensi] Province. Before Peng left Beijing, his case was closed by a verdict designating him a rebel. Peng Zhen is famous for being a dauntless man. He would not do anything against his conscience. Like Lu Dingyi and Yang Shangkun, he refused to sign the verdict.[11] His refusal to sign was a demonstration of moral integrity deserving high praise, though at the time it was without effect.

In Shaanxi, Comrade Peng lived in a small mat shed. When the old man met the local people, they addressed him cordially as "Elder Peng." He would chat with them informally, engaging in small talk. Who would believe that this man was of a class who had ridden in a Red Flag sedan!

Even in remote Shaanxi, Comrade Peng Zhen was a pillar of strength. Gold will always be gold; it can only shine.

DOCUMENT 50
DENG XIAOPING—I
From *Enlightenment*

[*Deng Xiaoping was purged and disgraced twice because of his opposition to the leftists but both times won eventual rehabilitation (1973 and 1977). This and the following documents reflect divergent views of the man.*]

Putting heaven and earth in order,
Opening the door,
Establishing discipline and great democracy,
Gathering in one hall for public discussion,
Abolishing and establishing rules:
Vice-Premier Deng is open-minded and humble,
And honored by the entire world.
His great and beautiful stature
And success in seizing the seat of government
Is hailed in the north and the south.
The cry of spring is heard.
The people show happiness.
All the young and strong dedicate themselves to the revolution
And contribute their entire lives to it.
Theirs are the true hearts; they are the true heroes.
They shake the heavens and move the earth
To contribute their hearts to help the nation,
To strengthen China, and engage in science and technology,
Anticipating the realization of the Four Modernizations.
The nation will be rich and strong;
The economy will be pushed ahead.[12]

DOCUMENT 51
DENG XIAOPING—II
From *Exploration*

[*This essay, originally entitled "Which Is Wanted: Democracy or a New Despotism," was written anonymously by Wei Jingsheng. It may have been the primary reason for his being sentenced to fifteen years imprisonment.*[13]]

Everyone now knows that lack of democracy has seriously thwarted Chinese social development in a number of respects. This is very serious. We now have two choices. First, we can move quickly to promote production and improve our livelihood, at the same time reforming our social system and thus advancing our society. Or, we can abandon the goals of democracy and modernization, limit production and the people's livelihood, and simply maintain the Mao Zedong-type proletarian dictatorship. So China stands at the crossroads.

Where are we heading? In what kind of social environment do the Chinese hope to live and work? Today's democratic movement springs from the longings of the people. The goal is to reform the social system and avoid any Mao Zedong-type dictatorship. This issue does not simply concern a few individuals. The invincible Chinese people seek the reorganization of the nation. Those who understand the situation and agree to work toward the common aim are at the forefront of the tide of history. Whoever stands in the way or uses trickery to lead the movement astray is history's villain. Those who suppress the true people's movement are executioners. It is not necessary to wait for the judgment of history. They will be found guilty immediately by the Chinese people, who comprise the jury. The public's judgment is severe and irrevocable. Maybe the power of this court cannot show itself immediately, since for now it is at a disadvantage, but history will reveal its unmatched power. Those who do not believe this should think back to the events of 5 April 1976. They will see that in the hearts of the people even the almighty himself [Mao Zedong] did not escape judgment.

Do some not fear such punishment? Of course; many people. There are would-be autocrats who forget [that the judgment of history awaits them], or who are blind to this and, drunk with power, take advantage of people's gullibility for their own petty ends. For example, in his March 16, [1979] talk to leading cadres of central ministries and commissions, Vice-Chairman Deng Xiaoping attempted to use the people's previous confidence in him to oppose the democratic movement. He made various charges against the democratic movement, attempted to blame it for the failure of the Hua-Deng regime to save China's economy and production, and tried once again to make the people the scapegoats for the failure of their policies.

Is Deng Xiaoping worthy of the people's trust? We hold that the people should not give any political leader unconditional trust. If he implements policies that benefit the people and if he leads them to peace and prosperity, we will trust him. We only have trust in his policies and the road he is following. If he implements policies that are detrimental to the people, and if he follows a dictatorial road and acts contrary to the interests of the people, the people should oppose him. Likewise, the people will only oppose his antipeople road and those policies that encroach upon their interests and normal rights. According to the principles of democracy, all authorities must bow before the people's opposition.

However, Deng Xiaoping has not bowed to the people's opposition. When people everywhere began asking why, after thirty years, China is still backward, and when they demanded an investigation into Mao Zedong's crimes against the Chinese people, Deng Xiaoping was the first one who came forward and said: "Without Mao Zedong, there could be no new China." In his March 16 talk, he not only stubbornly upheld this view but also publicly praised Mao Zedong as the banner of the Chinese nation. He said that Mao Zedong's mistakes and shortcomings are trivial matters hardly worth mentioning.

Is Deng afraid that an investigation of Mao's mistakes might lead to an investigation of some of his past collaborators, or is he preparing to carry on Mao Zedong's style of despotic socialist politics? If the first is so, then actually he has absolutely nothing to fear. The people are understanding enough to forgive him for his past mistakes, as long as he can lead the country to democracy and prosperity from now on. But if the second is so, then he should certainly not be forgiven. Even if he had been a paragon of virtue in the past, as long as his aim is to effect a Mao-style dictatorship, then he can only destroy the national economy and harm the people's interests. To forgive such a criminal would itself be a crime.

Does Deng Xiaoping want democracy? No, he does not. He does not want to understand the people's sufferings or to let people recover the powers that had been usurped by careerists and careerist groups. He says that the spontaneous struggle for democratic rights is just an excuse to make trouble, that it destroys the normal order and must be suppressed. Such a reaction to public criticisms and demands for progress truly reveals the strength of the people's movement.

We cannot help asking: What do you think democracy means? If the people do not have the right to express their ideas freely, how can one speak of democracy? If not allowing other people to criticize those in power is your idea of democracy, then what is the difference between this and what Mao euphemistically called the "dictatorship of the proletariat"?

The people have been holding rallies because they want to make accusations and report their plight. They want democracy. They have demonstrated because they are against hunger and despotism. This truly shows that they do not have democracy and that their livelihood is unprotected. The people are powerless. No wonder they are mistreated and lack even the most basic protection! Can this be called "the normal order"? If this "normal order" is one that protects the right of ambitious despots to act as they please and undermine the people's interests, then to whose advantage is it to protect this kind of order, the careerists or the people? Is it not obvious? We believe that normal order does not mean everyone marching in lockstep. Especially in politics, only if different kinds of ideas exist can the situation be called normal. If there are no different ideas, no variety of opinion, and no publications representing dissimilar viewpoints, then clearly you have political despotism. Such "order" is abnormal.

Abolishing the people's right of expression under the pretext of some social phenomena, such as disturbances by a few criminals taking advantage of opportunities, is a habitual practice of all new and old dictatorial fascists. We may recall the Tian-an-men Incident. Did not the Gang of Four wantonly suppress the people's revolutionary movement under the pretext of some cars that were burned? Deng Xiaoping has now also found similar pretexts. Is he going to use more crafty measures to carry out a similar suppression? The oppression must heighten their vigilance and no longer automatically believe in a ruler unless the ruler is subject to the people's supervision and control.

The people must maintain vigilance against Deng Xiaoping's metamorphosis into a dictator. Following his rehabilitation in 1975, Deng Xiaoping did not appear to be following the dictatorial system of Mao Zedong. Instead, he seemed to have given first place to the people's interests. Therefore, the masses of people warmly hoped he would continue to implement this kind of policy. They were willing to support him with their blood. (The Tian-an-men Incident is an example.) Do the people support Deng Xiaoping as a person? No, they do not. Without his fight for the people's interests, he himself has nothing worthy of the people's support. He now want to strip off his mask of protector of democracy and suppress the democratic movement. He is prepared to set himself against democracy and resolutely safeguard dictatorial politics. He is no longer worthy of the people's trust and support, because his actions have shown that he does not want to pursue democracy. He no longer safeguards the people's interests.

He is following a dictatorial road after deceitfully winning the people's trust.

It has been shown countless times in Chinese history that only after would-be dictators have fooled the people into trusting them can they have a free hand to do what they want. As the proverb says, "Once you have the people's hearts, you have your empire." When they have their power, their interests invariably conflict with those of the people, so they naturally concentrate on suppressing those who are fighting for the people's interests. What is important is not that this person should gain power rather than that person, but that the people not let *anyone* take away their power. The people must hold on firmly to the power, for this is what democracy means. Those to whom the people entrust power and the running of the government must be responsible to the people and subject to their restraint. According to the Constitution of the People's Republic, the only organizations and officials enjoying legitimacy are those elected by the people or subject to appointment and restraint by an elected government responsible to the people.

We would like to ask a question of senior government officials who have incited the arrest of people: Do you hold power legally or illegally? We would also like to ask a question of Chairman Hua and Vice-Chairman Deng: Do you hold your posts of premier and vice-premier legally or illegally? We would like to know if it is legal or not for a vice-premier and a vice-chairman to announce the arrest of people rather than for the courts and the people's representative organs to do so? We would like to ask two more questions: Which article of Chinese law says that "evil deeds" constitute a crime? What are the criteria for determining an evildoer, and whose views should the criteria reflect? If the answers to these few very simple questions are not clear, then we can say that China has no rule by law.

History tells us that there must be a limit to the trust placed in any one person. Without exception, anyone who seeks to gain the people's absolute trust is a careerist. One important question is what kind of person should be chosen for a position of public trust. But more important still is the question of how to make these people carry out the wishes of the majority. We cannot be easily persuaded that anyone will automatically serve the interests of others, still less that anyone will serve the interests of others at any cost to himself. We can only trust agents who are under our supervision and who are responsible to us. These agents must be appointed by us, not forced upon us. Whether or not one has the right to use governmental power must depend first of all upon whether or not one is encroaching, or is preparing to encroach, upon the people's basic democratic rights. Without exception, anyone who is not willing to accept the supervision of democratically-elected organizations, or anyone who is preparing to violate the people's basic democratic rights, can only be an enemy of the people. We think that it is this type of person alone who is fit to be called by names [which the government applies to dissidents, such as] "scoundrel." This is the standard of the people.

If the people want to remold the government and their leaders into servants of the people, they must first firmly control supervisory and mandate powers. The rights and procedures concerning voting and dismissal of officials from their posts must be guaranteed. A government and leaders which serve the interests of the electorate can only come about through genuine universal sufferage. If the government and leaders are truly subject to popular election and supervision, then a climate will exist that will check leaders' arrogance and hunger for power. Do not blame the leaders for letting power go to their heads and for not sincerely working for the people's welfare. Do not blame the people for being uninformed and for not daring to resist on behalf of their own interests. These problems arise because our society lacks a means for wise people to supervise wise officials.

Therefore, we hold that reforming the social system and leading Chinese politics to democracy constitute the precondition for solving China's various current social and economic problems. Only when the leaders are appointed by those whom they lead can they obtain the willing cooperation of the people and inspire them to action. Only when the people can fully express their ideas will they be willing to help the leaders to analyze and solve problems and develop everyone's knowledge. Only if there is cooperation and if everyone's knowledge and strength is combined can optimum working efficiency be guaranteed and the most ideal result be achieved. This is the only road that China can now take to succeed, even though under China's present conditions it is a road on which we will encounter great difficulties.

DOCUMENT 52
DENG XIAOPING—III
From a Wall Poster

[*The following is April Fifth Forum's response to the preceding essay.*[14]]

An article entitled "Which Is Wanted: Democracy or a New Despotism" in the March 25 *Exploration* has roused argument and general concern. We differ with some of the main points made in the article. We present our view here to engender further discussion with that author. We also invite criticism and suggestions from the people.

It is our understanding that the article was published as a result of these developments: (1) the speech of Comrade Deng Xiaoping [16 March 1979], (2) several articles published by official newspapers, and (3) the rumors of arrests and pending arrests. The public's reactions to all of this have been quite varied. Some opinions are restrained, some are radical. *Exploration* represents the more militant view. . . .

Probably due to the realities of the situation [discussed above in Document 36], the Party Central Committee and the government have discussed in the press several related topics and have also held meetings on the subject of the democratic movement. Word [about the latter] has spread quickly, giving rise to sensational rumors of a "clamping down" and of the arrests of the movement's instigators. In his March 16 speech, Comrade Deng Xiaoping discussed the various democratic groups and thus fed the rumors. The *Exploration* article can be regarded as a response to the situation in general and to Deng's speech in particular.

In the article, Deng Xiaoping was specified by name. We respect *Exploration's* view of holding no one sacred and of daring to speak their mind about anyone. We also agree that our economic shortcomings have systemic causes. But when it comes to speculation and inference, we must part company.

The *Exploration* article criticized "would-be autocrats" who "take advantage of people's gullibility for their own petty ends. For example, in his March 16 talk to leading cadres of various central ministries and commissions, Vice-Chairman Deng Xiaoping attempted to use the people's previous confidence in him to oppose the democratic movement. He made various charges against the democratic movement, attempted to blame it for the failure of the Hua-Deng regime to save China's economy and production, and tried once again to make the people the scapegoats for the failure of their policies." We doubt that this is correct. Judging both from history and the present realities, we do not find Comrade Deng "petty," much less a "would-be autocrat."

We have not yet heard what Comrade Deng actually said and did to "blame" the democratic movement for economic conditions. Perhaps *Exploration* made the above-quoted charges on the basis of more information than we ourselves possess. We wonder whether *Exploration* has evidence to sustain the view that Comrade Deng is "petty" and "a would-be autocrat." Can these people certify as to the accuracy and adequacy of the information? If so, we would join with them in opposing Deng Xiaoping. If they cannot so certify, we would deem their judgment invalid.

Lin Biao and the Gang of Four used to take a sentence or two [out of context] and use them to label people and oppress them. We must do everything we can to rid ourselves of this bad practice. Placing labels on people on the basis of a few sentences spoken is the wrong way to treat either a leader like Deng Xiaoping or a common person. Any charges that we do make should be based on a person's actions, not on mere words, and certainly not on unverified words. So far, Deng Xiaoping's actions do not reveal him to be "petty" or "a would-be autocrat," and we have the impression that *Exploration* has been hasty and unwarranted in throwing labels at him. Not that Deng Xiaoping is flawless. We admit that he, like Comrade Mao Zedong, does make mistakes. However, any criticism of him should be accurate and to the point. Making extreme judgments only leads to unfounded predictions and our losing touch with reality. In seeing Deng Xiaoping as "petty" and "a would-be autocrat," *Exploration* thus concluded that he would "strip off his mask as protector of democracy and suppress the democratic movement. He is prepared to set himself against democracy and resolutely safeguard dictatorial politics. . . . He is following a dictatorial road after deceitfully winning the people's trust."

What are the facts? These charges are refuted by what we have seen and by what we have not seen. A person who would establish himself as a dictator must trick people into trusting him before he has power. Once power has been seized, he can cast off people's trust and take firm control himself. Last November [1978], Deng Xiaoping, who had already secured considerable political power, was the first to support the new democratic movement symbolized by Democracy Wall. At that time, other powerful leaders with a limited understanding of the democratic movement were opposing it. Without the support of Deng and his followers, it would have been impossible for the democratic movement to develop as it has. So did he cheat those who trusted him? Surprisingly, he actually promoted a movement that would have made the so-called "autocracy" impossible!

Deng Xiaoping remains China's most powerful personage. If he really wants to suppress the democratic movement, he will have the support of many officials and could easily do so. But he has not done so, and the people are able to write what they wish and the publications are available at Democracy Wall.

What has actually happened in the past two years is that former "rightists" have had their labels removed; verdicts have been reversed for Peng Dehuai, the Sixty-one, and many others; the "four category" labels have been eliminated; [reconsidering] the Taiwan recovery question. . . [sic]. As for foreign relations, the Sino-Japanese Friendship Treaty has been signed, there has been the break through in Sino-American relations, and so on. As the Nantong She has pointed out, the changes in Chinese political life have been so dazzling that we are at a loss to determine where to go from here.

Recently, although we have indeed been going through a lot of changes, we are still unable to agree with *Exploration*'s conclusion. There are more examples than we can cite here.

A final comment on the "clamping down" rumor. The so-called "clamp down" [has been prompted by] several published articles on the democratic movement. We are convinced that some regulations are beneficial and necessary in a normal society. The public notice of the Shanghai Public Security Bureau stated, "Gatherings and demonstrations should be under the direction of the police. It is prohibited to obstruct railways or to attack public offices. Posting slogans, newspapers, and posters outside designated areas is prohibited." These regulations are issued to secure the normal development of the democratic movement, not to stop it. However, in the same public notice are regulations prohibiting "agitation for public disturbance" and "reactionary publications." These terms are ambiguous and must be defined and clarified. Otherwise, any lawful gathering could be deemed "agitation for public disturbance" and any perfectly constitutional pamphlet deemed "reactionary." Such ambiguity could be taken advantage of by those trying to thwart the democratic movement.

But no good end awaits anyone seeking to suppress the democratic movement. History will attest to that.

DOCUMENT 53
MAO ZEDONG
From a Wall Poster

[*Note: We know of very few essays that are expressly about Mao Zedong, although many essays mention him (see, for example, Documents 16, 26, 63, and 66). The final document of this section is one of the longer passages about Mao, taken from a five-page wall poster dealing with a variety of subjects. Even in this selection much of the criticism of Mao is only implicit, and the writer is primarily concerned with the procedures by which a national leader is selected and how rulers can be kept accountable to the people.*[15]]

For decades the Chinese people have endured the Great Leap and other things, while following the "communist ideal" of the Great Helmsman. Thirty years passed as one day. They taught us one thing: The people resemble a monkey who wants to grab the moon's reflection in a pond.

Isn't it clear that there is nothing to it? When Deng said that empty babbling should cease and work begin, the people demanded his return to power. Progress is measured by deeds. But many warned us: "Marxism-Leninism and the Thoughts of Mao Zedong are the foundation. Chairman Mao is the redeemer of the nation. Without him there would be no new China. Whoever has a different opinion is lost."

Others told us: "The Chinese nation needs a dictator. It needs democracy under a collective leadership. You can accept that or not. If you do not, then you go to prison."

Many say we are confused and would not understand anything anyway. They say we cannot understand how difficult the situation is and that, if we do not obey the leader, we can expect the consequences.

I advise everyone to ignore such political charlatans. We have been hardened in the Cultural Revolution, and we are no longer stupid. But what can we do? Why do we desire democracy? Human beings have discoursed on this for centuries. The readers of Democracy Wall have already analyzed the situation and have come to the conclusion that democracy in the long run is better than despotism. The people are really the masters of history.

Is that a fact or also just empty prattle? We have a Great Helmsman or a "wise leader" only because of the strength of the people. Neither of them would have made history by himself. Therefore, we can say: Without a new Chinese people, we would have no new China now. That sounds different from the epigram, "Without Chairman Mao, we would have no new China now."

Leaders come from the people. Democracy is what the people ought to have. If they demand democracy, they are claiming only the rights which are already due them. If those who lead us do not give us democracy, they are shameless thieves and worse than the bloodsucking capitalists of the past.

Does the nation have democracy today? No. Does it really want to direct its own history? Naturally it does. That is why the Communists conquered the Nationalists. Have our leaders done what they promised? The epigram about a people's democracy was realized by the dictatorship of the proletariat, and so a tiny majority achieved power. Then that was abandoned and the despotism of the Great Helmsman came about.

Then something else was contrived for us. Because our "great leader" was so great, trust in him would bring us more good fortune than democcracy would.

The public has again and again been compelled to swallow such fantasies. Are we really fortunate and well off? We cannot conceal that we are unhappy and that our society is still backward. Why? We must ponder that.

SECTION ELEVEN
CHINA'S GULAG

Until 1979 the world knew almost nothing about the prisons and camps where China's political prisoners were incarcerated, other than the fact that they existed.[1] *Then, in March 1979,* Exploration *carried two important descriptions of prisons in the Beijing area. The first essay below describes an institution where what might be called "normal" political prisoners are held. Fu Yuehua, for example, was held in it. The second essay, by Wei Jingsheng, describes a prison where more important political prisoners are held. It has been reported that Wei himself (the son of an official and well-known in his own right) was subsequently sent there.*

Aside from these institutions, China has innumerable labor camps, prisons, and jails, large and small, scattered all over the country. Most common are probably the detention houses in the communes. While not a great deal is known about these, we conclude this section with a very short description of the situation in one commune. It is likely that such jails house both political and criminal prisoners. (The distinction between the two tends to be obfuscated by Chinese law and official attitudes.)

DOCUMENT 54
THE "VIRTUE" OF VIRTUE FOREST
By Liang Yao

When "Virtue Forest Number One" is mentioned, anyone familiar with Beijing understands that the reference is to the old prison outside Desheng Gate. It is an ingenious, handsome old structure, designed in the late Qing dynasty in accordance with the *bagua tuxing* [the "eight diagrams" of the *I-jing* (Book of Changes)].

There is no way of knowing why it is called "Virtue Forest," but it certainly has been the embodiment of "virtue" since the day it was erected! It is said that its architect died there, thus becoming the first beneficiary of the prison's "virtue." Later, to suppress the tempestuous revolutionary movement, the Kuomintang reactionaries imprisoned innumerable revolutionary heroes and other virtuous people there and massacred uncountable sons and daughters of China. Li Dazhao [a founder of the Chinese Communist Party] lost his life there [1927]. Finally, in 1948, during the thundering liberation, the prison returned to the hands of the people.

However, it is the destiny of a shoe to be worn and the destiny of a prison to incarcerate. Virtue Forest is no exception. In the past, Virtue Forest served its function for the Qing dynasty and the Kuomintang reactionaries. What functions is it serving now that it has been returned to the hands of the people? We recently visited several individuals who were able to speak from personal experience. Let us look at the recent situation and see what "virtue" has been flowing from Virtue Forest!

Apart from filling its normal functions, a part of Virtue Forest Number One (originally called Beijing Prison Number Two) has become the Beijing Municipal Shelter. This "shelter" (so euphemistically named) is divided into three centers. Center Number One is a public security detention center where people who will be sent away are detained. The inmates in this center lead a prisoner's life. The great majority of them come from other parts of the country and had paid visits to upper-level [officials' offices]. Center Two and Center Three receive people of a "refugee" nature who are homeless and wander the streets. Enjoying freedom of action, they are better off than those in Center Number One.

The "shelter" has both men and women, some over sixty years old and others mere children accompanying their parents. Inasmuch as these people occupy different corridors, the total number cannot be known. There is no need to ascertain in detail which centers prisoners have been detained in. In view of the things done by this "shelter" which imprisons the innocent, we know the deeds and virtues of Virtue Forest.

One who was temporarily detained in Center Number One told us:

"This so-called 'shelter' is a prison which incarcerates many people from all over the country who have presented grievances or other concerns to upper-level [officials]. Instead of obtaining redress, they were arrested, detained, sent away, humiliated, and tortured. When one enters this prison's main hall, one is first stripped and searched. If one is even slightly less than humble, he is subjected to abuse at best, or trounced and beaten at worst. Some fourteen people live in small, low-ceiling, cold, wet, and dank rooms about eighteen meters wide. Here they eat, sleep, and discharge their waste. Therefore, when people enter this place it is as though they are entering a shack which has not been cleaned up. In the daytime, inmates collect their food in rotation. Each person is given two steamed, half-steamed, or rotten dumplings, one each meal, to be eaten with a bowl of dirty vegetable soup. Everyone sleeps on the bare, rough floor, with two people sharing a louse-infested bed cover which has not been washed in a year. Under these conditions, it is not unusual for people to become ill and die. In early 1978 a sick child in Center Number Three was neglected and died. When a doctor did come, he discovered many fat lice on the body.["]

A worker representative of the Lanzhou Railway Bureau who was imprisoned in Virtue Forest until February 21 [1979] has discussed his personal experiences there with us. Yuan Guoru, who used to work for the Lanzhou Railway Bureau had come to Beijing to make representations to upper-level [officials]. A certain leader had harbored a grudge against him and framed him because he had exposed the leader's mistakes. Yuan had been charged with being an "active counterrevolutionary" and sentenced to two years' imprisonment. Eventually he was found not guilty and released, but by this time his family had disintegrated; his wife had died and his children had scattered. After his release, he received no apology or compensation. Then he came to see the central authorities. Not only did they not resolve his problem, but the Letters and Visits Department of the Ministry of Railways first detained him, then sent him away, and finally jailed him. Yuan reports, "In collusion with Chen Shouyi of the Lanzhou Railway Bureau, this department's director, Guan Shaoliang, had me detained in Virtue Forest fifty-six times and in the Lanzhou 'shelter' sixty-four times. Every time they held me they made many charges against me, such as trespassing on Zhong-nan-hai [where China's top leaders live], trespassing in the Great Hall, mischief-making, holding up foreigners' cars, demanding money, trespassing in foreign embassies, and so on. It was as though I had committed heinous crimes. However, they always had to acquit and release me. During my confinement, I was brutally and callously tortured. They burned me with a poker, punished me by electric shock, and hung and beat me for as long as five hours, a number of times beating me until I was unconscious. But I never yielded. In fact, I broke three pair of handcuffs. Like they said, they never knew that someone like Yuan Guoru could be so obstinate.["]

Yuan was held in Center Number Two with Fu Yuehua and Xia Yuying. People who are detained in this "shelter" are nominally different from citizens who have been convicted of crimes. However, their treatment is worse than that of the convicts because (1) they have no definite discharge date, (2) they have no personal freedom, and (3) they have no right to be visited by their dependents and no freedom of communication. They lead inhuman lives.

Yuan continued, "People had to be searched when they walked into the old place. Inside, the sanitary conditions were worse than a pigsty. A cell was about the size of a storeroom. Prisoners lived and ate there, and slept on the cement floor. A Beijing University professor was incarcerated there for ten years, Lu Guanghui for five, and others for one, two, or three years. Each meal consisted of one *wotou* [a dumpling made of cornmeal and other cheap grains eaten by the poor in northern China] and a bowl of vegetable soup. One shirt could be exchanged for but one *wotou* and a pack of cigarettes. Prisoners who showed even the slightest discontent were cruelly beaten. Some people were badly beaten simply because they had said something to the effect that the food had not been properly cooked. A police captain (who always had an iron poker in his hands) did not even bother to provide any care for those injured as a result of the beatings. A beggar's child was beaten into unconsciousness because he had obtained an extra bun. One Ms. Zhang, who had come to Beijing to appeal to the authorities, was severely tortured. The reason was that she had called a civilian policeman a 'bandit' when he refused to return to her a handkerchief that she had left in her cell. There was also a man from Inner Mongolia who came to Beijing to appeal to the authorities. The police confiscated his appeal material and refused to return it. In anger, he broke a glass window. The police then suspended him in the air and beat him for more than three hours. Another woman, Xia Yuying, was jailed for fifteen days even though she had committed no crime. On one occasion, the police tied her up and beat her for three hours. As for the famous Fu Yuehua, after her arrest the police tried by every possible means to extract a confession from her, but they never succeeded. At one point, she was tortured so badly that she was covered with wounds and had to be carried back to her cell. Fu, faced with this kind of fascist torture, protested by going on a hunger strike. The police tried to force her to eat by prying open her mouth and stuffing it with rice. Finally, when this did not work, they gave her a shot of glucose."

In Virtue Forest, this sort of thing is a common occurrence.

Naive people may not believe that innocent citizens are treated so cruelly. But these citizens who have committed no crimes have indeed been hauled in and detained. Sometimes crafty methods have been employed to effect their arrests. People have been tricked by being invited in for "talks to solve problems" and then jailed. Their behavior was protected by the Constitution and they are not criminals. They should not receive such inhumane treatment, and certainly they should not be tortured. However, many can attest to the above facts from personal experience.

Some may say that such occurrences are events of the past. Since the smashing of the Gang of Four, the state has indeed formulated many new policies, systems, and regulations. It has announced that laws would be passed and has promised that the government would act in accordance with them, strictly maintaining them and punishing offenders. The state is not to act as it has in the past. These remarks are reasonable and represent the wishes of humanitarians and people of kindness and conscience. However, these hopes are not being realized because some people cherish feudal despotism, take the law into their own hands, and indulge in lawlessness. They do not have the slightest bit of humanity.

Yuan Guoru told us of another incident:

"A man named Zhang, who was the leader of Section Seven, Department Thirteen of the Public Security Bureau, made a speech in which he said: 'You have been sent here to be suppressed because you made trouble. . . . [sic] We have arrested you pursuant to reports from various units, and those units are responsible for any false arrests. We assume no responsibility.' With witnesses present, I then said: 'I Protest. The newspapers have all publicized the Constitution and the legal system. Have you ever heard of these?' Zhang got all excited and, almost losing his breath, cursed me as a rebel. 'We have five squadrons of a thousand police altogether. We live by arresting people. Acting on orders from above, we must carry out our duties. The press is a propaganda medium; reporters make their living by printing propaganda. It is like a trolley running on two tracks. Your disobedience does not frighten us. When you are insubordinate, we detain and suppress you. If your ox-head is not broken, we shall use more firewood to burn it.' "

So it is not that they do not know or understand the law, but that they simply ignore its existence. They have no intention whatsoever of putting law into practice. What they say and what they actually do are exactly contrary. As they themselves say, the trolley is running on two tracks at the same time.

All people of conscience regard people with morality, ability, and meritorious service as saviors. They hope they will bestow happiness on the world. However, the "virtue" of Virtue Forest has resulted in many people being killed. Its "virtue" has been erected on a mound of white bones.

Virtue Forest, Oh Virtue Forest, thou shalt not die. However, when will you, under the banner of a democratic legal system, insure "actions strictly in accordance to law and punishment for those who violate the law," with severe punishment for those who harm the country and people? When will you punish the *real* criminals and fulfill your true mission?[2]

DOCUMENT 55
A TWENTIETH-CENTURY BASTILLE
By Wei Jingsheng

If you ride along the main road of Changpng County near Beijing, you will discover a hot spring resort set in scenery as beautiful as a painting. This is the famous spa of Little Warm-Water Mountain, where (tradition holds) the Empress Dowager [1835–1908] used to come to take the waters.

If you continue further north a few minutes, you will come upon a table-sized sign declaring in several languages: Foreigners Not Admitted. Those not informed will assume that they have come to a prohibited military area. But a better-informed person will instantly feel a pang of terror, for just beyond lies the penitentiary for important political prisoners which is famous throughout the land: Qincheng Number One.

Actually, you will not find Qincheng on the map, and the most you will find on any list is "Number One." The local farmers have no knowledge of this huge maximum-security complex. There is only a vague and horrible rumor that once in the past the Japanese had constructed a prison in the area known locally as Qincheng.

In the northern section of the road there is a lonely but well-maintained asphalt road leading straight up to Qincheng prison. Both the main gate and the sentinel box look very ordinary. A stranger wandering there would not suspect that there is anything unusual. Through the open gate one can see a huge screen wall, so large that it totally blocks any view of the interior. On this huge wall is engraved a one-paragraph quotation from Mao Zedong's essay on the dictatorship of the proletariat. Behind the screen wall is a rectangular archway with a rusty iron gate. Some distance beyond is the central part of the prison, enclosed by a wall three meters high which is topped with electrical barbed wire.

Just imagine how many of those who rejected Mao's dogmatic policies have passed through this gate and never returned, not to mention his former comrades and devoted followers who, after being suspected of opposing him, did joyfully reemerge from the prison. The shock of hearing the news that one would be released could be fatal, so after 1975 it was common to send prisoners for short hospital stays before their release. Those who enter through the gates are usually atheists, but those who have been able to leave say that they have experienced a "modern hell." Thus people joke about this iron gate as being the atheist's gate to hell.

There are sentinel boxes on either side of the gate. If you have obtained permission to visit the prison, you will continue on to a T-shaped (*ding-ze-xing*) asphalt road with walls on both sides. The road rises gradually as one heads north. The east and west sides are landscaped with orderly gardens. To the west there are many fruit trees and, to the east, one sees newly-constructed housing. These modern garden apartments (*you-fang*) were built during the Cultural Revolution to accommodate the rapidly increasing number of high-ranking political prisoners.

Each building is entered directly from the road. At the end of the road is a walnut grove on a small hill. During spring and summer the surroundings are a lush green. Considering the well-designed housing, it all could be considered glorious. Such a tranquil environment would be ideal for one seeking relaxation. But the beauty of the scenery only heightens the agony of those families whose loved-ones are kept there, and the prisoners themselves will never forget the dreadful memories.

Qincheng is strictly isolated from the outside world. Only former prisoners, their families, and close friends know about it. The prison is administered by the Fifth Section of the Ministry of Public Security, whose members are solely responsible for it. Regular policemen do not know the nature of Qincheng. The guards are carefully selected. One criterion is age; prisoners report never seeing guards over twenty. They are replaced at regular intervals.

Prisoners are divided into four classes according to whether their food costs eight, fifteen, twenty-five, or forty *yuan* [per month]. Actually, corruption on the part of both personnel and the institution prevents the prisoners from receiving what they are officially allotted. For example, if the official monthly ration is 17.5 kilograms, a person who never exercises actually cannot eat even half of that. The entire amount is nonetheless purchased, even though what is left over cannot be stored. It is said that the guards feed it to their pigs, which are then sold to supplement the guards' own diet.

When it comes to dispensing food, the Qincheng guards are reported to be quite ingenious. Food is withheld as a means of punishment. One of the lightest and most common punishments is first to starve the prisoner and then give him or her a bowl of very greasy noodles as "compensation." Most, of course, become ill as a result and have to miss the next few meals as well.

Each inmate occupies a separate one-by-three-meter cell containing a basin of water, a chamber pot, and a plank bunk with a thin bed cover. The black prison uniform is replaced every six months.

Certain prisoners are granted special privileges, such as the right to read Marxist-Leninist works or *People's Daily*. Ordinary prisoners whose attitude is deemed "cooperative" may engage in a number of unpaid activities such as making rope or hats out of straw, or exercising to keep the body from becoming stiff. But those who make a bad impression on the prison staff are subjected to all sorts of punitive or restrictive measures, including being denied the right to exercise. They may not take walks or even engage in movements within the cell. These restrictions are imposed for as long as half a year. A former deputy director of the People's Liberation Army Institute, who had been deputy chief of staff during the Korean War, was kept immobile here for six months, after which he was no longer able to walk.

Quite separate from the cubicles is an exercise area of approximately one hundred meters square. It is laid out in rows of connected squares like rice paddies in southern China. The endless walking and running by the prisoners destroyed much of the grass, leaving a bare circular dirt path. The exercise area used to be divided by bamboo partitions. Then, during the late 1960s, this arrangement was replaced, and now a high brick wall separates two rows of connected exercise cubicles.

The inmates' lives are governed by all sorts of irrational regulations. They have to face sleeping the door. To turn one's back to the doorway is not permitted, and if one happens to do so while sleeping, he is awakened, over and over if necessary, until the prisoner learns to face the glass pane. There was a Tibetan who, after sleeping on one side of his face for more than ten years, developed a swollen ear that became infected and numb. He tried sleeping on the other side, but was repeatedly awakened and scolded by the guards until, driven beyond endurance, he went berserk and tried to strangle them. Only then was he granted special dispensation to roll over in his sleep.

Sanitary conditions are poor. Soap is not provided, and bathing is permitted only once a month, regardless of the season. A few privileged prisoners are given semiannual physical examinations.

All of this is filled with irony. These prisoners are gifted individuals who had joined the Communist Party to fight for the freedom and well-being of China and of mankind; they devoted the better part of their lives to obtaining and maintaining the Party's political dominance. But Qincheng is enough to strangle one's will. The place could almost be called a dungeon, or a psychiatric institute. In Qincheng, even those who were once imprisoned by the enemies of the Communists are victims of modern techniques to destroy body and mind.

The torments of daily life alone would not suffice to break the will of these stalwart people. Indeed, Qincheng is said to be equipped with modern instruments of torture. For example, former prisoners recall that they had been subjected to a strange instrument which caused terrible pain in the head. When the pain became unbearable, the torture suddenly ceased, but then it would resume again until either a confession was extracted or they concluded that the procedure would not be effective. There are other less modern but still effective methods of torture. For example, a prisoner may be exposed night and day to a strong light; after a while he feels that he is going crazy.

One person who was tortured at Qincheng was Wang Guangmei. [Ms. Wang, scion of one of China's leading families and widow of former Chief of State Liu Shaoqi, was rehabilitated in 1979.] She is said to have suddenly gone out of her mind one day while eating her bread and cabbage soup. When visited by the wife of an official, her appearance was almost inhuman. The sight was such that the visitor could not rest with the memory and, at considerable risk to herself and her family, she protested to Mao Zedong. Her letter to Mao, together with a general feeling of indignation among cadres, eventually led to a change in command. The public security people were replaced by Unit 8341 and, after the Cultural Revolution, Qincheng became "relatively civilized."

The most common form of torture is simple beating. The prisoner is summoned and surrounded by a group of men who slug and kick until he is bruised, bloody, and completely breathless. Even more common is for prisoners to be so heavily drugged that they become mentally unstable. The justification for administering these drugs is to cure "mental illness." Sometimes people are sent to the hospital for further "treatment." One person who had received the treatment recalls that after taking the medicine he had talked to himself constantly for days on end. Naturally, such monologues were recorded for use during the next interrogation. Among the hospitals that participate in such practices are the Fuxing Hospital, Hospital 301, and Anding Hospital. Officials are kept in what are called "high-echelon cadre treatment centers." Anding's center is located in the suburban town of Desheng-men and is called Zone Five. A visitor there once saw a stocky middle-aged man with a blank expression on his face and many scars on his head walking aimlessly in a straight line. He had to be intercepted by a guard or he would have bumped into the wall. These prisoners, who had since youth fought against dictatorship and dedicated themselves to the cause of freedom and righteousness, have now been tortured to the point where they have lost their sense of reality. Torture at Qincheng has been even worse than that which used to be carried out by the Nationalists in the 1940s.

In the movie *Zhuipu* the villain gets punished in the end. But in Qincheng the scenario is very different. The evil deeds there are committed under the direction of the government. The institution is more real than any movie. Even high government officials are ever under threat of being "invited" there for a "visit." Nearby, carefree foreigners are enchanted as they visit the Great Wall. There is nothing carefree about an official who is going to visit Qincheng. On the contrary, he will tremble with fear.

Wardens will not accommodate prisoners' requests. Some inmates, unable to endure such conditions, attempt suicide. Others go on hunger strikes. For example, the Panchen Lama [from Tibet] once refused food. He declared that he did not wish to live any longer and that his remains should be "delivered to the Central Committee of the Party." But usually after a prisoner has been on a hunger strike for a week he is given a severe beating, often damaging his teeth. Prisoners are also forced into a tight rubberized suit, which is inflated with air to restrict body movement and prevent breathing. The rubber suit is so effective that it is called a "pacifying jumpsuit." And if these methods are not effective, prisoners are force-fed large quantities of liquid.

Prison terms at Qincheng have generally run more than ten years. Indeed, hardly anyone was ever released before the 1970s, which is why one never heard of the place. Before the end of the Cultural Revolution it was extremely rare for anyone to be permitted to visit there. Relatives did not know where the inmates were or what their condition was. (Even wardens have been ignorant of the true identity of prisoners, who were identified by number rather than name.) A family, when unable to obtain information from the Ministry of Public Security, normally considers that the person has permanently disappeared. Likewise, prisoners are not given any information about their families, though they can assume that the families are encountering political difficulties. The state of mind of a political prisoner can only be comprehended by those who have had the same experience.

A human being is more than just flesh and bones. Even atheistic materialists must recognize the existence of man's spiritual side. What does Qincheng do for its prisoners to provide for the well-being of the mind? Some former inmates recall not being allowed to converse with anyone. Sometimes, even at the risk of being punished as a "troublemaker," an inmate would curse a warden just to spark some conversation. Only during the interrogation sessions did inmates have an opportunity to talk. One man, after ten years of confinement, was so overwhelmed when he finally heard his name called out that he was literally unable to speak. Even those who have not actually been subjected to prolonged physical and mental torture still show hidden signs of disorder after their release. Some, including those of strong character, could not speak fluently for two years after a decade of solitary confinement.

But even when denied any external stimulation, the human mind continues to function. Whoever invented this "mental therapy" understood quite well that a prisoner, for example, is bound to be concerned about his family and friends. In particular, he worries about his wife and children. The most effective way to break a prisoner's will is to keep him in an unbalanced state of mind. Unable to obtain any information about his family and friends, a prisoner worries that they are being discriminated against and is frustrated by his inability to assist them. He realizes that their suffering is a result of his own "offenses" against the authorities.

The proverb "psychology works better than force" is borne out by reports from many released prisoners, who had been told such things as: Your wife has remarried and is well adjusted in her new home. Your son has violated socialist order; he was not convicted, but was simply sent to a labor camp for reeducation. Your attractive daughter has had many suitors. Your son has been ill, but the government is doing everything possible to treat him. Etc., etc., etc. It has been common for prisoners eventually to discover that the stories were untrue. Why had the stories been told? The answer is to be understood in the context of the anguish which such stories cause. . . . In short, Qincheng officials have utilized every conceivable means of squeezing "the last drop of surplus value" out of these hapless souls.

In 1975, many of these long-time Party members suddenly had what they thought was a stroke of good luck. As part of the "reversal of verdicts" movement, they were released at Deng Xiaoping's suggestion.

But a sudden and overwhelming joy can sometimes be dangerous. To "insure safety and health" the Central Committee adopted a policy of exile. Those who left Qincheng that year had to first spend some time in the hospital to absorb the shock of reentering society. Two years later, hospitalization was no longer considered necessary. Instead, the prisoners were sent to remote villages, whose quiet surroundings supposedly serve likewise to soften the violent shock of liberation. The locations are selected according to three criteria: (1) parolees should not be kept in a large city; (2) they should not be kept near any transportation junction, and (3) they should not be kept where they had ever lived or worked. Perhaps most of the political prisoners have been exiled pursuant to these rules, with the exception of the Panchen Lama and some close friends of Party leaders.

Before leaving [Qincheng] you are made to shoulder a number of groundless accusations. A final "case summary" is then drawn up showing why your decade of imprisonment was well deserved. Upon your release, you are taught to be thankful for Chairman Mao's leniency, for, after all, a "contradiction between us and the enemy" is being treated merely as a "contradiction among the people" [that is, an intolerable offense is now deemed tolerable]. Therefore, you will not complain if your activities are restricted and you are sent to a faraway village. Former Beijing Mayor Peng Zhen, former State Planning Chairman Bo Yibo, and many other prisoners have been dealt with in this manner. Bo Yibo is more courageous than most. "In the past I erred in following the directive of the Central Committee," he admitted, but he added: "Now shall I commit another error by obeying the Central Committee? To avoid making any more mistakes, I refuse to go into exile." Bo thus refused to leave Qincheng. Since then, it is said, the prerelease accusations have been dispensed with, and political prisoners are sent directly into exile.

Once he sets foot in Qincheng, a prisoner loses any sense of well-being. So when he leaves prison he is greatly relieved, for he assumes that even exile will be comfortable by comparison. But is there really much difference between conditions in Qincheng and those in exile? The food ration continues according to a four-grade system: 200 *yuan*, 120 *yuan*, 80 *yuan*, and 60 *yuan*. In Qincheng, prisoners are constantly guarded by armed wardens; in exile they are constantly watched by local Communist Party officials (in the name of providing care for them). Take, for example, Li Sa, the Russian wife of Li Lisan. [Li Lisan led the Chinese Communist Party for a few years beginning in 1928.] She was accused of being a Soviet agent and sent to Qincheng for seven or eight years. Upon her release she was sent to Yuncheng in Shanxi Province. The local commune provided two educated youth to attend to her needs. As she was an old woman, she requested transfer to Beijing where she could live with her daughter and granddaughter. Permission was not granted until December 1978.

These two instances are relatively mild. Some exiles, it is said, are still not allowed to receive visits from their friends and relatives. So it is really an extension of Qincheng Prison, showing the continuity of the Party's policy toward prisoners.

*   *   *

I have revealed the terror of Qincheng not merely to plead for innocent prisoners, although those who devoted their youth to the Chinese revolution and then dared oppose Mao's barbaric dictatorship do indeed deserve our respect and emulation. The real lesson that we learn from this prison is that the dictatorship of the *proletariat* does not exist in our country. Rather, the dictatorship is used as a tool to *oppress* the proletariat. The tool has been used so effectively that all of the dictator's opponents have been eliminated, even "comrades-in-arms" from the era of the Long March.

It is quite natural for dictators to resort to barbaric measures to govern a country. Dictatorship cannot survive unless it has strong methods to suppress the people. Not only must the masses be repressed; the instruments of repression must also be aimed at any opposition in the inner circle. Even toward comrades who once fought at their side, dictators show not a bit of mercy. One can almost say that those who lost their lives during the revolution were the lucky ones. Besides being honored as heroes who fought for freedom and peace, they had *peace of mind*. They did not have to worry about themselves and their relatives being oppressed by their comrades. They did not constantly tremble with fear at the prospect of being tortured.

Dictators have many excuses for eliminating their opponents. There are "class enemies," "counterrevolutionaries," "rebels," and "traitors." Dictatorship requires such labels, and it requires Qinchengs. . . . In order to avoid the disaster of dictatorship, one has to eliminate the conditions that make it possible, including dehumanizing political prisons.

Through a hundred years of bloody struggle, the proletariat obtained freedoms of expression, press, assembly, organization, religion, and the right to strike. Why did these freedoms disappear after the so-called proletarian Community Party gained power? Why do all "proletarian" governments dictate to their masses and repress those who really speak for the masses? It is because their basic approach to government is incorrect. If the majority benefits from democracy and freedom, why do we go to such extremes to maintain dictatorship? Why is it necessary to arrest people who simply express their opinions? Qincheng proves that our government is not the people's government, because it has deprived the people of free speech. Those who have been tortured are usually the masses' friends, whereas the prosecutors are the enemies of the people. Only those who lack the support of the people have to resort to making false charges and torturing their opponents in order to perpetuate their dictatorship.

We must get rid of Qincheng forever. We must be permanently rid of all political persecution and imprisonment. At stake are not simply a few unfortunate victims, but rather the basic political and personal rights of an entire people. Do you believe that every individual has the right to express his or her opinion on national policy? If you do, then you must oppose the arrest of those who have expressed their political views. If you do not believe others have the right to express *their* opinion, then how can you argue that *you* have any rights? After all, your opinion might be absolutely correct, but having the right to express it is another matter.

We might ask the former officials emerging from Qincheng: When you used to suppress the rights of others, what did that do to help secure your own rights? When you engaged in political persecution yourself, did you foresee yourselves being subjected to the same kind of persecution? The masses realize now that freedom of speech can only be secured through the abolition of political imprisonment and oppression. People's rights cannot be protected by a dictatorship which strips people of their rights. They can only be secured by the mutual protection of everyone's rights.[3]

DOCUMENT 56
COMMUNE PRISONS
From *Beijing Spring*

Our correspondent reports:

The Longhua Commune in the northern part of Gaoyang County, Hebei Province, has established fifteen commune-operated detention houses. They hired some of the dregs of society as wardens. . . . The wardens use all kinds of tortures to extract confessions, referring to the procedures by the fine-sounding phrase "criticizing capitalist management methods."

One of these detention houses was officially opened on 15 April 1978. It houses over 130 prisoners. We have a description of the place by Duan Qingfen, a secretary of the Party branch at the commune farm-machine depot, who himself was held there and escaped. He says that there are still over twenty people incarcerated there, all farm-machine workers. They are detained in a room of twenty square meters. All the doors and windows are blocked up.[4]

Section Twelve
AMERICA: A MODEL FOR CHINA?

Although the participants in the democratic movement evinced a degree of patriotism and nationalism (see Section Thirteen), they were also quite willing to appeal to foreigners for at least moral support. They were delighted to have their activities covered by Western and Japanese journalists. According to one poster, "Foreigners . . . who are concerned with the democratic movement and show sympathy and real interest, are the true friends of the Chinese people. . . . We thank them from the bottom of our hearts."[1]

As China's democrats searched for models for a new political system, two foreign countries seemed to have special appeal. One was Yugoslavia, which is mentioned quite frequently in the various dissident essays. However, these writings reveal very limited knowledge about that country, and it is unsurprising that there is no extensive treatment of it.

More seemed to be known about the United States, as is evidenced by an appeal to President Jimmy Carter, which a group of self-styled workers wrote shortly before Vice-Premier Deng Xiaoping's visit to Washington (Document 57). This letter was not unique, but was perhaps more pro-Western than most movement writings. Its sentiments were highly controversial and gave rise to rebuttals such as that in Document 58.

DOCUMENT 57
LETTER TO PRESIDENT CARTER
By Gong Min[2]

Esteemed President Carter:

How are you?

Today, 1 January 1979, is a memorable and historic date. It is the date when China and the United States, our great country and your great country, have established formal diplomatic relations. With the establishment of diplomatic relations between China and the United States, the strong desire which has long existed between the peoples of the two countries has been realized. Diplomatic relations have opened wide the door for the promotion of friendship, cooperation, and understanding between the peoples of the two countries. This will not only strengthen the exchange of culture, science, and technology, and enhance and develop economic relations between the two countries, but will also vigorously promote and stabilize peace in Asia and the whole world. We believe every Chinese and American will say in his heart: "It is excellent. This should have been done long ago."

Esteemed President Carter, on this occasion please allow us, as human beings, to extend our hands to you, as another human being, and to express our greetings through you to all the American people. To us you are not only a president but also an ordinary American citizen and an ordinary person among the broad masses of people on earth. We are the younger generation of China, a generation which has painfully struggled amid disappointment, despair, and hope. For a long time we have admired your country and the American people—our blue-eyed brothers. How we have desired to learn about what is happening there in "America," another continent under the same sky, under the brilliant stars and stripes, in the 1970s, and what lies in store for your country in the 1980s! What are the Americans thinking about, talking about, and doing?

Unfortunately, even though we hold many ideas in common, many here have had guilty consciences for holding these ideas. We would have liked to have sung, "I sing for thee, Americans," but we did not dare. An invisible iron curtain blocked us. A political, cultural, and psychological Great Wall, made up of plain prejudice and stupidity, stood between our two nations, between our two sectors of humanity.

Ever since our childhood, people have described you to us as "tigers," "wolves," "freaks and monsters"; so you have left us with a very strange and horrible impression. We have attempted to peep through the gaps of the spiritual wall, to peep at the outside world through the breach caused by the wall's degeneration and collapse: "What kind of monster is the

United States?" However, we could never see the true picture. Now that our republic and your United States have established formal diplomatic relations, the iron curtain has been lifted, the spiritual wall which separates the peoples of the two countries is being demolished and will be completely removed, and it is quite possible for us to stand on the horizon and look at you and the world. We will hear the happy "hello" from young American friends, and the young American friends will also see the smile on our faces—the smile of China and the smile of friendship and understanding.

Esteemed President Carter, we are a group of Chinese workers, the younger generation of the Chinese proletariat. On this occasion, when our countries have established diplomatic relations, we would like to have an unprecedented, friendly conversation with you—our American friend. We would like to talk with you about the human rights issue and the issues concerning our democracy and legal system.

Under the leadership of the Party Central Committee headed by Chairman Hua, our country is carrying out the new Long March. Working with one heart and one mind, it is now vigorously developing the Four Modernizations and at the moment has shifted the emphasis of the work of the Party to promoting the Four Modernizations. This has marked the beginning of a new period in our country, a prelude to great political and economic change in the life of our nation. Alongside the progress of the Four Modernizations, new changes which are suited to the Four Modernizations will also occur in the political, economic, legal, moral, and ethical ideas to which we have been accustomed. We completely support the grand plan of the Four Modernizations. We also support the present stability and unity, so essential to the achievement of the Four Modernizations, which are the common desire of the whole Party and all Chinese.

But the *keys* to the realization of the Four Modernizations are human rights, democracy, and a sound legal system. Without human rights, without true socialist democracy, and without a sound legal system (which includes specific legal demarcations regarding political mistakes and insures the specific implementation of the Constitution), the Four Modernizations are but empty talk. Now, even though we have started advocating and implementing democracy, we do not have much democracy. We should have more and still more. This is by no means so-called "liberalization."

Enhancing human rights, appealing for democracy, and strengthening the legal system are not things to be afraid of, and they are not "upheavals" at all. They are not reactions to stability and unity but are indispensable component parts of the Four Modernizations. They will only strengthen stability and unity and will bring longer peace, happiness, and ease of mind to a generation. Otherwise, even if the Four Modernizations are realized, their fruits will again be appropriated by bureaucrats, and the people will not be able to taste their sweetness. Here we are, citizens of a republic, and yet we have not enjoyed socialist democracy and human rights; we have not had freedom of thought, speech, press, assembly, and association, and the various personal freedoms that one should have in a socialist country, and which are stipulated in our Constitution. It is precisely for this reason that we make our appeal.

Political frauds used to regard human rights as alien elements. They disdained human rights and democracy. They were afraid of them and feared them. They turned the concept of "democracy" upside down and changed it into "rule over the people." They became the natural masters of the people! They were afraid of the two words "human rights" and steered clear of them. They dared not mention this thing, and they did not have the courage to face it. This is because, given this thing, people will have real political freedom, and ill-gotten power will be done away with. However, human rights is the trend of social development, and these are what the people strongly desire. In the previous period when Lin Biao and the Gang of Four ran rampant, although our republic did not have the outward form of a feudal despotism, everyone who was physically and mentally sound could plainly feel and understand the existence of feudal despotism or feudal socialism.

"The political freedom of a citizen is a kind of peace of mind. This peace of mind is derived from the view that everyone feels safe and secure. To enjoy this kind of freedom (Note: In England, even if a man's enemies are as numerous as the hairs on his head, nothing will happen to him. This is really something excellent, because mental health and physical health are both essential. "Notes on England."), it is necessary to establish a kind of government under whose rule a citizen shall not fear another citizen" (Montesquieu, *De l'esprit des lois* [1748]).

However, even as citizens of a People's Republic, we find much to fear. We fear trumped-up charges, we fear secret reports, we fear our "immediate superior," and we fear the bureaucratic mentality. We even fear saying something sincerely and honestly.[3] Where is there so much as a shadow of human rights and democracy in this? Inasmuch as the legal system is unsound and human rights and democracy have not been insured, not only have the masses been victimized, but so have many high-ranking leaders, including many revolutionary elders.

There have always been plenty of movements in our country, and our generation has more or less been brought up on them. However, the purpose of some movements was solely the struggle of special interests for power. A large-scale "movement" or "revolution" could be launched simply at a person's will, without regard to whether the "movement" or "revolution" was really necessary, whether it was advantageous to enhancing the productive forces, or whether it was going to bring great calamity to the nation. In a rather prolonged "movement" or "revolution" launched in a certain period, neither democracy within the Party nor the normal democratic life of the masses were insured. Those who were the targets of the movement lost their legal protection, while those who launched the movement stood beyond the reach of law and were not subject to the limits of law. All matters go through a process of exposure and understanding; the longer the lapse of time, the more clearly are matters understood. Now, as we review certain struggles within the Party, what we see is that personal autocracy existed under the fiction of the "Party." There were exclusion, suppression, and relentless blows by hook or crook, dealt at those who were outside and differing. For instance, it is clear to everyone that Liu Shaoqi, Peng Dehuai, and Comrade Tao Zhu (whose remains are yet to be found), as well as our esteemed and beloved Vice-Chairman Deng [Xiaoping], were all victims of the absence of democracy within the Party.

In various political mass movements [words illegible] the masses mobilized in the movements. Like spinning tops, they rubbed against and collided with one another in various movements. Lin Biao, the Gang of Four, and frauds of their ilk unscrupulously enmeshed the people in the theories of class and class struggle, and they instigated ceaseless conflicts between one group and another. Some people held that law may only be used to control one group of people and should not be applied to the others, and that they could override the law, pursue "rule by the voice of one man alone," exercise dictatorial power, destroy democracy, and trample upon human rights. Because of the poison of the feudal despotism and autocracy in China during the past several thousand years, and because of the influence of the reactionary ideological system of Lin Biao and the Gang of Four, the idea of special privileges and the concept of gradation still exist in the minds of some people. They have always held that they are taller, bigger, and more special than other people. They disdained independent intellectual life, personality, natural desires, and proper rights. In a word, they disdained human rights, and they behaved as though they were "special creatures among the human race." However, they did not know that a mouse and a king are of the same value when dead!

Under the imposing power of Lin Biao and the Gang of Four, our generation experienced great suffering. The republic has been established for so many years and, as a matter of fact, the old economic relations which produced class differences have long been changed. The system of private ownership has been changed into the socialist system of public ownership, and the exploiters have been forced to work and support themselves. However, they claimed that there still existed "classes" among the people. They did not work to develop production and the socialist economy but shouted for "class struggle" all day long. They detached themselves from the objective social reality and artificially created a kind of "class concept." They staged class struggle just for the sake of staging class struggle, with the purpose of covering their [words illegible] to struggle for power and interests. To them there were "class struggles" everywhere, "new directions in class struggles" could be found everywhere, and everywhere there were hypothetical "enemies" who in fact existed only in their minds. They used this to confuse the opinions of the masses in order to uphold their vicious rule.

Their "enemies" were numerous. Writers and artists who did their own thinking were their enemies. Scholars, professors, and editors who dared "contend" and air their views were their enemies. Musicians, painters, and film actors and actresses who had originality and dared express their own personalities were enemies. People who were not blindly faithful to the idols and were brave enough to uphold the truth and explore the forbidden zones were their enemies. In short, courage and conscience were their enemies, and everyone who was unwilling to be among the "enmeshed," who were bold enough to think, to speak up, and to work, and whose thinking really broke through the cage were their enemies. Those groups of people could be persecuted and suppressed in large numbers. [The leaders] just wanted people to think in their meshes, live in their meshes, and spend their lives in their meshes. Otherwise you were "antiparty and antisocialist" and you were "rightists," "counterrevolutionaries," and "bad elements."

Even we who have been wearing our red neckerchiefs and have grown up together with the republic were caught in their meshes. We have lost our youth, we have no ideals, we do not have bright memories, and we do not have a rich and varied intellectual life. Our years were spent with "today being but a repeat of yesterday," and our lives passed aimlessly in tiresome uniformity and monotony. They put up idols everywhere and "idolized" the leaders. They forced people to bow their heads toward them and worship them, distorting the significance of man beyond recognition. It was just as our Party press—which described those dark years and made numerous exposures—reported: Whoever damaged a [Mao] badge, or damaged a portrait of the Great Man, or uttered a complaint would be convicted on the charge of being a "current counterrevolutionary," and a basic-level unit could, therefore, ignore the legal system and willfully pass its verdict and stigmatize a citizen. The victim would wear the stigma from youth to adulthood, and even to the grave. Without going through the courts, one could be stripped of all lifelong political and economic interests.

The legal demarcation concerning political errors must be clearly set out. Human rights cannot be trampled on at will, and a citizen of a nation cannot be willfully sanctioned by law and unlawfully persecuted. The line should be formulated to insure the real implementation of the specific articles of the Constitution of the nation; otherwise, the provisions of the Constitution on the rights of people will become empty talk. Freedom of speech will be regarded as "reactionary speech" and "counterrevolutionary speech"; ideological freedom will be branded as "nonproletarian viewpoint" and "reactionary ideology"; a free association will be seen as "reactionary organization" and "counterrevolutionary clique"; freedom of assembly will be used as a pretext for "bad people" and "class enemies" to sneak in, and citizens will be apprehended at will; freedom to strike will be distorted as "intentional sabotage of production"; freedom of demonstration will be denounced as "disturbing social order"; as regards freedom of publication, the "golden rule" will be applied to strangle works, and the people's will and social practice will not be regarded as the sole criteria for analyzing and testing works; freedom of the individual will be regarded as "bourgeois liberalism" and "individualism" and "anarchism," and the form of "organization" will be used to forcibly interfere and harshly suppress.

Esteemed President Carter, we have frequently thought about why there is so little democracy and why democracy is so lacking in a socialist country like ours. What we have always had was simply "all-round dictatorship." Why have we not mentioned human rights? Why have we long disregarded this central subject on the agenda of the world in this century? Why has the great banner of human rights been hoisted by a capitalist country like the United States and not by us, with an advanced social system? Can it be that human rights are merely something for your bourgeois country? Why should we preach "prevent the emergence of revisionism and oppose revisionism" and "prevent the restoration of capitalism"? Why does a developed capitalist country not have to preach "prevent the occurrence of proletarian social revolution"? Why can a socialist country peacefully evolve to be capitalist and revisionist (like the first socialist country, the Soviet Union, which has restored capitalism? Why can a proletarian country not prevent her own degeneration? Why does capitalism not evolve into socialism? Why does a capitalist country not need to prevent her degeneration? Can it be that the proletariat and laboring people in capitalist countries are so content with things as they are,

are so short of class consciousness and rebellious spirit and have no demand for changing reality? Is not all this worth consideration and deep thought? Do we not need to find the positive answers to these problems? In our country we have often heard sermons on democracy and held that proletarian democracy is the supreme, typical democracy. However, this is merely a concept, not an established fact. For so many years we saw that Lin Biao and the Gang of Four did not embody democratic state leadership. Actually, we have never had a ballot in our hands. A fact which we must not disregard is that democracy is a word derived from a foreign country. It originated in Greece and means "people's political power." The bourgeoisie has had the democratic system for more than three centuries, and the proletarian democratic system which has existed for only several decades is far from being mature and has many shortcomings. For instance, there exist in our stagnant, despotic dictatorship: bureaucracy, carrying on official business for private gain, persecution of the masses, the blossoming of only one flower and only one school of thought. People have no freedom to select employment, change residence, or publish their own opinions and works. Citizens dare not criticize leaders and their own government, dare not run counter to the "opinions of their superior officers," and so forth.

On balance, the proletarian democratic system is not as perfect as bourgeois democracy. The proletarian democratic system has not become a strong lever for the advanced development of social sciences, technology, literature, art, and productive forces. In the period of Lin Biao and the Gang of Four, our economy was on the verge of collapse, people's living standards could not be raised but fell, science and technology were extremely backward, and literature and art were nearly dead. In a developed capitalist country like the United States, the comparatively perfect democratic system is always linked with the high material development and development of civilization and spirit. Although your American democratic system also has its defects, these defects are only compared with each other here. We are convinced that, so far as its intrinsic significance is concerned, the socialist democratic system is likely to fully mobilize the wisdom, talents, and creative spirit of all members of society and to impel at high speed the development of social productive forces, so that it will become the supreme, typical democracy. (Such a democracy is quite compatible with the Four Modernizations.) Up to the present we have far from achieved this ideal. The various defects that exist in our democratic system have become serious obstacles to and shackles on material and spiritual production in society. To realize the Four Modernizations, we must begin, and have begun, to eliminate these defects. Meanwhile, the proletarian "democratic system" cannot really serve the social interests of the proletariat and laboring people and cannot prevent the degeneration of a proletarian country.

In this sense, our concern is not so much preventing the restoration of capitalism as preventing the restoration of feudalism. Our republic has developed from an embryonic semifeudal semicolony and has never really experienced the stage of capitalist development. The period when Lin Biao and the Gang of Four ran wild entailed the restoration of a feudalism that was darker, more terrible, and more brutal than the Middle Ages. They could restore feudalism in China because they took advantage of the immaturity, imperfection, and numerous defects of the proletarian democratic system. Therefore, preventing a restoration of feudalism is a cardinal task which we cannot now, could not in the past, and must not in the future disregard.

Esteemed President Carter, whether or not a country respects human rights and upholds democracy depends very much on the question of whether or not it has a sound legal system, and the most important factor is its social structure. A king who attempts to practice despotism will generally first concentrate in himself all posts and powers, as is the present situation in some countries in the East. They centralize the state's legislative, judiciary, and executive powers in one person, and terrible tyranny therefore rules over everything. Just as Montesquieu pointed out in *The Spirit of the Laws:* "When the legislative and executive powers are combined in the same person, or in the same body of magistrates, there can be no liberty, because apprehensions may arise lest the same monarch or senate which enacts tyrannical laws execute them in a tyrannical manner." Again: "There is no liberty if the judicial power is not separated from the legislative and executive. Were it joined with the legislative, the life and liberty of the subject would be exposed to arbitrary control, for the judges would then be the legislators. Were it joined to the executive power, the judges might behave with violence and oppression."

It is exactly because of this that our generation has never enjoyed any real human rights. We do not have our independent character and lifestyle. The various democratic parties of our country have existed as a mere formality. Some of their members are aged, some have died, and some have been struck down. Is there any "long-term coexistence and mutual supervision" [between the Communist Party and democratic groups]?[4] As for the election of government officials, all leaders, from the people's representatives down to leaders at all levels, are appointed, assigned, or elected on instructions. They are by no means truly elected by the people, not to mention the dismissal and replacement of incompetents.

These government officials can remain beyond the supervision of the masses, and they have turned from being public servants to being the masters of people's minds. As a powerful and dignified socialist country in which the people [ostensibly] were the masters, China wore the cloak of a republic but in essence was a despotism and autocracy. It has fundamentally violated the great principles of the first political Party of the proletariat—the Paris Commune—and does not have the courage to put into practice the principles of the Paris Commune.

Esteemed President Carter, we know that your country has its Declaration of Independence, of which your American people are very proud, and you have a glorious chapter in your American history—the American War of Independence. When appraising the Declaration of Independence, Marx noted that "for the first time the great thinking of a democratic republic was produced" in the United States; and when referring to the American War of Independence, Lenin said that it was "the earliest and the greatest genuine war of liberation in the history of mankind." The Declaration of Independence proclaimed "that all men are created equal, that they are endowed by their Creator with certain unalienable rights, that among these are Life, Liberty and the pursuit of Happiness. That to secure these rights, Governments are instituted among Men, deriving their just powers from the consent of the governed. That whenever any Form of Government becomes destructive of these ends, it is the Right of the People to alter or to abolish it, and to institute new Government." Your young United States of America was established on this foundation.

Today our two countries have established formal diplomatic relations. We hope to understand the United States, and to understand it still more realistically and fully. If it is not wishful thinking, we hope very much that we can go to the United States to look around as ordinary Chinese citizens (and not always have those government-designated officials acting on our behalf). Let the people organize an "ordinary Chinese citizens' visiting delegation" to visit the United States to see what kind of a "monster" it really is and thereby make comparisons among different countries of the world before we determine our choice with respect to: What are the things we need? What are the things we do not need? What are the things we should forsake? And what are the things we should retain?

Of course, the United States and the American people are not totally strange to us. We have a long list of brilliant names in our heads: They are Washington, Franklin, Jefferson, Paine, Lincoln, Whitman, Edison, Jack London, Mark Twain, Ford, Nixon, and so on and so forth. Some of them have made outstanding and beneficial contributions to progressive politics, science, and culture, and some have exerted active and diligent efforts for the great historical achievement of the establishment of diplomatic relations between China and the United States.

Esteemed President Carter, our esteemed and beloved Vice-Premier Deng has accepted your invitation and is going to visit your country. He is going to take with him good wishes to the American people on behalf of the 800 million Chinese people. He is a man most trusted by the people of our time. He is a broad-minded and generous man, a most informed man, and a man who seeks truth from facts. This is what our people have found out about him through observation and practice.

China has been cut off from the world for decades, yet the minds of the people of our two countries are by no means cut off from each other. The Chinese people have a favorable impression of the American people, and they feel happy over the establishment of diplomatic relations between China and the United States. The United States is the world's most prosperous country, and it is quite certain that its high civilization will harmonize with its high degree of democracy; therefore, relatively speaking it is the most democratic country in the world.

In the United States people have attached importance to and have properly explored the value of man and "what kind of person a man should be." They are now expounding its undoubtedly very profound and rich meaning. There is no doubt that the American people enjoy a very high level of material life, and they have enjoyed far greater intellectual freedom than the people of any other area of the world. An ordinary American citizen will never have to fear another citizen, no matter how great the powers this other citizen holds. Americans will not be charged with "committing a crime" simply because they criticized in an upright manner the head of their own country, and they will not be arrested and called "counterrevolutionaries" or "bad elements." The supreme head of state also will not be excused from legal sanctions if he ever violates the criminal code. This is because, like any ordinary citizen, he is also subject to the limitations of law, and the law commands an even higher authority than he does.

Today human rights are generally highly treasured and respected among the American people. The United States has a very high degree of popularization of culture, and the American people are very well educated. They have no shortage of democratic capacity and disposition. We firmly believe that they all have the same hope: that their other brothers on earth can also enjoy what they enjoy. Human rights is a traditional term to the American people, and we have noticed the brilliance of these two words from the earliest Declaration of Independence of the United States up to President Carter's recent speeches. Whether to the Chinese people or the American people or the people of any other country in the world, "human rights" have the same significance. On this planet where mankind lives together there is no distinction as to race, nation, or state boundaries regarding human rights. They are the common desire of all the progressive peoples of our time.

Our country is a developing country, and its philosophy is Marxism. This philosophy, however, does not oppose human rights but is in line with human rights. Our young generation has attempted to use the basic principles of Marxism to search for a kind of developing philosophical concept—the philosophy of practice; and we have attempted to search for its basic principles in the future development of Marxism. The truth of Marxism does not fear any test. The principle that matter is in constant motion, and the principle of the inherent laws of dialectics concerning the motion of matter, can also be supplied to Marxism itself. People have kindly painted a beautiful picture of the future for us: By that time people will be living in a common sociopolitical system and the world will become a social structure of universal harmony. Several generations of Chinese people have firmly believed that this is the inevitable law of historical development. The purpose of reviewing the past is to sum up in the best way possible historical experience, thus to face the future. As we review our past, however, and test the ideal of harmony, objectively according to a practical philosophical viewpoint, we discover that both in China and abroad harmony has not been realized. We cannot ignore the fact that the objective situation has not developed in the direction of great unity and uniformity, but that it has scientifically revealed and set forth diversified movements of great variety in the world, and that people have generally searched for opportunities and conditions to express and develop their characters.

We have come to realize that there is no artificial or inherent law that governs the world and that can determine the direction of world movement. In every epoch it is only the kind of special inevitability of history which arises from within the epoch itself that gives impetus to the society to move forward. The American War of Independence and the Declaration of Independence, which Marx called "the first declaration of human rights," were aimed at opposing the tyranny and merciless looting of the British. The emergence of the "Declaration of the Rights of Man," which proclaimed for the first time that "men are born, and always continue, free and equal in respect of their rights," was of antifeudal and progressive significance. So there was the bourgeois revolution in France. Later, the key document of the proletariat, the Communist Manifesto, was promulgated, calling on workers of all countries to unite. This document served as a practical guide during the great October Revolution in Russia. It was not that an inevitable law of history, which we used to hold to be of universal theoretical significance, was playing its role, but that these events were all determined by the true inevitability of history which arose from within the particular epoch itself, each of which had its own special contributing factors. As a matter of fact, no theory is "designed" and no revolution is "predetermined." They are not subject to the limitations of a certain artificial concept of "law," and they must all be tested through social practice. In the present historical epoch, human rights constitute a torrential tide. It is a loud cry by mankind of this century demanding a reassessment of the value of man. It is one form of expression of a new awakening in man's consciousness, and it is the central theme which focuses on the views of all progressive people. This tide can never be resisted!

Although the Chinese people, the American people, and the peoples of other countries live in different lands and have different beliefs and ways of life, human rights are the thing that the whole of mankind understands. The problem of human rights in any country must arouse the intense concern, sympathy, and support of the whole world.

Finally, what is worthy of special emphasis is that, since the founding of our republic, the Constitution has expressly provided that people have the rights of speech, publication, assembly, association, parade, and demonstration. However, these rights have not been exercised in real life. Although the Constitution of our country has been revised, our human rights have not increased because of the revision. The more the Constitution was revised, the more have human rights been whittled down. The end to this situation in which the people have no rights began with the new Constitution formulated at the Fifth National People's Congress, personally presided over by NPC Chairman Ye Jianying and guided by the line and spirit of the Eleventh Party Congress. Under the protection of the new Constitution, which is different from any previous constitution, we have begun to exercise our rights.

The Enlightenment Society was established in Beijing (Peking) on 24 November 1978. The Enlightenment Society is a people's association which was spontaneously organized by the masses, the first such society since the liberation of our country. It has not been hindered, interfered with, suppressed, or strangled since its establishment more than a month ago. This has proved incontrovertibly and for the first time to the Chinese people and the peoples of the world that the new Constitution formulated at the Fifth NPC is a great constitution which really upholds people's democratic rights and is not a constitution enacted on the basis of one person's say-so. Today we can enjoy the right of association and possibly can win the right of freedom of publication. We must thank the Party Central Committee headed by Chairman Hua, NPC Chairman Ye, and

Vice-Chairman Deng, who have protected people's democratic rights and won the people's trust and support!

People want democracy.

Even more, people want leaders who defend democracy.

Such democracy and such leaders are appearing in our country. We hope that now and in the future such democracy will not be forfeited by anyone and that such leaders will not disappoint the people.

Greetings to you and the great American people!

May Sino–U.S. friendship flourish forever!

The future belongs to progressive mankind!

DOCUMENT 58
AMERICAN DEMOCRACY: A CRITIQUE
From a Wall Poster

On January 26 I* posted an essay entitled "Is the United States a 'Democratic Paradise?' " The piece has prompted reproach from quite a few people, including Jie Jun, who recently wrote an article disagreeing with me.[5] I am delighted, for this is what I have been expecting. Otherwise what is Democracy Wall?

Before Comrade Deng Xiaoping's visit to the United States there appeared on Democracy Wall and at Tian-an-men a number of one-sided articles that eulogized American democracy. They deviated markedly from the principle of "making foreign things serve China." They implied that China has never enjoyed democracy and only the United States has. Socialism could never bring democracy, only capitalism could. China could only be saved by completely adopting American democracy. No other type of democracy could solve our problems.

The Enlightenment Society went the farthest. Pretending to be guided by Marxism-Leninism, it in fact went contrary to Marxist-Leninist class struggle and contrary to the theory of proletarian dictatorship. The Society actually begged President Jimmy Carter to give "human rights" to the Chinese people. Jie Jun says that the letter from the Enlightenment Society to President Carter conveyed nothing but the wish for friendship with the American people. Was the matter so simple? They wrote in black and white: "Inquire about the human rights movement in China." I think Jie Jun does not need to be reminded of the political and emotional meaning implied in such a diplomatic expression as "inquire about" something.

Many of the people gathering in front of Democracy Wall are youths in their twenties. Since they reached the age of understanding, they have witnessed the so-called Great Proletarian Cultural Revolution. For the fourth and longest time since 1949, China was guided by the heinous influence of the left-opportunist line. For ten years the gravest harm was done; Marxism-Leninism was emasculated, socialism trampled upon, the friend-enemy relationship reversed, and right confused with wrong. Evil people ran amuck while good people could hardly survive. The country was ruined, and the people suffered bitterly.

It was not wrong for the people to oppose this so-called "socialism" that they were experiencing. [But some democratic activists (?)] have mistaken the feudal, autocratic "socialism" of Lin Biao and the Gang of Four as

---

* Author not identified. See note 5.

Marxist-Leninist scientific socialism. This is understandable, because these youths experienced neither the bright period in the history of our Party and state, nor the admittedly imperfect socialist democracy and legal system; they saw only the phony aspects.

As far as social and ideological development are concerned, the change from feudal autocracy to bourgeois democracy represents progress. However, the wheel of history can never be reversed. Should the Chinese people, who removed the great mountains of imperialism, feudalism, and bureaucratic capitalism, throw away socialism as well and go back to the road along which capitalism emerged, grew up, monopolized, and perished?

I was born before the victorious conclusion of the War of Resistance against Japan. During the past few decades I have experienced the brilliance of Marxism-Leninism-Mao Zedong Thought and the brilliance of socialism. After ten years of the so-called Great Proletarian Cultural Revolution, I am more than ever convinced that socialism can save China. Of course, by socialism I do not mean the "socialism" of the Cultural Revolution. Nor do I mean the socialism which we have today. What I mean is scientific socialism which is imbued with the boundless vitality of democracy. We must creatively apply Marxism-Leninism, transform the Chinese Communist Party, rely on the people of the entire country, humbly learn all good things from foreign countries and from human civilization, and struggle arduously. I believe that if we do all of this, we will finally be able to gradually establish a people's democratic system based on socialism and, by the end of the century, realize our wish to build a powerful socialist country with modern industry, agriculture, science, and technology, and national defense.

Therefore, I strongly object to the idea of turning to worship a foreign Buddha the moment we have done away with our "despot" and abandoning socialism in favor of capitalism. . . .

The article by Jie Jun reads: ". . . 'a dying person who . . . like the sun setting beyond the Western Hills, will soon be relegated to a museum' is a portrayal of the past. . . . In the United States, scientific development, economic growth, and modernization in daily life have caused both philosophical and psychological changes. . . . America is a democratic paradise." He agrees that the United States was once an imperialist country and "the world's policeman," but claims that it has changed now because of scientific development, growth in social wealth, and general modernization. He does not describe in clear-cut and direct language the results of this change. Yet, from his question of whether I had adopted a realistic approach and from his own answer to this question, it can be deduced that he holds that, instead of being imperialist in nature, the United States has developed into a "democratic paradise."

Let us tell the story from the beginning. The United States used to be an imperialistic country. Then, as a result of two or three decades of development, that is, scientific development, growth in social wealth, and modernization in daily life, as Jie Jun has said, the country changed ideologically and psychologically. So, we may ask: Has the United States changed its imperialist nature? Does the monopoly bourgeoisie there no longer desire to suppress, exploit, and plunder other classes? Has there been any change in the system of private ownership of the means of production? Have the laws and the state machine which protect this private ownership been changed? Have the realities of class oppression, class exploitation, and class antagonism altered? Has the United States stopped plundering the colonies and semicolonies in the Third World? Is it no longer true that "it is money that makes everything run"?

It is Jie Jun's conclusion that all of this has changed and that now the United States is not imperialistic but, rather, "a democratic paradise" for everyone. So I want to ask: Is there a single imperialistic country in the world? And especially I want to ask: When and how did the United States accomplish this great change characteristic of a proletarian revolution? . . .

I think that the United States has indeed undergone great changes in recent decades. In addition to developments in science, technology, economics, and production, there have been changes determined by the laws of history. This historical change cannot but have predominance in the overall development of society. . . . As a result of the struggle waged by the world's people, including the American people, the United States has forever lost the status of "world dominator" and has gone downhill day by day. To lease class struggles at home and abroad and to concentrate the various forces to vie with the USSR for world hegemony, it has to change its strategy and tactics. However, its imperialistic nature has not changed a bit.

As a result of social development, material progress, and the masses' heightened consciousness, gone forever are the days when the U.S. monopoly bourgeoisie can rely on force alone to plunder and exploit the masses. Tempered in workers' movements in past centuries, the working masses have learned to protect their economic interests by fighting against the monopoly capitalists. As the strength of the working class has continued to grow, the monopoly bourgeoisie has had to grant the workers more legal rights, higher wages, and greater social welfare. The capitalists know very well that they cannot keep increasing their profits without paying this price. This new aspect of exploitation exists not only in the United States but in all other countries as well.

Internationally, U.S. imperialism is also on the defensive. In its contention with Soviet revisionism for world hegemony, it may adopt some methods appropriate for defense. For instance, it may withdraw its military forces from some areas, it may clamor in opposition to the USSR, it may ask Moscow to give "human rights" to dissidents, and so on. This new situation does not reflect any good intentions of the United States; it is only the new face of American imperialism under changed conditions. It is not that the United States no longer seeks hegemony, but simply that it is assuming a position suitable to its weakness in the struggle for hegemony.

Today, in the United States and elsewhere, no one can save American imperialism from its inevitable decline. Rejuvenating this imperialism is only a daydream. Therefore, we must see through current superficial phenomena and perceive the essence of the matter. Otherwise, we shall deviate from objective reality, make erroneous judgments, and go astray.

A cursory reading of history tells us that America's democracy was full of vitality during the period of its establishment and growth. Compared with other capitalist countries, the United States has had the most complete democratic revolution and has one of the highest civilizations. The reason for this is the dogged militant spirit and rich creative power of the American people. This has had a great influence on political, economic, cultural, educational, scientific, and technological development, and is one of the reasons why the United States has long been the most advanced capitalist country. Although the economic and political system continues to serve the monopolistic bourgeoisie, there is still much of value which we can study to our benefit. For example, we can learn a great deal from America's legal system. Furthermore, the bourgeois-democratic political system is so well developed that there has never been a dictatorship or a coup d'etat. We should give serious thought to the reasons for this.

According to the U.S. state system, the bourgeoisie may replace their agent, the president, if he fails to live up to its expectations. The proletariat cannot do this in our socialist state, even though it is supposed to enjoy even greater democracy. Should we not ponder this? And one could give many other examples. Our socialist democracy is still full of vitality; it can be nourished through our learning from the American experience. I do not hesitate to say that inheriting the fruits of the advanced thinking of mankind does not shame but actually glorifies communism.

As a product of history, the United States surely has numerous achievements to its credit which reflect the progress of mankind. However, this in no way alters America's imperialistic character. Many of our young people were born after liberation and even after the war to resist the Americans in Korea. They have not shed blood fighting U.S. imperialism. They do not see that there are still people in other parts of the world who are shedding blood resisting U.S. imperialism. Perhaps they might have heard these things but have forgotten. . . . Of course, I do not mean to oppose friendship between the American and Chinese peoples or to oppose the general line of our foreign policy.

But some people, when they talk about friendship between our two peoples and allying with the Americans against the USSR, seem to want to silence others who would point out the good points of socialism and the Communist Party. When you do make these points the "democracy fighters" call you "a guard in a blue coat." They do not allow others to disclose the reactionary nature of capitalism and the evils of imperialism. If you do, you are accused of violating the friendship between the Chinese and American peoples and opposing our Party's general foreign policy line. It is a checkmate situation! What striking contrast there is between their love and their hatred! This is thought-provoking.

But we needn't worry! I may have said some unpleasant things about the Americans, but they have undergone a long testing and are quite intrepid. The United States has seen some of civilization's greatest achievements. Yet, it has passed the zenith of its prosperity and is rapidly going down the road of decline and decay. This eloquently demonstrates that the United States is not a "democratic paradise" and that Jimmy Carter is no foreign Buddha.

THE QUESTION OF TAIWAN

*Although the spirit of humanism pervades most of the writings in this
volume, when it comes to the question of Taiwan most of the groups come
across as full-blown nationalists. On February 22, for example, the Human
Rights League posted a three-page appeal "To Guarantee Peaceful Unification and Protect Our Country's Territorial Integrity." The League
called for "the Chinese government and Taiwan to construct a new,
united, peaceful, and democratic" China. (The League also strongly supported the current war effort against Vietnam.)* [1]

*On the subject of Taiwan, we have already seen the views of the Thaw
Society (Document 15). The two documents in this section are from* Enlightenment *and* Masses' Reference News. *The articles are rather unusual
in that they speak somewhat favorably of the Chiang family which has
ruled Taiwan. But they are typical in their lack of awareness that many
Taiwanese would prefer to be ruled neither by the Chinese Nationalists
nor by the Chinese Communists, but rather want independence and self-
government.*

DOCUMENT 59
SOLEMN STATEMENT
Issued by the Enlightenment Society

It is said that the responsible persons of the Beijing Communist Party Committee have suppressed democracy on the pretext that "a Taiwan broadcast openly asked the XX[2] journal to contact them." In view of these developments, the Enlightenment Society wishes to make the following statement. We believe that our views are in keeping with the spirit of the message which the Standing Committee of the National People's Congress sent to the compatriots on Taiwan on New Year's Day.

Taiwan Province is a part of the sacred territory of China. The compatriots on Taiwan are our kith and kin. The peaceful reunification of the motherland is our lofty aspiration as well as our sacred duty. This society is willing to serve as a bridge between the mainland and Taiwan Province Therefore:

(1) Should Mr. Chiang Ching-kuo or his representative, or people from other public organizations, wish to come to Beijing to discuss democracy, human rights, and the great cause of the peaceful reunification of the motherland, they will be warmly received by this society.

(2) Should Mr. Chiang Ching-kuo or his representative, or people from other public organizations, wish to invite members of this society to Taiwan to discuss democracy, human rights, and the great cause of the peaceful reunification of the motherland, this society will not refuse their invitation.

DOCUMENT 60
THE CHINESE NATIONALISTS RECONSIDERED
From *Masses' Reference News*

The establishment of formal diplomatic relations between China and the United States was announced on December 16 [1978]. As president [of the Republic of China on Taiwan], Mr. Chiang Ching-kuo issued a declaration the next day denouncing the United States for being perfidious and scrapping the [US-ROC mutual defense] treaty. He also reiterated that his stand on recovering the mainland remains unchanged. On December 18, as chairman of the Kuomintang (Nationalist Party), he convened the Party's Central Executive Committee. He also declared that he was opposed both to an independent Taiwan and to an alliance with the Soviet Union. This "opposition" has shown that Mr. Chiang Ching-kuo, very much like his late father, is still filled with national moral integrity. For this, Communist China should respond with applause to express its praise.

Suppose Mr. Chiang favored the independence of Taiwan or an alliance with the Soviet Union. We can imagine how much trouble that would cause Communist China. With one heart and one mind, Communist China is speeding up the realization of the Four Modernizations. It urgently requires a peaceful environment for a relatively long time. No matter what kind of subjective will it is based on, the fact that Mr. Chiang has forsaken both the independence of Taiwan and an alliance with the Soviet Union has more or less objectively given Communist China a great help. It seems that peace talks between the Kuomintang and the Chinese Communist Party are inevitable. It is only a matter of time. This is because Mr. Chiang actively laid one of the most important foundations for peace talks: He himself will not engage in the independence of Taiwan and an alliance with the Soviet Union, and he also opposes other people doing so.

It seems that Deng Xiaoping has made all the concessions he should make. What he cannot concede appear to be the two major issues of the official name of the country and the national capital. If Mr. Chiang treasures national unification and reunification of the people, and cooperates and gives concessions on the two issues, then he will not only receive warm applause from Hong Kong, Taiwan, and abroad, but also certainly from the mainland.[3]

THE CRACKDOWN

*Although the final demise of the democratic movement was not sig-
naled until Deng Xiaoping's speech of 16 March 1979, in fact dissidents
had been feeling pressure from the authorities almost from the beginning.
In this connection, it should be recalled that the democratic activists who
are the subject of this book were not the only political dissidents who had
been active. Toward the end of 1978 the government found it necessary
to arrest many leftists who were given the elastic designation "counterrevolutionaries." Such arrests took place from one end of the country to
the other.[1] But the first known democratic activist was not detained until
January 18. The case of Fu Yuehua has been recounted in the introduction. The dissidents' reaction to her arrest was immediate. First, two general statements were issued that asserted the need to protect diisidents'
rights (Documents 62 and 63). When these failed to effect Fu's release, two
more pointed analyses of her case were published (Documents 64 and 65).
Finally, however, the official rhetoric reached a crescendo, as did that of
the more militant dissidents (see Document 51, above, for Wei Jingsheng's
response).[2]*

*We begin this section with a few paragraphs that reveal that even be-
fore the crackdown was manifest, publishing unofficial journals was a task
fraught with difficulty (Document 61).*

DOCUMENT 61
THE PUBLICATIONS' DIFFICULTIES
From *Beijing Spring*

In order to search for truth and to exercise the democratic rights provided by the Constitution, many courageous young people have decided to test the law by publishing their own magazines. . . . Unfortunately, the printing houses have all said that without the approval of the higher officials they cannot accept any printing orders. Thus, these magazines have pursued the same path as once did Deng Xiaoping, Doctor of Mimeography.* But even mimeographing is as difficult as the passage over the snowy mountains and great plains [an apparent reference to the Long March, 1934–35]. Although their wages are no more than thirty to forty *yuan,* these young people manage to "squeeze out some money between their teeth" in order to buy the necessary materials. But sometimes even money is not enough. Printing supplies are under tight control and are always in short supply. If you buy a large quantity of paper, you must certify its use. Mimeograph machines are supplied only to official organizations and schools. Ink cannot be bought by ordinary citizens. (*Fertile Ground* was obliged to resort to printing the journal in red ink.)

The editorial boards of these magazines are hard to locate. Most of them are "phantom boards." The daring ones use their home addresses for subscribers and contributors to write to. The timid ones have to use some other way, for the plainclothesmen may already be keeping an eye on them.

All work has to be done after working hours. Who would dare be a minute late getting to work because he had been working on his magazine? One's superiors are all-powerful. At best, they make you feel uncomfortable; at worst, they could have your publication banned.

Alas, "democratic rights" are just words on paper. Without the material conditions and real legal protection, they are meaningless.[3]

---

* Deng Xiaoping was a student-worker in France between 1920 and 1925, at which time he edited the mimeographed Chinese Communist weekly *Chiguang* (Red Light). At the time he was whimsically given the "degree" of "Doctor of Mimeography."

DOCUMENT 62
JOINT STATEMENT

In order to implement and defend Articles 45 and 52 of the Constitution of the People's Republic of China,* our various mass societies and publications of Beijing hereby issue the following joint statement:

1. Various mass societies, newspapers, and journals run by the people are determined to persevere in carrying out a long-term struggle to realize socialist democracy and promote the development of social productive forces. The people's organizations and media should combat any speeches, comments, or actions that contravene the Constitution, beginning by making our position known in posters, and so forth, on Democracy Wall.

2. With regard to those citizens and members of various mass societies, newspapers, and journals who participated in certain activities within the constitutional framework and who were arrested and persecuted by organs of the dictatorship under pretexts or according to rumors and trumped-up charges, the mass societies, newspapers, and journals should jointly demand that judicial organs publicly give their reasons for the arrests. They should also ask that court hearings be held.

3. If citizens and members of various mass societies, newspapers, and journals are persecuted to death as a result of participating in activities within the constitutional framework, various mass societies, newspapers, and journals are duty bound to publicize it to win public support.

4. Various mass societies, newspapers, and journals will carry out long-term rescue work for the persecuted citizens and will ask to visit them in prison. We are duty bound to pay comfort visits to and offer material support to family members of the persecuted citizens.

We hope that citizens in all walks of life will support the above four points.

(Signed)   *April Fifth Forum*
Exploration
Masses' Reference News
Human Rights League
Enlightenment
People's Forum
Today

---

* Article 45 guarantees freedom of expression and other civil liberties. Article 52 provides for freedom in "scientific research, literary and artistic creation, and other cultural activities," all of which are to be "encouraged and assisted by the state."

Document 62 was published in *Exploration (Tansuo)*, no. 2, 29 January 1979; translation: JPRS 73421.

DOCUMENT 63
STATEMENT BY THE CHINA HUMAN RIGHTS LEAGUE

The China Human Rights League makes the following statement on a speech allegedy given by a responsible municipal Party committee person on behalf of the Beijing Municipal Party Committee, a speech dealing with material appearing on Democracy Wall:

A responsible municipal Party committee comrade made a speech referring to the posters on the streets. He said they commented on Chairman Mao either by singing his praises or maliciously attacking him. The China Human Rights League resolutely supports the right of the people to discuss Chairman Mao by name and to openly evaluate his strengths and weaknesses. We have done so in the past and will insist on doing so in the future. We will also emphasize exploring aspects that some leaders write off as insignificant. We must make as fair and objective an assessment of Chairman Mao as possible. We also have sufficient reason to demand the right to openly assess any state leader. We believe that this is not only the sacred and inviolable right of the citizens of the People's Republic of China (PRC) but also the sacred duty of every Chinese citizen wholeheartedly devoted to modernization. We also have sufficient reason to believe that assessing Chairman Mao's strengths and shortcomings scientifically rather than in a superstitious way is a prerequisite to realizing China's socialist modernization.

Referring in his speech to the notices posted on Democracy Wall, the responsible comrade called them "other publications." He cited *April Fifth Forum* and three issues of *Enlightenment* as examples. We think this responsible comrade has used very improper words. Can people's publications posted on Democracy Wall, like *April Fifth Forum* and *Enlightenment,* be anything other than openly published works? It is clearly specified in Article 45 of the PRC Constitution that the citizens have freedom of speech, freedom of correspondence, freedom of publication, freedom of assembly, freedom to form associations and hold parades, freedom to strike, and the right to argue things out thoroughly and put up posters. Since the notices on Democracy Wall are openly published and legitimate, why should they be called "underground publications"? Are steps being planned to ban them? If they are to be banned, please listen to reason. Bona fide Communists are open to reason and are above doing anything unreasonable.

In his speech, the responsible comrade accused people of setting up "underground organizations," making "petitions," inciting others to stage parades, and talking with foreigners. We think the accusations made by the responsible comrade on behalf of the responsible persons of the Beijing Municipal Party Committee are against the democratic spirit of the Constitution. We know that following the appearance of Democracy Wall, editorial departments of such magazines as *April Fifth Forum, Today, Fertile Ground, Masses' Reference News, Exploration,* and *Beijing Spring* have arisen along with such organizations as the Enlightenment Society and the China Human Rights League. The viewpoints of these organizations are all aired in an open rather than secret manner. The existence of these organizations is in line with the PRC Constitution. Why should they be called "underground organizations"? As far as the China Human Rights League is concerned, we will base ourselves on the sacred democratic rights vested in us by the Constitution—rights such as freedom of speech and the freedom to form a society. We will continue to speak out and to develop and expand our organizations. We also retain such sacred and inviolable democratic rights as holding parades and demonstrations bestowed on us by the Constitution. As we did before, we will act according to the will of the people. We will only uphold historical dialectics and historical materialism. Never will we simply follow the will of our superiors. Those superiors who do not act according to the democratic spirit of the Constitution or to the will of the people will naturally be rejected by the people.

Although we are "citizens of the world," we are first of all "citizens of China." We are not only zealous internationalists but also devoted patriots. We firmly believe that contact between the citizens of China and foreigners (whether friends or enemies) is normal. We believe that as long as murder, arson, encroachment on human rights, criminal activities, or involvement in espionage activities are not involved, any open form of civilian contact between Chinese and foreigners should receive government support. Such a government will naturally win the support of the people and the praise of the world. History shows that such a government is naturally powerful and those blessed with such a government are naturally happy and free people.

If the leadership uses the appearance of our city as an excuse to ban Democracy Wall, we find such leadership unworthy of respect. It is insincere to say the very least. If the leadership of the Municipal Party Committee is sincere, we suggest that it order the allocation of funds to build a Democracy Wall that will blend in well with the city's appearance.

In his speech, the responsible comrade said bad people were mixed in with the good people who put up posters. He said a solution should be sought by distinguishing between enemies and friends. We believe that not only is it likely that bad people have put up posters but they have possibly also found their way into the Party Central Committee Political Bureau and to the side of Chairman Mao (as in the past), or to the side of

Chairman Hua (now) and into the Municipal Party Committee. However, bad people are bad, but this is not because they put up posters on Democracy Wall. Similarly, Lin Biao and the Gang of Four were bad, but not because they found their way into the Political Bureau and to the side of Chairman Mao. We can more reasonably claim that Lin Biao did bad things because there was no Democracy Wall then and because he had not joined the people in putting up posters (even if he had done so to spy on them). Instead, he had become involved with a plot called Project "571" [coup d'etat attempt in 1971]. Putting up posters in itself is not only legal but glorious. It shows that we are exercising a right to which we are entitled as citizens. It also indicates in many cases that putting up posters is fulfilling a citizen's glorious obligations—such as showing real courage in being concerned over the future of the motherland and the destiny of the nation and over the happiness or unhappiness of the whole body of citizens.

As thoroughgoing materialists or dialectical materialists, we of the China Human Rights League are above efforts to conceal our own viewpoints. We adhere to the view that publication of our viewpoints is not only a sacred and inviolable right but also a glorious obligation not to be vilified. We do not hesitate to sacrifice our own blood and lives to safeguard such rights and fulfill such obligations. Finally, the China Human Rights League will never negate any good deeds that any leader does. Nor will we ever give up the right to criticize any bad deeds committed by any leader.

The China Human Rights League[4]

DOCUMENT 64
FU YUEHUA'S ARREST: AN INVESTIGATIVE REPORT
By Representatives of the Various Publications

Place: Guang-an-men Police Station [Beijing].
Interview of: Officer in charge.
Time: 8 February 1979, 11:25–11:50 A.M.

Q: Ah, has Fu Yuehua been taken away from here?

A: Yes, police headquarters wanted to question her. She was removed on their authority.

Q: What is the problem? Can you tell us what she is supposed to have done?

A: We are not sure ourselves, and neither is the [Xuanwu] district office. So we really have no business discussing it. We have no right to discuss a case when we are unclear about the underlying considerations.

Q: Was there an arrest warrant?

A: We are not really sure. As far as we know she was brought in for questioning. The police from headquarters came, and we led [them to her].

Q: Was an arrest warrant shown? Was the reason for the arrest given at the time?

A: We are not sure.

Q: We would like to know about the procedures used in her arrest.

A: You say you put out people's publications. Judging from what we hear from our superiors, we are not clear that you are legitimate. If you want to interview public security officials, you need a press card or letter of introduction. You people set up your own organizations, so I can hardly deal with you.

Let me explain. If you were to come as representatives of the masses, we would welcome you. But you are coming as "reporters" with no letter of intent or press card, and we know nothing about your organization.

This person Fu Yuehua was disturbing the peace and disrupting social order. The Public Security Bureau has the right to take her in [literally, "give her shelter"] for questioning. At an appropriate time a public announcement will be made. As to what aspect of it will be announced and under what circumstances, I suggest that you trust that the people's government and the public security organs will deal with this problem correctly. Do not come and interfere. Okay?

Q: Has Fu Yuehua been arrested?

A: It is not an arrest. She is being questioned. She is being provided shelter for questioning.

Q: Is she being "provided shelter" because she "disturbed the peace"? Can you give us a definite answer on this?

A: We are in the middle of questioning her now. When necessary, we will state the relevant aspects of the case. It is not necessary to discuss it now.

Q: You think it is not necessary to talk about it now? Fu Yuehua lives in Beijing and has a home. Why is it necessary for you to "provide shelter" for her? In fact, she was taken from her home. What kind of "shelter" are you providing her! She is no vagrant. Clearly you have detained her.

Were there any other [arrest] procedures?

A: Of course we have our department's procedures.

Q: Was [the procedure in this case] in accord with the spirit of the Constitution?

A: There is no need to keep asking about this. If we did arrest her, I did not make the decision personally. We have superiors, you know!

Q: So you are saying that she was taken into custody by the Xuanwu District Office?

A: Yes, we did.

My remarks have been carefully considered.

When, in the future, it is appropriate to discuss all of this, we will do so.

Q: Can you give us a definite time?

A: No definite time. When it is necessary to do so.

If you have come here as part of an organization, I can refuse to receive you. Furthermore, although some questions can be discussed, some cannot because they are off limits. Now we have to keep within limits, and I hope that you will not ask any more questions.

Q: Is there a specific law that provides for "giving shelter"?

A: We have taken Fu Yuehua into custody for questioning. Our public security organ has the authority to do this. You should understand that the decision was not made by individuals. The detention of Fu is absolutely legal.[5]

DOCUMENT 65
IS FU'S DETENTION LEGAL?
From *Exploration*

On February 8 a delegation of reporters from various journals and civic organizations in Beijing visited the Xuanwu police precinct office to acquaint themselves with the actual situation in the Fu Yuehua case. During his meeting with the delegation a . . . responsible person was most discourteous toward the reporters of mass organizations and nongovernmental journals. He answered the reporters' questions vaguely . . . .

All the *Exploration* editorial department comrades believe that this kind of attitude not only shows an enmity against the spirit of the Constitution but also contempt for the masses. This is a shameless provocation against democracy. It is therefore necessary to state the following:

1. Even after Chairman Hua and Vice-Chairman Deng had called for democratization, the Xuanwu Police Bureau nonetheless detained a comrade who was active in the democratic movement. The masses have been told: "It is not necessary for you to understand the reasons for the detention." First, this represents a hostile attitude toward the democracy movement. Secondly, this represents a stand that runs counter to the spirit of giving full play to democracy as promoted by Chairman Hua and Vice-Chairman Deng. Thirdly, this represents a line directly opposite to bringing democracy into full play and promoting the Four Modernizations as adopted by the Third Plenum of the Eleventh CCP Central Committee.

2. The Xuanwu Police Bureau has said that a so-called "internal procedure" had been followed [in the Fu case] and that its use has been escalated. However, even the head of the Guangan police substation does not clearly understand the "internal procedure." Since this procedure is so internal that even a head of a police substation does not know anything about it, what then is the essential difference between applying this procedure to arrest people and wantonly arresting people? Does it mean that one may wantonly arrest people by following an "internal procedure"? Is this a normal legal procedure?

3. When we did our reporting work at the Guangan Police Substation on February 8, the head of the substation still did not know the actual reason for the arrest of Fu Yuehua. On the afternoon of that day the Xuanwu police precinct office brazenly fabricated a case of "taking into custody for screening"! . . . There is no prescription empowering a policeman to go to the person concerned and take him or her into custody. We would like to ask responsible people of the law enforcement organs who have a "thorough understanding of the law" to answer two questions: Which legal article mentions "taking into custody for screening" and what

is the basis for going to the home of a citizen to take him or her into indefinite custody?

4. A responsible person by the name of Zhang of the Xuanwu police precinct office announced that Fu Yuehua had committed the crime of disrupting public order. He declined to give an explanation. If a public security bureau can arrest people without evidence and decline to explain the reasons for such arrests, then we would like to ask: Is the Public Security Bureau a dictatorship enforcement tool *of* the proletarian masses or a tool to enforce dictatorship *over* the proletarian masses?

Thus, we believe the unreasonable arrest of Fu Yuehua carried out by the Xuanwu Police Bureau is a deliberate disruption of the legal system. Higher level judicial organs should attach importance to this serious disruption of the legal system carried out by a law enforcement organ. We demand that the Beijing Municipal Court and Procuratorate deal with this case, immediately release Fu Yuehua, . . . and take action against those criminal elements in this incident.[6]

DOCUMENT 66
RESPONSIBILITY FOR THE TROUBLE
From *Exploration*

On February 12 [1979] a *People's Daily* commentator's article stated: "We should impose legal sanctions on some individuals who had ulterior motives in deliberately creating trouble and causing serious consequences." In the same paragraph, the commentator also told us: "There is a small number of people who neither innocently suffered from the persecution of the Gang of Four nor are jobless. However, they have deliberately created excuses, unscrupulously left their production posts, and put unreasonable demands on the state to achieve their personal aims." In the same article, the commentator also specifically told us that those involved are only "a very small number of people in some individual localities who have instigated people to make trouble by making use of the democracy that the Party and state have brought into play."

Thus, we can clearly understand that what the comrade commentator was referring to was the democracy movement or poster movement which is currently being launched with great vigor and vitality in various major cities in China. Moreover, according to the commentator's views, this movement has been taken advantage of by a very small number of people. Their aim, of course, is to sabotage public order, the Four Modernizations, and ultimately the well-being of the people.

How wonderfully has this series of labels been concocted, and how full of internal logic they are! However, we regret to say that the logic is not much different from the logic of the Gang of Four. You can find similar wording in an April 1976 issue of *People's Daily*. The charges then were that a very small number of *provocateurs* had put forward unreasonable demands and sabotaged public order, deliberately created trouble, and caused serious consequences to achieve their personal aims. The only difference is that there is no mention today that "the spearhead was pointed at the Party Central Committee and Chairman Mao." This is probably because this commentator realizes that the masses regard his Great Helmsman as stinking.

The masses are dissatisfied because state leaders have won the people's trust by fraud and have not tried to solve their problems. The country has encountered difficulties because leaders have not tried to carry out beneficial construction or listen to people's views even though they control state power. If "socialist order" is only intended to insure the power of a small number to suppress the people and ignore their demands rather than insure their democratic rights, then there is no point in the people upholding this kind of "order," because upholding it means upholding the people's enemy.

Do the people have the right to express their will by "holding processions and assemblies, forming associations, striking, publishing, and speaking up," and by "speaking out freely, airing their views fully, holding great debates, and writing big-character posters"? Of course they have. The Constitution expressly stipulates that the people have these rights. So what the people are doing is merely performing their rightful duties. Constitutional clauses, such as "take care of and protect public property . . ." and so on, deal directly with the interests of the people themselves. These interests need to be protected by the people by exercising the above-mentioned rights. Nevertheless, the *People's Daily* commentator believes these clauses by themselves protect the rights of the people.

I would like to ask the comrade commentator what things he thinks the Constitution insures? Should the state submit to the will of the people or should the people submit to the will of a small number of people who control state power? What is the overall situation? The people's interests and the will of the people constitute the overall situation. If part of the people cannot represent the entire people, then who can represent the people? Is it you people who are always ready to suppress the people and do away with their democratic rights?

What has caused all the discontent? It is the reactionary policies of the Gang of Four and the current antipeople policies you want to continue. It is those privileged people who have, through their incorrect policies, forced people to live in hunger and cold and to march down dead ends. It is those executioners who have not hesitated to sacrifice the people's lives and cause the economy to slump while fighting among themselves for power and personal interests. They thought that it was their right no matter what evil deeds they might have done. The people have no right to sabotage the "order" involved in their doing evil things. They also thought that although they have not done any good deeds for the people and are not welcomed by them, they will be able to maintain their rule over the people as long as they maintain order.

Yes, at that time they were correct in their thinking; however, they are wrong today. People will no longer believe their lies. Our view is that we must first eliminate those bureaucrats and masters and realize people's democracy before it is possible to realize the socialist Four Modernizations.[7]

POETRY OF THE DEMOCRATIC MOVEMENT

The movement for democracy, like most great events in Chinese history, generated much poetry. While many men and women took up their pens, one poet towered above the others: Huang Xiang. Huang was born in Hunan Province. At the age of eleven, after receiving only four years of education, he became a worker. He earned his living by chopping wood and working as a porter. Eventually he moved to Guiyang in Guizhou Province, where he became involved in the democratic movement.

We reproduce here three of his poems often cited by other writers. These poems were actually written earlier than most of the other documents in this volume and bear the dates 1976, 1969, and 1976–77, respectively. However, they are believed not to have appeared in any publication will until October 1978 and thus are associated with the democratic movement of 1978–79.

Following each poem is a commentary by Li Jiahua.[1]

DOCUMENT 67
NO, YOU HAVE NOT DIED
By Huang Xiang

Dedicated to the heroic day of 5 April 1976*

Why do you hide your face and cry, Tian-an-men?
Why do your whitened lips shiver, Tian-an-men?
Why, why is your bosom bleeding, Tian-an-men?
Does your body shake violently? Answer me, Tian-an-men.

From the burning flames and lava in your heart.
From the shouts and angry cries that have shaken the sky and the universe.
Do you mean to say you are dying silently just like this,
Do you mean to say you are closing your phobic eyes?
No, you have not died. And you shall not die.
The entire world has seen the angry expression on your face.
In front of bayonets and rifle butts,
You were not scared away.
You were abused and trampled by animals while not having any weapons.
You held fast without giving in.
You heroically lay in the pool of blood.

No, you have not died. And you shall not die.
Your flag was not blown away, nor did it fall.
Your signs that were torn and destroyed did not lower their fiery
                    red wings.
Your fliers and poems whose throats have been choked
Are still voicing scratchy calls.
Your fist that is as heavy as a hammer
Still challenges and fights in silence.
Your body that has been wounded beyond recognition
Still cries *"j'accuse."*
Death does not belong to you.
You are invincible.
Yes.
I believe freedom will not stop breathing.
Truth will not be tongue-tied.
There will be a day

---

* The dedication refers to the demonstrations in Beijing on the date indicated. The people were demonstrating primarily against the leftists. The event is now seen as the harbinger of China's contemporary democratic movement. See the Introduction.

When you will rise again from the pool of blood.
You will be tenfold, even a hundredfold and a thousandfold stronger
        than today.
You will again raise the flag of awareness.
Win victory over that which once pointed its gun at you,
To announce loudly and majestically the rights of man.

COMMENTARY BY LI JIAHUA

In 1976 dark clouds filled the sky over China, and the muffled rumbling of thunder could be heard from afar. People lived in turmoil and felt uneasy, disturbed. They looked up to the sky and, in their anxiety, beseeched: "Violent storm, please come quickly!"

On April 4 [1976] nearly a million people, sad and indignant, dashed through a blockade set up by the Gang of Four and assembled at Tian-an-men Square. Of their own accord, they held a "grand offering by the people to our respected and beloved Premier Zhou [Enlai]." The square was an ocean of humanity and a mountain of wreaths. Numerous poems and spirited speeches expressed the admiration and respect for Premier Zhou felt by hundreds of millions of people, as well as their hatred for the Gang of Four.

However, their just action met with interference and disruption! The beautiful wreaths offered to Premier Zhou were removed, and the poems and songs the people had written in tears were torn away. . . . What was the source of this interference? The Chinese people clearly know the answer.

The lion in the path must be driven off; the stubborn dragon barring the way must be kicked away! To remove this big obstacle, on April 5 the people put up appeals in every street and lane of the ancient city and distributed protest leaflets. Defying death and violence, they stood on the base of the monument and made heroic speeches. They shouted: "Gone for good is Qin Shi Huang's feudal society!" . . . This was a violation of the "sacred taboo" and led to a bloodbath.

In the awe-inspiring melee that ensued, the people used their firmly clenched fists against the loaded guns of the police and their tired and blood-spattered bodies against the glinting knives. When light came with the dim light of the moon, they violently knocked at the palace gate and shouted with their weak and choked voices: "Give me back my youth! Give me back my human rights!" They exposed the very essence of the contradiction of the age and voiced the cause of the people's misery. They punctured the fetishes of the East which had benumbed the broad masses and poured out what everyone had in his heart but dared not express. Just for this they became victims of a bloody massacre and, with hatred lingering in their hearts, they fell below the clean white memorial and in front of the tightly closed palace gate.

Following these people's glorious deaths, the banner of awakening was hoisted in everyone's mind! This brand new banner then began to spread, expand, and pervade. It solemnly told all Chinese people: "In China, where Jiang Qing and her cohorts are running amuck, people cannot enjoy even the most rudimentary form of democracy and human rights. The Constitution merely remains a piece of paper!"

The bloodshed on April 5 was a revolutionary movement against autocracy and dictatorship. It was also a case of the counterrevolutionaries' suppressing the revolutionaries and darkness overshadowing brightness. It was the ugliest performance by autocrats that has been exposed in twentieth-century China. It was like the final refulgence of a setting sun for the patriarchal and dictatorial systems which had lasted thousands of years.

The April Fifth Movement is the continuation, intensification, and development of the May Fourth [1919] Movement. If the May Fourth Movement is regarded as a banner to oppose imperialism and feudalism, then the April Fifth Movement can be called a movement against autocracy and dictatorship and for basic human rights and democracy in socialist China.

The April Fifth Movement is a movement of socialist mass democracy and the initial attempt by people in their quest for basic human rights. Although this attempt was brutally suppressed by the notorious Gang of Four, it nevertheless raised a banner to lead the 800 million people in a socialist republic to attack the remnants of autocracy, and it served openly as a serious face-to-face challenge to all perverse actions that are against the people's will and defile public opinion. The April Fifth Movement proclaimed: The broad masses of Chinese people, who have been seriously hoodwinked and fooled, have awakened with surprising speed!

> *There will be a day*
> *When you will rise again from the pool of blood.*
>   (From "No, You Have Not Died")

The Gang of Four have been smashed! The former verdict of the bloody affair at Tian-an-men has been reversed. The ice which locked China's great earth is now slowly and quietly melting. However, the melting is too slow. In order to speed up the melting, we put up the *Enlightenment* poster on 11 October 1978. On the following morning I visited Tian-an-men Square. Under the brilliant clear sky, the place where rivers of blood had flowed in the past was now very quiet. Here I looked around, recalled the past, and listened carefully. Suddenly I heard the voice of those who, two years before, had died demanding vengeance. A loud call thundered out at Tian-an-men.

> *Arise, victims of injustice and humiliation.*
> *Today is the day of your rehabilitation.*
> *Let us rally together once again!*
> *Hold the banner still higher.*

DOCUMENT 68
SONG OF THE TORCH
By Huang Xiang

The poets say that my poems belong to the future,
In the anthologies of another century.

I

Moving at the edge of the sky far, far away,
Swinging on the expansiveness of the sky of dark blue.
It is a shining troop,
It is a silently flowing river of fire.
It lights up the ever-drawn curtains,
Flowing into those shining doorscreens that reflect each other.
Gathering on every street . . . .
Filled by the night . . . .
Fluctuating in each pair of heated irises,
Burning the charred and thirsty life.
Ah, torch, you extend a thousand shining hands,
Open up ten thousand shining throats.
Awaken the great road, awaken the square,
Awaken all people of the entire generation.
Those who have been forgotten by time and those who have forgotten
        about time,
Those whose thoughts are as dull as the machine.
Those who are emotionless as if frozen like ice,
Those whose blood is cold as ice,
Those on whose faces are written anger and silence,
Those on the corner of whose mouths are carved unconsciousness
        and hopelessness.
Those whose lives are as prosperous as spring,
Those who are filled with youthful activity.
And those whose footsteps are sluggish and whose feet are soiled and
        full of mud,
And those shadows that gather in gangs and roam about.
Together with those eyes covered by sand,
And the soiled hearts filled with soot.
Ah, torch, you use the shining finger
To knock open the dark rooms of each soul.
Let strangers understand each other,
Let those who are estranged become reconciled.
Let those who hate become friendly,

Let the suspicious never doubt anymore.
Let the hated listen to the voice of goodness,
Let the ugly see beauty.
Let the dirty become pure and clean,
Let the black become white.
You have brought a world ruled by light and heat,
All is so clear and bright, high and far, sacred and pure.
In the irresistible and magical ring of your fire,
Mankind is allowed to experience the trembling of eudaemonia.

II

A troop of millions of torches flows,
Like an upturned melting furnace, like a burning sea.
The light of the fire illuminates the thousand-year-old giant,
That is the Master of masters, the King of kings.
They are a group of idols, the disgrace of mankind.
The cause and result of all disaster.
Thus, under the shining light of the fire that penetrates the sky,
People for the first time have voiced the questions of man.
Why can they control the will of millions,
Why can they manipulate the life and death of the populace?
Why do we have to show respect and worship the idol,
Let superstition imprison our living will, emotion, and thoughts?
Do you really mean to say the idol is more beautiful than poetry
          and living?
Do you really mean to say the idol can cover up the glow of truth
          and science?
Do you really mean to say the idol can suffocate the thirst for love,
The cry of the heart?
Do you really mean to say the idol is the universe and the entirety
          of living?
Let the people restore the dignity of man,
Let living again become living.
Let music and kindness make up the souls of mankind,
Let beauty and nature again belong to man.
Let each pair of eyes become a poem,
Let every person dismantle the barrier to his feelings.
Let respect and glory be buried in the dust of time,
Let time and man be forever great.
Let the living be true,
Let living be the cause of being true.
Let youth experience the quiver of sweetness and beauty,
Let the latter years of life be as peaceful and quiet as dusk.

Let us not all be on guard against each other,
Let everyone be regarded as a human being.

In the darkest of night we forget not the dawn,
But long for its light all the more.

Let our words blaze forth to the world:
Life must be arranged anew.

III

Sound the great gong of truth, the torch is saying.
Light the bright lamp of science, the torch is saying.
Return to mankind a human face, the torch is saying.
Death to violence and dictatorship, the torch is saying.
Eradicate those temples of the mind
Where idols are worshiped, the torch is saying.
Replace them with glorious, modern palaces, the torch is saying.

Such upright and fiery calls,
Such holy and fiery beliefs,
Such heavy and fiery breaths,
Such red-hot and fiery language.
The fiery troops have expanded,
The river of fire has flooded,
The furnace of fire has become white hot,
The sea of fire has boiled.
The flaming hands have pulled up the curtain of the night,
The light of fire is master of the entire universe.
Man is baptized in fire,
The earth is remolded by fire.
The old is being incinerated,
A new and crying one is jumping out from the cradle.

13 August 1969 10 A.M.   Thinking in doubt.
15 August 1969.   Written in streaming tears.

COMMENTARY BY LI JIAHUA

In the darkest of night we forget not the dawn,
But long for its light all the more.

A small torch fire is gradually growing bigger before my eyes . . .
Oh! The big far-reaching fire!

From the crackling flames of this burning torch,
From the very heart of the burning fire turning white,
I see a kernel breaking out of its shell, responding to the calls,
And a green sprout growing despite the fire!

The "Song of the Torch" expresses the author's imagination. It is like an imaginary revolution and at the same time the last revolution in human society. It is a product of the author's lofty spiritual world and reveals his beautiful inner thoughts.

In this revolution all human sufferings will be eliminated, and the dews of brilliance, which are real, good, and beautiful, will permeate every part of the world as well as all aspects of people's spiritual life. There will not be any "highest" or "lowest" in the world, because the highest will be burned down, while the lowest will be held high by the mighty hand of revolution. The fire will eliminate all the vulgar practices and rotten ideas of the people and give them new aspects of life, so that every person will become an indispensable component of society. It will give full scope to everyone's ability and wisdom and bring great glory to society. The fire will enable people to completely shake off brutality and hatred, and there will be no quarrel among them. They will share the same views and principles and have identical ideals. In lofty and harmonious unity, they will produce, live, think, invent, pioneer, and explore together. With these dynamic forces they will enrich their own social life and cultivate their big earth.

In this revolution the banner of human dignity will be planted once again. The people will no longer suffer from unbridled enslavement and ravages, but with their personal traits and styles free of interference they will take their place independently in society. [words illegible] Life will be worth living, because it is beautiful. [several lines illegible] Everyone with his youthfulness will cheer in "pleasant surprise" in the majestic bosom of nature and, in the face of love, taste that "sweetness" which touches people's hearts. Old people will no longer wear the torn clothing which does not fit their children or worry about having no one to care for them when they are alone and helpless. Their last days will be as tranquil as the surface of an autumn lake and as beautiful as a summer evening. There will be no spies or special agents, beggars, greedy misers, or millionaires. All around them will be beautiful, good, and great people.

In this revolution, those who have passed their time aimlessly now realize the value of time and therefore seize the opportunity to study, work, and create; those whose way of thinking has been as mechanical as a machine are now wide awake and able to see the huge world, human feelings—both vigorous and relaxed—and wings exploring the sky. Those "whose feeling is as solid as a block of ice and whose blood is as cold as water" will be stirred mentally and physically by the burning flames, and the blood will suddenly begin to circulate. Those with "sullen and long faces" will shout at the approach of fire. Those "who are dejected, with despair showing at the corners of their mouths," will find renewed vigor because of the fire. Those who are like "shadows loafing around in groups" will be guided by the fire to their path of advancement. Those "whose eyes are blinded by dust" will wash away their past falsehoods and ignorance as demanded by the fire. In this unprecedented big fire, strangers become intimate friends, while those who have parted company because of prejudice are now signaling for mutual understanding. In the fire I see "those who were distant from one another" become close again, while hatred which has lasted for generations is now changed to closeness. Those who were suspicious and jealous need doubt no more. In this fire "the hated ones" are now loved, while the "ugly" welcomes the arrival of the beautiful and true. The "dirty ones" have washed away yesterday's dirt, and the darkness in the heart has given way to brightness.

The revolution of fire once again sounds the "bell of truth," which has remained silent for thousands of years; it lights the "lamp of science" which serves to advance human welfare. It returns to people what they have lost, and under the impetus of fire everyone's beautiful natural character, rich hypothesis, and colorful imagination in various forms are for the first time won back from the hands of violence. The "temples in the heart for offerings to gods" are now promptly destroyed, while the gorgeous palace of truth is being meticulously "built" and "carved."

This is the sunrise of human spirit and wisdom and a revolution by mankind which is now fully awake. This is the final revolution. Decadent beliefs and decadent civilization, along with old prejudices and fetishes, are totally "disintegrated"; and during the disintegration of the old world a new one, like a baby full of vitality, is born. [many lines illegible]

This portrayal of the future society by the poet is based on his [two words illegible] and strong conviction in the future of communism. Similar portrayals can be seen in Thomas Moore's "Utopia," Campanella's "City of the Sun," Owen's "A New View of Society," and other similar works. The philosophy of these authors has in different forms and varying degrees given impetus to the society of yesterday and today. It is true that a world of lofty ideals may not be realized in one historical period. However, this is certainly a reflection of the poet's conscience and conviction and the hope of mankind—a mankind full of inquisitive and progressive spirit—for the future.

DOCUMENT 69
THE GOD OF FIRE
By Huang Xiang

Millions of planets are whirling beneath your feet,
Many skies and suns are engulfed in your body.
Ah, God of Fire, I know you have already approached me,
In the darkness of space I quietly listen to the sound of your footsteps.
My heart fondly listens with happiness and surprise,
You have come from the deep and dark of the universe.
From behind the lost and countless number of years,
From the end of endless millennia of time.
You reveal the black veil that space has refused to unveil for a long time,
You reveal your bright toes in front of my eyes.
You move about slowly, you sway slightly back and forth,
You unreservedly expose your naked body to me.

Your hot breath is boundless,
Your hot golden rays shine through the sky.
Your thunderous footsteps shake the world,
The clouds in the sky are your expansive wings.
The dew covering the land is your tears of happiness,
You stir up layers and layers of light waves, rolling up fiery flames.
Invisibly you strike upon the patient and waiting hearts,
You wear the corona of dawn and you show the glow of dawn on
          your cheeks.
Your form is the reality of dreamy shadows, the dreamy shadows
          of reality.
You have come, consolidating the light and glow of the sun, moon,
          and stars.
You gather the power of lightning and thunder of all the skies,
In the upper reaches of the sky, you wave your shining arms.
Sprinkling boundless rain of fire.
Allowing all living beings to cleanse themselves in the heavenly fire.
Burning the world of irrational and erroneous structures to ashes.

Ah, God of Fire, the unknown that is known to all,
Where you have descended, people rejoice.
Countless hearts are filled with your milky light.
You roll up the layers and layers of curtains covering the hearts,
And stroll toward the deep and far corners of people's souls.
You shake the inner halls of superstition

And the irrational and erroneous deep inner palaces.
You sweep away the remnants of broken beliefs.
Ah, you are Prometheus, you are the liberator,
You liberated yourself
And also broke the spiritual chains that bound the world.
Where the chains are loose, the old scars
Are allowed to be seen by those who do not wish to be liberated.
Where the chains are tight, let those who wish to be liberated

Be born again in a quiver of happiness.
You have come, as a flood of light, a massive wave of heat,
You have drowned the sandy dams
Of yesterday's conservative and narrow emotions.
Let strangers become friends.
Let the separated open up the door to understanding.
Let those who are hostile
Build a bridge of generosity, thanks to you.
May mutual suspicion end,
And the ancient chasm be closed.

You belong to all time,
You transcend the planets,
All peoples know your language.
Each faith and religion understands what you say.
From those who are insincere and flatter you
I see you turn away in disgust.
To those who worship you, I see you humbly blush.
To those who fear you and rely on you,
You raise your proud head.
To those who are dying and still resisting you,
They humiliate themselves under your fearsome stare.
You have found a place in society for those who have been bullied.
For those who have been kept from the truth
You have opened the door to knowledge.
You have broken down the well-guarded gate
That locked people behind walls of ignorance and prejudice.
You have removed the pathological veil
From those who resist freedom more than tyranny.
Those cheated and thus themselves untrustworthy
Have regained their trustworthiness because of you.
The hopeless have regained hope
And courage because of you.
Thanks to you, science is no longer sacrificed

Before the altar of tyranny.
Wisdom no longer must breathe heavily
And kneel at the feet of violence.
The will of a person can no longer represent the will of all.
Ah, God of Fire, Master of Time, Master of Space,
You are the personification of universal law,
You are the will of justice.
You are yourself the standard of truth and falsehood,
You are the measure of right and wrong.
Ah, sitting at the seat of the chief judge in the tribunal of practice,
You investigate and give judgment to all truth.
The idol of the past is now tied to the pillar of torture by fire.
Among confusion and misconception of ancient times,
The voice of doubt has now been excited.
Your solemn judgment resounds throughout the universe.
"All that have been upturned are now upturned anew."
Ah, God of Fire, God of Fire,
You have come, come, come.
You have ignited throughout the sky to save the world.
Your glory and a new mankind have fused together.
You shall live in everlasting life, you shall die in that which never dies.
You are the gift of time, you are the pride of the world.
From your name
Man doubts all that which is known,
Gains unknown explanation.

COMMENTARY BY LI JIAHUA

"Poet, you are the first to hear the distant rumbling of thunder, the first to hear the crying in the dark, the first to see the coming brightness" (From my *New Art of Poetry*).

The poem "God of Fire" symbolizes light, and "The World Bathed in Storm" [not included in the present volume] the whirlwind. The former shows the ardent hope and pursuit of our age for brightness, while the latter represents an urgent call for change—these are the political and philosophical contents of the two poems which the author wanted to expound. Here we will talk mainly about the political aspect.

When Lin Biao and the Gang of Four were on their rampage and autocratic darkness was choking the people, society was in a turmoil and people lived in fear. All young people felt that this was the end of everything. However, even in these dark hours of despair, when the people's appeals met with no response from any quarter, the poet had a strong faith in truth and was full of hope for the future. He fought, resisted, pondered time and again, and lived on unyieldingly in the firm belief that truth and science would ultimately triumph over falsehood and fetishes. He also firmly believed that the people would certainly rise to "kick tyranny and totalitarianism out of the world," thus bringing brightness to the dark world and to the passive way of living.

As Ah Qing wrote in *On Poetry*: "The predictions of the poet are utterly simple and unaffected—what he says will come, will come. He does not conceal the conviction that the decadent will soon perish; that the end of night means dawn; and that the world cannot be perpetually dark as long as the earth keeps on rotating."

Finally, that day came. In October 1976 the Party Central Committee headed by Chairman Hua, representing the will of the broad masses and responding to their demand, smashed with one blow the Gang of Four—who had committed crimes and caused disorder—and set right the course for the development of history.

Following the arraignment of the Gang of Four before the tribunal of history, the poet heard a call of the new epoch. He said with emotion: "I know you are approaching. I am quietly listening. . . ." True, "I can hear the noise and see the shadow." "Oh, our long-expected new epoch, your arrival is so late and yet so sudden!" "Huge crowds are hailing you on the spot of your arrival!" The darkness of yesterday has become brightness, thanks to you. Yesterday's life of despair is now gladdened by you; those who have died or are still living in disgrace because of injustice have been rehabilitated, and the wounds of poisoned hearts have been healed by you! To build a bright China and to champion the cause of innocent children, you have resolutely "shaken up the palace of fetishes and falsehood and swept away the broken fences of these discredited beliefs." "Those who have been estranged from one another" are led by you to "open the door of understanding." Those children who were sworn enemies because of their childishness and prejudice have now become close friends and brothers because of your kind and warm call. "Those who were pushed around" have been guided by you "to the seats of democracy among the masses." For "those who were driven by suffering and the necessities of life to knock at the door of truth, violently and indignantly," you have "opened the door of wisdom." For those who are brave in advancing and scaling heights, you have provided a ladder of science. For those who are brave in crossing deep and wide gullies, you have built a network of bridges . . . Because of your arrival, "those who have been de-

ceived into believing falsehoods are now retracting these beliefs." Those
who have long been afraid to express their hopes are now beginning to
express them bravely because of you. . . .

Oh, you have come! Today "you are sitting on the bench of practice
in a tribunal" and are "conducting strict tests and passing judgments on
all fabricated or disguised 'truths.' " You are "tying the idols to burning
pillars of torture" and letting them be consumed in flames. You are "setting right all that has been turned upside down." In the large hall of justice of practice, I see you

"Pulling down those who stand highest,
Lifting up those who have been pushed down to the bottom,
Pushing down those who are deep-rooted, and
Steadying those who have lost their support."

I have also personally seen you promptly raising your mighty hand of
wisdom to help the miserable people of this age by

"Tolling the great bell that has long remained silent,
Clearing the singing throats choked by tears,
Blowing out the flickering light on divine altars,
Removing the eye bandages used to keep people from seeing,
Pushing open the locked iron gates one by one, and
Kicking away the barricades used to keep souls apart."

So you have come! You have come! You have come holding high the
big banner of practice. You have come holding high our long-expected
great banner of democracy. You have given us strength and courage,
warmth and confidence. You are leading us to smash the "divine seats outside our bodies and the altars inside our hearts." You direct us to pull
down the gilded idols from their pedestals and "kick tyranny and totalitarianism out of the world."

You are a liberated force—a force of the Chinese people which has
long been suppressed. You are the voice loudly calling for emancipation; a
"pleasant surprise" in suddenly bringing brightness after a long dark
night; the ancient deluge of democracy and freedom which no disintegra-
ting autocracies can resist; and a lofty faith of the new generation emancipated from the fetters of feudal fetishes.

Oh, you have come! I can clearly see your coming. You symbolize big
storms and heavy rains. You are the personification of light and fire. I
can see you standing majestically in the East. You are towering over the

earth of old China. In a kind voice with southern accent familiar to the 800 million people, you said to us: "Pioneer, discover, reform, and create!" Your voice is transformed into layers of gorgeous clouds and brings unparalleled beauty to the East. You are transformed into sparks of fire to light up the lamp of science and produce great brilliance. Your words bring good messages which enlighten every heart, and your powerful hands smash yesterday's dark prison. You are "a beam of light in the kingdom of darkness" and a phenomenon welcomed by our age. Your name forms a glorious page in our long history, and your existence provides democratic China a strong bulwark.

Oh, you have come! You have come! You are so small and yet so big; so low and yet so high; and so plain and yet so abstruse. You appear in China "as fresh and majestic as a rising sun" and are full of vitality. You are a banner towering over 9,600,000 square kilometers—a banner signifying that our 800 million people cannot be insulted or destroyed.

Today we have heard your voice waking us up for reform. In response to your upright and selfless call, we have already lit the torch of *Enlightenment*. Yesterday, on the Huaihai battlefield,* "your metallic voice traveled over thousands of miles of gunsmoke." Now, with your unflinching steadfastness and your full warmth, you are leading us on our march to the goal of prosperity, wealth, democracy, and freedom. . . .

In the fast-changing twentieth century, when science has already enabled us to reach the stars and outer space; at a time like today, when the existence of matter, or existing matter, and the principles of its motion are all revealed; and during the large-scale revolution in the superstructure and the economic base, and in human spirit and feeling, the poet deeply feels that in the unlimited history of the human world "every step taken can be considered a start as well as a conclusion." The "conclusion" means yesterday, the disappearance of falsehoods and the abandonment of people's spiritual world of the past. The "start" means the definite beginning of an indefinite tomorrow and the knowledge and affirmation of what is definite on this side and indefinite on the other side. It also means our getting close to truth in our pursuit for it at varying speeds.

Under the illumination of "The God of Fire," mankind is now forging ahead with full confidence in a big storm.

---

* The battle between Nationalist and Communist armies for Xuzhou, November 1948– January 1949.

NOTES

INTRODUCTION (Pages 1-26)

1. Two scholars who have insisted on the importance of human rights concerns for the Chinese are John K. Fairbank and Jerome A. Cohen.

2. "Recent wall posters and mini-demonstrations in Peking have stimulated some naive speculation about whether China is moving toward Western-style democracy. It is not." A. Doak Barnett, *New York Times*, 12 December 1978.

3. Robert W. Barnett, "Human Rights in China," *Worldview*, March 1978.

4. *See Asiaweek*, 14 December 1979, p. 8.

5. *SPEAHRhead*, no. 2, Summer 1979, p. 14.

6. *See*, for example, Burton Watson, "Chinese Protest Poetry: From the Earliest Times Through the Sung Dynasty," *Asia*, no. 17, Winter 1969–70.

7. Confucianism can be seen as a group of schools of thought lying along a continuum between authoritarianism and relative liberalism. For an interesting article that takes this approach (emphasizing economics), *see* Yeh-chien Wang, "State Control or 'Laissez-Faire': A Dichotomy in Confucian Tradition," in *Si yü yen* (Thought and Word), Taipei, May 1968.

8. Seymour, p. 72. (Books cited in "Suggested Reading" are indicated in abbreviated form in the Notes.)

9. The main proponent of this view was Yan Fu. *See* Benjamin Schwartz, *In Search of Wealth and Power: Yen Fu and the West* (Cambridge, Mass.: Harvard University Press, 1964.)

10. *See* Chow Tse-tsung, *The May Fourth Movement: Intellectual Revolution in Modern China* (Stanford, Calif.: Stanford University Press, 1960).

11. The official Communist view places more emphasis on the "liberation" wrought by the movement, than on its liberalism. *See Renmin ribao* editorial on the ,subject, 5 May 1979; abridged translation in *Beijing Review*, 18 May 1979.

12. For the historical background on the subject of the Communists' treatment of their opponents, *see* Patricia E. Griffin, *The Chinese Communist Treatment of Counterrevolutionaries, 1924–1949* (Princeton, N.J.: Princeton University Press, 1976), and Lyman P. Van Slyke, *Enemies and Friends: The United Front in Chinese Communist History* (Stanford, Calif.: Stanford University Press, 1967). For a sophisticated study of the Communists' attempts at mind control in the early 1950s, *see* Robert Jay Lifton, *Thought Reform and the Psychology of Totalism: A Study of "Brainwashing" in China* (New York: W. W. Norton, reprinted 1963). For a discussion on the subject of estimating the number of political killings during this period, *see* Seymour, p. 102, n. 92.

13. There was also a modest thaw in the early 1960s. *See* Merle Goldman, "The Unique 'Blooming and Contending' of 1961–1962," *China Quarterly*, no. 37, January–March 1969.

14. This figure is given by Agence France Presse reporter Georges Biannic, citing "a well-informed Chinese source" in Beijing. The years indicated are 1966–69. U.S. Foreign Broadcast Information Service, *Daily Report*, 5 February 1979.

15. Seymour, p. 171, quoting *Xuexi*, 18 June 1968.

16. For more on the subject of posters, *see* Alan P.L. Liu, *Communications and National Integration in Communist China* (Berkeley and Los Angeles: University of California Press, 1971), pp. 102-105; and Frederick T.C. Yu, *Mass Persuasion in Communist China* (New York: Frederick A. Praeger, 1964), pp. 137–142.

17. A complete translation appears in *Chinese Law and Government* 10, no. 3, Fall 1977.

18. *SPEAHRhead,* no. 1, Spring 1979, p. 24.

19. The actual names of the writers are Li Zhengtian, Chen Yiyang, and Wang Xizhe. For further information on the later aspects of the case, *see SPEAHRhead,* no. 1, p. 1, and no. 3, Fall 1979, p. 5. Two *Beijing zhi chun* discussions of the subject are translated in report no. 73728 of U.S. Joint Publications Research Service (hereafter cited as JPRS).

20. Estimate made by a correspondent of the Hungarian news agency MTI, quoted in *China Quarterly,* no. 67, September 1976, p. 661.

21. *See SPEAHRhead,* no. 2, p. 16; and *Beijing zhi chun,* no. 2, 27 January 1979; translation: JPRS 73728.

For a student participant's recollections of the April Fifth incident, *see* Chen Ximing, ". . . Test of the Times," *Beijing zhi chun,* no. 1, 9 January 1979; translation: JPRS 73728.

22. One of the journals of the democratic movement (*Siwu luntan*) was named after the April Fifth Movement. An editorial noted, "The current mass democratic movement . . . is a continuation of the April Fifth Movement of 1976." *Siwu luntan,* no. 9, 29 April 1979; translation: JPRS 73731.

An official account of the April Fifth Incident appeared in *Renmin ribao,* 5 April 1979; abridged translation: *Beijing Review,* no. 15, 13 April 1979, pp. 9-13.

23. For an official explanation of the new state Constitution, *see* Ye Jianying, "Report to the First Session of the Fifth National People's Congress," *Beijing Review,* no. 11, 17 March 1978.

24. *See* Hua Guofeng, "Report to the First Session of the Fifth National People's Congress, *Beijing Review,* 17 March 1978.

25. *Renmin ribao,* 21 October 1978; translation: U.S. Foreign Broadcast Information Service, *Daily Report,* 26 October 1978.

26. *Ibid.*

27. *SPEAHRhead,* no. 2, p. 13.

28. *See* "Communique of the Third Plenary Session of the Eleventh Central Committee of the Communist Party of China," *Beijing Review,* no. 52, 29 December 1978.

29. For excerpts of Ulanhu's speech, *see SPEAHRhead,* no. 2.

30. *Renmin ribao,* 29 January 1979.

31. *New York Times,* 26 and 27 November 1978. *See also* Document 26.

32. *New York Times,* 27 November 1978.

33. *New York Times,* 29 November 1978.

34. For some examples of leftists being arrested, *see SPEARhead,* no. 2, pp. 11, 13, 16; and no. 3, pp. 10, 12.

35. *New York Times,* 27 November 1978.

36. *SPEAHRhead,* no. 3, p. 5.

37. For more complete information, *see* Appendix, below.

Most of the information in the following paragraphs is taken from Gan Weiming, "Pioneers of the Democratic Movement: Democratic Fighters Fu Yuehua and Wei Jingsheng," *Huang he* (Yellow River), no. 6, April 1979; and Hong Xin, "Unofficial Publications in Beijing," *Zhong ming,* no. 19, 1 May 1979 (both in Chinese).

38. *Washington Post,* 29 October 1979.

39. *Washington Post,* 30 October 1979.

40. *New York Times,* 27 December 1978. On 4 January 1979, they were given an interview with Wang Zhen, a deputy prime minister. Although Wang promised to look into their situation, he admonished them to dedicate their lives to the nation. Later,

the official media reported that the problems had been resolved and that the youths were all working hard. *Renmin ribao*, 10 and 11 February 1979.

41. In addition to Fu, various other dissidents were arrested at this time, the best known being Zhang Xifeng. Agence France Presse, 2 February 1979; translation: U.S. Foreign Broadcast Information Service, *Daily Report*, 5 February 1979.

42. U.S. Foreign Broadcast Information Service, *Daily Report*, 25 January 1979.

43. *New York Times*, 27 December 1979. The official media was also acknowledging that Mao's instructions had contained shortcomings.

44. Bai Jia, "April Fifth Forum in Guangzhou," *Dongxiang*, no. 7, 16 April 1979 (in Chinese).

45. Gan (*see* note 37).

46. U.S. Foreign Broadcast Information Service, *Daily Report*, 24 January 1979.

47. Agence France Presse, 24 January 1979, U.S. Foreign Broadcast Information Service, *Daily Report*, 25 January 1979.

48. *Renmin ribao*, 12 February 1979. *See also Zhongguo qingnian bao*, 13 February 1979.

49. *New York Times*, 25 May 1979.

50. *Renmin ribao*, 16 March 1979.

51. *Gongren ribao*, 22 March 1979.

52. *Beijing ribao*, 22 March 1979.

53. *Zhongguo qingnian bao*, 17 March 1979.

54. *See* Xiao Weiyin, Luo Houzhai, and Wu Zheying, "Human Rights Problems from the Marxist Perspective," *Honqi*, 5 May 1979 (in Chinese). For a later discussion, *see* "Commentator" article in *Guangming ribao*, 26 October 1979; translated excerpts in *Beijing Review*, no. 45, 9 November 1979.

55. Wei Lang, "Has the Political Climate in Beijing Changed?" *Dongxiang*, no. 7, April 1979 (in Chinese).

56. Hong (*see* note 37).

57. *SPEAHRhead*, no. 2, p. 5.

58. *Renmin ribao*, 1 April 1979.

59. *New York Times*, 2 April 1979.

60. *SPEAHRhead*, no. 2, p. 5.

61. *SPEAHRhead*, no. 1, p. 21.

62. Hong Yan and Lin Tse, "April 5, 1979 at Tian-an-men," *Dongxiang*, no. 7.

63. Gan (*see* note 37).

SECTION ONE (Pages 27-41)

1. DOCUMENT 1 is from *Qimeng*, no. 2, 24 November 1978; translation: JPRS 73215.

2. DOCUMENT 2 is from *Qimeng*, no. 1, 11 October 1978; translation: JPRS 73215.

3. DOCUMENT 3 is from *Zhongguo renquan*, 22 March 1979. Our Chinese text is from *Zhongguo ren* (The Chinese) 1:5 (1 June 1979); translation: Chinese English Language Service.

4. We have omitted the sixth item because its meaning is unclear, possibly due to a misprint in the original. (There is a reference to a "battlefront," but this is before the Sino-Vietnam war broke out.)

DOCUMENT 4 is from a Beijing poster advertising *Masses' Reference News*. Our Chinese text is taken from *Huang he* (Yellow River), no 6, April 1979; translation: Maddy Lynn.

5. DOCUMENT 5 is *Exploration's* publication statement of 9 January 1979. It ap-

peared in *Tansuo*, no. 1, March 1979. Our Chinese text is taken from *Huang he*, no. 6; translation: Chinese English Language Service.

6. DOCUMENT 6 was originally entitled "Realizing the Four Modernizations, Democratic National Construction, and the Contending of the Hundred Schools." It originally appeared in *Minzhu yu shidai*, no. 1. Our Chinese text is taken from *Zhongguo ren* 1:5 (1 June 1979); translation: Chinese English Language Service.

7. DOCUMENT 7 is from *Jintian*, no. 1. This translation is reprinted by permission from *Index on Censorship* (London), September 1979.

8. DOCUMENT 8 originally appeared as the Foreword to *Beijing zhi chun*, no. 1, 9 January 1979; translation: JPRS 73421.

9. The word "enlightenment" is taken from the eighteenth-century European movement. *See* Zheng Yan, "On the Historical Significance and Practical Importance of the Enlightenment," *Qimeng*, no. 1 [sic], 29 January 1979; translation in *SPEAHRhead*, no. 4–5, Winter–Spring 1980.

The first part of DOCUMENT 9 is from *Qimeng*, no. 2; translation: JPRS 73215.

10. The second part of DOCUMENT 9 is a "provisional draft" of goals as issued by the Guiyang headquarters of the Enlightenment Society. It was published in *Qimeng*, no. 3, 1 January 1979; translation: JPRS 73215.

11. DOCUMENT 10 originally appeared under the title "Thaw Society Announcement." It was posted on Democracy Wall in Guiyang, 27 February 1979, and in Beijing in March. Our Chinese text is taken from *Huang he*, no. 6; translation: Chinese English Language Service.

The Thaw Society published a sixteen-point Manifesto in the March 8 issue of *Jiedong*. A translation can be found in *SPEAHRhead*, nos. 4–5, Winter–Spring 1980.

SECTION TWO (Pages 43-80)

1. For details and sources, *see* "Elections for China?" in *SPEAHRhead*, no. 3, Fall 1979, p. 4.

2. DOCUMENT 11 is excerpted from *Qimeng*, n.d.; translation JPRS 73421.

3. The word "autocrats" has been supplied; the original word was unclear.

The author of DOCUMENT 12 is indicated as "Jin Sheng," a pen name for Wei Jingsheng. Part I is dated 5 December 1978, and was posted on Beijing's Democracy Wall. Part II is undated and apparently was written some time thereafter. Both appeared in *Tansuo*, no. 1, December 1978; translation: JPRS 73756. Part III appeared in *Tansuo*, no. 2, January 1979; translation: JPRS 73787.

4. DOCUMENT 13 is from *Qimeng*, March 1979; translation: JPRS 73421.

5. DOCUMENT 14 is excerpted from *Beijing zhi chun*, no. 1, 9 January 1979, and no. 2, 27 January 1979; translation: JPRS 73421.

6. Shaoshan is the name of the village where Mao Zedong was born. The reference here is apparently to Maoist economic policies, according to which localities were to be self-reliant.

DOCUMENT 15 is a manifesto which was adopted at the first plenary meeting of the Thaw Society, held in Guiyang on 8 March 1979. Our Chinese text is taken from *Huang he*, no. 6, April 1979; translation: Maddy Lynn.

SECTION THREE (Pages 81-95)

1. DOCUMENT 16 is excerpted from *Zhongguo renquan*, February 1979; translation: JPRS 73421.

2. DOCUMENT 17 was originally entitled "Those Who Speak Up Should Be Absolved from Incriminating Charges." It is taken from *Siwu luntan*, no. 6, 25 February 1979; translation: JPRS 73421.

3. DOCUMENT 18 is from *Qimeng*, n.d.; translation: JPRS 73421.

4. DOCUMENT 19 contains excerpts from "Local News Examined," *Beijing zhi chun*, no. 1, 9 January 1979; translation: JPRS 73728.

5. DOCUMENT 20 was originally "Did You Know? On 'Letter Inspection.'" It appeared in *Siwu luntan*, no 4, 1979. Our Chinese text is taken from *Zhongguo jen* 1:5 (1 June 1979); translation: Chinese English Language Service.

6. DOCUMENT 21 is from *Qiu shi bao*, February 1979. Our Chinese text is taken from *Zhongguo ren* 1:5 (1 June 1979); translation: Chinese English Language Service.

7. DOCUMENT 22 is from *Tansuo*, no. 2, January 1979; translation: JPRS 73421.

SECTION FOUR (Pages 97-105)

1. DOCUMENT 23 is a letter dated 28 February 1979, from an untitled pamphlet published by the China Human Rights League (Zhongguo renquan tongmeng), 22 March 1979; translated in part by JPRS (no. 73421) and in part by James D. Seymour.

2. The first part of DOCUMENT 24 is an open letter by the Legal Study Group of the Human Rights League addressed to "The Legal, Investigation, and Public Security Organizations Concerned with the Fu Yuehua Incident," dated 19 February 1979. The three points at the end are by the league's Tianjin Legal Study Group. Both parts were published in *Zhongguo renquan*, no. 2. Our Chinese text is taken from *Zhongguo ren* 1:5 (1 June 1979); translation: Chinese English Language Service.

3. DOCUMENT 25 was originally entitled "The Principle of 'Assumption of Innocence' Must Be Implemented." It appeared in *Siwu luntan*, no. 6, 25 February 1979; translation: JPRS 73215. For a useful official commentary on the question of assumption of innocence, *see* article by Tian Cai which appeared in *People's Daily*, 17 February 1979; translation: U.S. Foreign Broadcast Information Service, *Daily Report*, vol. 1, 7 March 1979.

SECTION FIVE (Pages 107-127)

1. The author of DOCUMENT 26 is described as a "worker." After appearing in Guiyang, the essay was posted in Beijing's Tian-an-men Square. This summary appeared in *Lien-ho pao* (Taipei), 26 November 1978. Our translation is taken from *SPEAHRhead*, no. 2, Summer 1979. Reprinted with permission.

2. The editor has omitted the words "complete and centralized" at this point, the author's meaning being unclear.

DOCUMENT 27 first appeared in *Qimeng*, no. 3, January 1979; translation: JPRS 73215.

3. The editor has omitted five paragraphs dealing somewhat repetitively with the subject of human rights. In the omitted section mention is made of the need for "firmness, unity, determination, and faith."

SECTION SIX (Pages 129-137)

1. DOCUMENT 28 is a paraphrase of an extract from a five-page poster which appeared in Beijing in December 1978 and was first published in the West in *Die Welt* (Hamburg). A translation from the German appeared in *Freedom at Issue*, May–June 1979. (Used with permission.)

2. In the original, this sentence began: "In April 1959 . . ." This was when Liu became state chairperson. However, it is questionable whether one can say that Mao "pulled back to play a secondary role" before the Lushan Plenum.

An earlier version of this essay was posted on Beijing Democracy Wall on 11 January 1979. DOCUMENT 29 is a revised version which appeared in *Qimeng*, no. 1, 29 January 1979; translation: JPRS 73421.

SECTION SEVEN (Pages 139-151)

1. We have checked our Chinese text (see below) and this translation agrees. However, we suspect that the author originally wrote, or intended to write, just the opposite. Marx, after all, insisted that economics is decisive. If Wei did intend to say what appears in the text, it is a tribute to the thoroughness of Mao's eradication of the essence of Marx's teaching.

DOCUMENT 30 is comprised of excerpts of an essay which originally appeared in the March 1979 issue of *Tansuo* under the name "Jin Sheng," a pen name of Wei Jingsheng. Translated in part by JPRS (no. 73421), in part by James D. Seymour, and in part by the International League for Human Rights. (Chinese text from *Huanghe*, April 1979.)

2. DOCUMENT 31 originally appeared on Beijing's Democracy Wall. It was reprinted in *Beijing zhi chun*, no. 1, 9 January 1979; translation: JPRS 73421.

3. For the source of DOCUMENT 32, *see* Section Six, note 1.

4. DOCUMENT 33 is an extract from "Local News Examined," *Beijing zhi chun*, no. 1; tranlsation: JPRS 73728.

5. DOCUMENT 34 is from a longer story entitled "A 'Miracle' Which Is Not a Miracle." It was written in late 1975, but was not published until 1979. *Beijing zhi chun*, 9 January 1979 (no. 1) and March 5 (apparently incorrectly numbered "1").

SECTION EIGHT (Pages 153-167)

1. DOCUMENT 35 is from *Minzhu yu shidai*, no. 1, March 1979. Our Chinese text is taken from *Zhongguo ren* 1:5 (1 June 1979). Translated in part by the Chinese English Language Service and in part by Mab Huang.

2. DOCUMENT 36 is mostly comprised of an extract from a Beijing poster by *Siwu luntan*, 28 March 1979. It is in response to an attack on Deng Xiaoping by Wei Jingsheng (*see* Document 51). Our Chinese text is taken from *Bei-Mei ribao* (North American Daily, New York), 2 July 1979; translation: Chinese English Language Service.

We have inserted in the middle of this document six sentences drawn from another *Siwu luntan* piece, "The People's Democratic Movement and the Style of 'Upright Officials' the People Expect," by Shi Huasheng. Specifically, this portion includes paragraph 4, sentence 3 ("The country's ownership system . . .") through paragraph 5 (". . . counterparts in other countries."). This appeared in no 9, 29 April 1979; translation: JPRS 73731.

3. For the source of DOCUMENT 37 *see* Section Six, note 1.

4. DOCUMENT 38 is part of an essay which originally appeared under the title "Democracy in Economic Management and Democracy in Politics," *Beijing zhi chun*, no. 2, January 1979; translation: JPRS 73728, revised somewhat on the basis of the Chinese text in *Zhongguo ren* 1:15 (1 June 1979). The author is identified as a worker in the Number Two Municipal Housing Repair Company and as a delegate to the Tenth Central Committee of the Communist Youth League.

5. The original title of DOCUMENT 39 was "Do Away With the Power of Administrative Leadership of Basic-Level Organizations in Factories, Mines, and Other Enterprises." From *Beijing zhi chun*, no. 2, 27 January 1979; translation: JPRS 73421.

SECTION NINE (Pages 169-176)

1. The question itself is illegible.

DOCUMENT 40 is from the story cited in Section Seven, note 5. The story ends happily, with the man (who turns out to have been a very high military official) restored to office and the narrator marrying his daughter.

2. The Chinese text here becomes illegible.

3. DOCUMENT 41 originally appeared under the title "Destitute Petitioner Forced to Sell Cotton Padded Quilt." *Beijing zhi chun*, no. 1, 9 January 1979; translation: JPRS 73728. The author is identified as a staff reporter of the journal.

4. DOCUMENT 42 is an extract from the "National News" section of *Beijing zhi chun*, no. 2, 27 January 1979; translation: JPRS 73728.

SECTION TEN (Pages 177-205)

1. *Beijing zhi chun*, no. 2, 27 January 1979; translation: JPRS 73728.

2. Lan Sheng, "Criticizing Metaphysics and Metaphysical Criticism," *Siwu luntan*, no. 6, 5 February 1979; translation: JPRS 73421.

3. The reference is to Jiang Qing, Wang Hongwen, Yao Wenyuan, and Zhang Chunqiao.

The poem in DOCUMENT 43 (originally entitled "Shocked to Hear of the Premier's Death") appeared in *Qimeng*, no. 3, 1 January 1979; translation: JPRS 73215. It is intended to be sung to the tune of "Manjianghong."

The three paragraphs at the end of the document are a paraphrase of part of an essay entitled "View the Necessity of a Radical Social Change from the Perspective of What Happened to Zhou Enlai in his Later Years," by Xu Shu. The essay appeared first in *Siwu luntan*, no. 3, 6 January 1979, and was reprinted in the no. 8 issue of the same journal (1 April 1979); translation: JPRS 73987.

For other democrats' views of Zhou, *see* "Long Live the Spirit of Zhou Enlai," and accompanying poems, in *Beijing zhi chun*, no. 1, 9 January 1979; translation: JPRS 73728.

4. DOCUMENT 44 is excerpted from Qi Dai, "Comrade Shaoqi Should Be Reappraised," *Beijing zhi chun*, no. 2; translation: JPRS 73421.

For additional comments on Liu, *see* Document 15. Regarding his posthumous standing, *see Asiaweek*, 14 September 1979, pp. 17–18; *Dongxiang*, September 1979, translation: JPRS 74396; and Wang Guixiu and Zhang Xianyang, "On the Criticism of 'Peace Within the Party,'" *Hongqi*, no. 2, 16 January 1980 (in Chinese); and *SPEAHRhead*, nos. 4–5, page 12.

5. The county in which Dazhai is located.

DOCUMENT 45 is comprised of excerpts from "View Dazhai from Chen Yonggui (Is This Proper?)," by Jin Zhiqing, *Qimeng*, n.d., pp. 7–11; translation: JPRS 73421.

6. Parenthetical note as in original.

7. Ms. Nie was a member of the Philosophy Department and a leading antagonist of Beijing University President Lu Ping.

DOCUMENT 46 was originally titled "Who Was the Big Traitor Inside the Party?" The author is only identified as "a veteran Communist Party member who knew the ins and outs of the matter and was persecuted." From *Beijing zhi chun,* no. 1; translation: JPRS 73421.

8. DOCUMENT 47 originally appeared as a note entitled "Personalities: Jiang Qing Is in Qincheng Prison," in *Zhongguo renquan,* February 1979; translation: JPRS 73421.

The definitive study of Jiang is Roxane Witke, *Comrade Chiang Ch'ing* (Boston: Little, Brown and Company, 1977).

9. DOCUMENT 48 is excerpted from "Chen Yun, an Exemplary Truth Seeker," by Xue Xi, *Beijing zhi chun,* no. 2; translation: JPRS 73728.

10. This conflicts with one account (in *Beijing zhi chun,* no. 1, *see* below): "The welcoming crowd did not applaud or shout; instead, one heard the sobbing of the widows and orphans of those lost during the Great Cultural Revolution."

DOCUMENT 49 is comprised of extracts (which have been reorganized and reintegrated) from the following: "A Report on Comrade Peng Zhen's Return to Beijing," *Beijing zhi chun,* no. 2; Li Ying, "Comrade Peng Zhen, the People of Beijing Hope You Will Be Back Soon," *Beijing zhi chun,* no. 1; and Li Ying, "Peng Zhen's Experience," *Beijing zhi chun,* no. 2.

11. The author is not altogether consistent on this point. Elsewhere (*Beijing zhi chun,* no. 1, p. 14) it is stated that Peng "obeyed the decision of the superior Party organization to obtain his release by making a newspaper announcement and a written statement of repentance . . . [but they nonetheless] refused to release him."

12. DOCUMENT 50 is comprised of lyrics intended to be sung to the tune of "Manjianghong," from *Qimeng,* no. 3; translation: JPRS 73215.

13. DOCUMENT 51 first appeared as an editorial in a special edition of *Tansuo,* 25 March 1979. Translated in part by JPRS (no. 73421) and in part by Maddy Lynn. Our Chinese text is from *Bei-Mei ribao,* 1, 2, and 5 June 1979.

14. DOCUMENT 52 is excerpted from a poster which appeared in Beijing on 28 March 1979. Our Chinese text is taken from *Bei-Mei ribao,* 2 and 4 July 1979. Translated in part by the Chinese English Language Service and in part by James D. Seymour.

For more on Deng Xiaoping, *see* Document 57.

15. For the source of DOCUMENT 53, *see* Section Six, note 1. After the period covered in this volume, there were relatively direct commentaries about Mao. Examples are: "Emancipate the Mind and Clarify the Truth," and "Greetings to a Beautiful Spring," both of which appeared anonymously in *Siwu luntan,* November 1979, translated in *SPEAHRhead,* no. 6, Summer 1980.

SECTION ELEVEN (Pages 207-223)

1. The best sources on political prisoners in China are Bao Ruo-wang's book and the Amnesty International report (*see* Suggested Reading, below). On efforts to remold prisoners, *see* Robert Jay Lifton, *Thought Reform and the Psychology of Totalism: A Study of "Brainwashing" in China* (New York: W. W. Norton, reprinted 1963); and chapter 9 of Martyn King Whyte, *Small Groups and Political Rituals in China* (Berkeley and Los Angeles; University of California Press, 1974).

2. DOCUMENT 54 originally appeared in the March 1979 issue of *Tansuo.* Our Chinese text is taken from *Huang he,* no. 6, April 1979. Translation in part by Steve K. Chen and in part by James D. Seymour.

3. DOCUMENT 55 originally appeared in the March 1979 issue of *Tansuo.* Our Chinese text is taken from *Huang he,* no. 6, April 1979. Translation by Arthur Li.

4. DOCUMENT 56 is an extract for the "National News" section of *Beijing zhi chun,* no. 2, 27 January 1979; translation: JPRS 73728.

SECTION TWELVE (Pages 225-244)

1. *SPEAHRhead,* no. 1, Spring 1979, p. 2, citing Agence France Presse, 24 January 1979.

2. *Gong Min* means "citizen."

DOCUMENT 57 originally appeared in *Qimeng,* no. 3, 1 January 1979; translation: JPRS 73215.

3. Parts of this and the preceding sentence have been omitted because of illegibility.

4. In 1956 leaders called for the noncommunist parties such as the Democratic League to coexist with the Communist Party on a long-term basis. (According to Maoist theory, all parties are ultimately to wither away.) The democratic parties were also invited to "supervise" the Communist Party. The experiment, however, was short-lived, and after 1957 the democratic parties existed in name only. *See* James D. Seymour, "Communist China's Bourgeois-Democratic Parties" (M.A. essay, Columbia University, 1960).

5. The reference is to Jie Jun, "The United States Is a Democratic Paradise," *Qimeng,* n.d., translated excerpt: JPRS 73987.

DOCUMENT 58 evidently originally appeared as a poster, under the title: "Further Discussion on Whether the United States Is 'A Democratic Paradise'—A Talk with Jie Jun." The article was signed: "Quan," a pen name meaning "rights." In the 29 April 1979 (no. 9) issue of *Siwu luntan,* it was republished "without the permission of the author . . ., with slight abridgment"; translation: JPRS 73731.

SECTION THIRTEEN (Pages 245-248)

1. Agence France Presse, 22 February 1979, U.S. Foreign Broadcast Information Service, *Daily Report,* 4, 23 February 1979.

2. The designation "XX" refers to a two-character name of a publication, possibly that of the Enlightenment Society itself.

DOCUMENT 59 appeared in *Qimeng,* no. 1 [sic], 29 January 1979; translation: JPRS 74321.

3. DOCUMENT 60 first appeared under the title "Mr.. Chiang Ching-kuo Merits Praise," in *Qunzhong cankao xiaoxi bao,* no. 1, 24 March 1979; translation: JPRS 73421.

At about the same time as China's human rights movement, there was a human rights movement in Taiwan (subsequently repressed). Although largely oriented toward the development of an *autonomous* society, and thus out of step with the sentiments expressed in these two essays, a few participants were influenced by developments on the mainland. There was even established a "Democracy Wall" in Taipei, notice of which was duly taken by Beijing dissidents. *See* "Patriotic Wall and Democracy in Taiwan: Heated Controversy at Taiwan University," *Qunzhong cankao xiaoxi bao,* no. 4, 24 February 1979; translation: *SPEAHRhead,* nos. 4–5, p. 31.

SECTION FOURTEEN (Pages 249-261)

1. *See SPEAHRhead,* no. 2, Summer 1979, p. 11.

2. Later commentaries are not within the purview of this volume. On the arrests of Wei Jingsheng and Ren Wanding, *see Siwu luntan,* no. 9, 29 April 1979; translation: JPRS 73731. For further postcrackdown materials, *see SPEAHRhead,* nos. 4–5, Winter-Spring 1980.

3. DOCUMENT 61 appeared in the second issue of *Beijing zhi chun,* 27 January 1979, under the title "The Many Difficulties of the People's Publications." Our Chinese text

is taken from *Bei-Mei ribao*, 12 June 1979. Translation: Chinese English Language Service.

4. DOCUMENT 63 is excerpted from *Zhongguo renquan*, February 1979. The statement is dated 21 January 1979; translation: JPRS 73421.

5. The full title of DOCUMENT 64 was: "A Record of an Investigation into the Fu Yuehua Case." It is not known whether this transcript was published in China. Our text is taken from *Huang he*, no. 6, April 1969. Translated by Mab Huang and Maddy Lynn.

6. DOCUMENT 65 is by the editorial department of *Tansuo*. *Tanuso*, no. 3, 11 March 1979; translation: JPRS 73421.

7. DOCUMENT 66 first appeared as an editorial in *Tansuo*, no. 3, 11 March 1979, under the title "Who Created the Troubles? Who Caused the Serious Consequences?" Translated in part by JPRS (no. 73421) and in part by James D. Seymour. Our Chinese text is taken from *Huang he*, no. 6.

SECTION FIFTEEN (Pages 263-279)

1. The poems in this section are from *Qimeng*, no. 1, 11 October 1978; translation: JPRS 73215. The commentaries are from *Qimeng*, no. 2, 24 November 1978; translation: JPRS 73215. Ellipses in this section are as found in JPRS.

Another poem by Huang Xiang is "Eulogy to Democracy Wall," a translation of which appeared in *SPEAHRhead*, nos. 4–5, p. 3.

ORGANIZATIONS AND PERIODICALS

The following is a list of organizations and serial publications known to have been part of the 1978–79 democratic movement. In a case where an organization and its journal have similar names, only the journal is listed.

April Fifth Forum (Siwu luntan), Beijing (Peking); formed by a merger of
    April Fifth News and *People's Forum*
April Fifth News, see above
Autumn Fruit (Qiu shi) Beijing
Beijing Spring (Beijing zhi chun), Beijing
China Human Rights (Zhongguo renquan), Beijing and Tianjin
China's April Fifth (Zhonghua siwu)
Democracy and Modernity (Minzhu yu shidai)
Enlightenment (Qimeng), Beijing and Guiyang
Exploration (Tansuo), Beijing
Fertile Ground (Wotu)
Four Modernizations Forum (Si hua luntan), Beijing
Future (Weilai), Guangzhou (Canton)
Human Rights, see *China Human Rights*
Hundred Flowers (Bai hua), Beijing
In Search of Truth (Qiu shi bao), Beijing
Light, southern China
Livelihood (Shenghuo)
Masses' Reference News (Qunzhong cankao xiaoxi), Beijing
New Democracy Promotion Association *(Zhongguo xin minzhu cujin hui)*
New Sprouts (Xin lei), Guangzhou
People's Forum (Renmin luntan), see *April Fifth Forum*
Red Bean (Hung dou), Guangzhou
Sichuan Democratic Alliance, Sichuan
Sino-American People's Friendship (Zhong-Mei renmin yuhao bao),
    Beijing
Spring Grass (Chun cao), Guangzhou
Thaw (Jiedong), Beijing and Guiyang; a spin-off of *Enlightenment*
Today (Jintian), Beijing
Us (Wo-men), Beijing
Voice of the People (Renmin zhi sheng), Guangzhou
Wuhan April Fifth Study Group *(Wuhan siwu xue hui),* Wuhan

SUGGESTED READING

Amnesty International. *Political Imprisonment in the People's Republic of China*. London: Amnesty International Publications, 1978.

Bao Ruo-wang (Jean Pasqualini) and Chelminski, Rudolph. *Prisoner of Mao*. New York: Coward, McCann & Geoghegan, Inc., 1973.

Goldman, Merle. *Literary Dissent in Communist China*. Cambridge, Mass.: Harvard University Press, 1967.

Huang, Mab. "Human Rights in a Revolutionary Setting: The Case of the People's Republic of China." In *Human Rights: Cultural and Ideological Perspectives*. Edited by Adamantia Pollis and Peter Schwab, New York: Praeger Publishers, 1979.

Index on Censorship (London) 9: 1, February 1980, special issue on China.

Moody, Peter R. *Opposition and Dissent in Contemporary China*. Stanford, Calif.: Hoover Institution Press, 1977.

Seymour, James D. *China: The Politics of Revolutionary Reintegration*. New York: Thomas Y. Crowell Co., 1976.

SPEAHRhead: Bulletin of the Society for the Protection of East Asians' Human Rights (quarterly). P.O. Box 1212, New York 10025.

INDEX

An index can be of only limited value as a guide to the main themes of a book such as this. Furthermore, no useful purpose would be served by a listing of either the most common or the most obscure terms (such as "Gang of Four" on the one hand, or little-known place names on the other). To maximize the usefulness of this index, certain nonobvious analytical categories have been included. Among these are: arrests of dissidents, economic justice, elections, equality, family, foreigners (attitudes toward), historical background, home (sanctity of), information (public access), Marxism-Leninism, movement (freedom of), official attitudes toward the human rights movement, ownership systems, parties (political, systems of), publishing by dissidents (general information about), and sexual equality. These precise terms will not necessarily appear on the indicated pages.

Page numbers in boldface type refer to definitions or major discussions of the indicated subject. Italicized page numbers denote essays written by the individual or published by the organization or in the publication named.